Anonymous Communication Networks

Protecting Privacy on the Web

OTHER COMMUNICATIONS BOOKS FROM AUERBACH

Advances in Biometrics for Secure Human Authentication and Recognition
Edited by Dakshina Ranjan Kisku, Phalguni Gupta, and Jamuna Kanta Sing
ISBN 978-1-4665-8242-2

Anonymous Communication Networks: Protecting Privacy on the Web
Kun Peng
ISBN 978-1-4398-8157-6

Case Studies in Enterprise Systems, Complex Systems, and System of Systems Engineering
Edited by Alex Gorod, Brian E. White, Vernon Ireland, S. Jimmy Gandhi,and Brian Sauser
ISBN 978-1-4665-0239-0

Cyber-Physical Systems: Integrated Computing and Engineering Design
Fei Hu
ISBN 978-1-4665-7700-8

Evolutionary Dynamics of Complex Communications Networks
Vasileios Karyotis, Eleni Stai, and Symeon Papavassiliou
ISBN 978-1-4665-1840-7

Extending the Internet of Things: Towards a Global and Seemless Integration
Antonio J. Jara-Valera
ISBN 9781466518483

Fading and Interference Mitigation in Wireless Communications
Stefan Panic
ISBN 978-1-4665-0841-5

The Future of Wireless Networks: Architectures, Protocols, and Services
Edited by Mohesen Guizani, Hsiao-Hwa Chen, and Chonggang Wang
ISBN 978-1-4822-2094-0

Green Networking and Communications: ICT for Sustainability
Edited by Shafiullah Khan and Jaime Lloret Mauri
ISBN 978-1-4665-6874-7

Image Encryption: A Communication Perspective
Fathi E. Abd El-Samie, Hossam Eldin H. Ahmed, Ibrahim F. Elashry, Mai H. Shahieen, Osama S. Faragallah, El-Sayed M. El-Rabaie, and Saleh A. Alshebeili
ISBN 978-1-4665-7698-8

Intrusion Detection in Wireless Ad-Hoc Networks
Nabendu Chaki and Rituparna Chaki
ISBN 978-1-4665-1565-9

Intrusion Detection Networks: A Key to Collaborative Security
Carol Fung and Raouf Boutaba
ISBN 978-1-4665-6412-1

MIMO Processing for 4G and Beyond: Fundamentals and Evolution
Edited by Mário Marques da Silva and Francisco A.T.B.N. Monteiro
ISBN 978-1-4665-9807-2

Modeling and Analysis of P2P Content Distribution Systems
Yipeng Zhou and Dah Ming Chiu
ISBN 978-1-4822-1920-3

Network Innovation through OpenFlow and SDN: Principles and Design
Edited by Fei Hu
ISBN 978-1-4665-7209-6

Pervasive Computing: Concepts, Technologies and Applications
Guo Minyi, Zhou Jingyu, Tang Feilong, and Shen Yao
ISBN 978-1-4665-9627-6

Physical Layer Security in Wireless Communications
Edited by Xiangyun Zhou. Lingyang Song, and Yan Zhang
ISBN 978-1-4665-6700-9

Security for Multihop Wireless Networks
Shafiullah Khan and Jaime Lloret Mauri
ISBN 978-1-4665-7803-6

Self-Healing Systems and Wireless Networks Management
Junaid Ahsenali Chaudhry
ISBN 978-1-4665-5648-5

Unit and Ubiquitous Internet of Things
Huansheng Ning
ISBN 978-1-4665-6166-3

AUERBACH PUBLICATIONS
www.auerbach-publications.com
To Order Call: 1-800-272-7737 • Fax: 1-800-374-3401
E-mail: orders@crcpress.com

Anonymous Communication Networks

Protecting Privacy on the Web

Kun Peng

CRC Press
Taylor & Francis Group
Boca Raton   London   New York

CRC Press is an imprint of the
Taylor & Francis Group, an **Informa** business

CRC Press
Taylor & Francis Group
6000 Broken Sound Parkway NW, Suite 300
Boca Raton, FL 33487-2742

© 2014 by Taylor & Francis Group, LLC
CRC Press is an imprint of Taylor & Francis Group, an Informa business

No claim to original U.S. Government works

Printed on acid-free paper
Version Date: 20140210

International Standard Book Number-13: 978-1-4398-8157-6 (Hardback)

Library of Congress Cataloging-in-Publication Data

Peng, Kun.
    Anonymous communication networks : protecting privacy on the web / author, Kun Peng.
        pages cm
    Includes bibliographical references and index.
    ISBN 978-1-4398-8157-6 (hardback)
    1. Internet--Security measures. 2. Computer networks--Security measures. 3. Privacy, Right of. 4. Data protection. 5. Online identities. I. Title.

TK5105.59.P463 2014
005.8--dc23   2014001317

Visit the Taylor & Francis Web site at
http://www.taylorandfrancis.com

and the CRC Press Web site at
http://www.crcpress.com

Contents

Chapter 1

Anonymity in Network Communication

Anonymity is a fundamental right of a democratic society. In most democratic nations, anonymity is very important and the laws and government regulations have been set up to protect information privacy in every aspect of society including the fast-developing computer and communication network. Users' anonymity is one of the most important requirements to information privacy. According to the Privacy Act Regulations [3], anonymity is an important property in applications of network communication. Due to wide application of IT and network techniques, user anonymity in network applications has become a critical challenge of security of our society, especially in areas like finance and terrorism and crime prevention. According to the Australian Federal Privacy Commissioner, the number of complaints and enquiries about anonymity remains high [1] and IT and Internet issues have become very important [2] in recent years. There are various motivations for this. Many participants of network applications like e-finance, e-commerce and e-health want to conceal their activity and identity so that their personal privacy can be protected. In some other applications like e-voting the participants do not want their identities to be linked to their activities. In all these applications, anonymity has to be implemented although their requirements for anonymity may be different. A complicating factor is that computers and computer networks make it quite easy to maintain and distribute digital information. Millions of bits can be transferred without error, stored, and analyzed in seconds. People are aware of the potential danger of this information processing power and are afraid of losing control of their personal data in both their private and business lives. Yet, their behavior is often inconsistent with that fear.

Without a satisfactory solution to anonymity of network communication, many network applications cannot gain customers' confidence and thus cannot replace the traditional counterparts. For example, coins and notes in

1

traditional cash are indistinguishable and do not reveal consumers' identities while each e-cash coin is a distinguishable string and may be linked to a consumer. So a customer used to traditional cash and traditional shopping manner may worry about his anonymity and be reluctant to use e-cash and on-line shopping. In another example, in traditional paper-based election systems a scrambled ballot box can guarantee anonymity of the voters. If no electronic scrambling is provided, the voters will be concerned about their anonymity and be unwilling to vote, which is especially serious in a nation with compulsory elections like Australia. In e-health systems, medical information must be transfered, shared and viewed while the patients' anonymity must be protected. When anonymity is implemented, a good balance must be kept with other security and practical properties like integrity, efficiency and information recovery (in abnormal situations). For example, digital signature is a normal tool to guarantee information integrity, but often violates users' anonymity. In some network applications, special digital signature techniques like group signatures and ring signatures are employed to achieve integrity and anonymity simultaneously. However, group signatures and ring signatures schemes are usually too inefficient for practical systems. So integrity, anonymity and efficiency are contradictory in some applications. Another contradiction is between personal privacy and national security. Individuals want to reserve anonymity in communication while the government may want to monitor suspicious communication. With a democratic social system facing a serious terrorism threat, a government must achieve a good balance between anonymity and national security. After September 11, the American government began to limit usage of encryption in communication. However, this is not necessarily a good solution. A more flexible method is to design recoverable anonymity such that messages through private communication can be recovered with a court order.

1.1   Right to Be Anonymous

Privacy and anonymity are essential parts of today's society. In some environments, such as medical treatments and banking, the privacy and anonymity of individuals are protected by law. Other aspects of modern life may not have such clear protections. Today, people are increasingly using computer networks to accomplish activities that were always assumed to be private or anonymous in the non-virtual world. The current protections provided by law and law enforcement are slowly being driven to adapt to this new life in the virtual world.

Computer and telecommunication technologies have generated great concerns regarding the protection of privacy and anonmymity on global networks. Many scholars, policymakers and "netizens" have discussed appropriate methods to protect privacy in electronic transactions and to ensure protection of personal identity on networks. International organizations, such as the

Organization for Economic Cooperation and Development (OECD), have also been active in providing relevant principles. As a result, various laws and government policies, industry self-regulation, technological solutions and private contract-based approaches have been suggested as appropriate methods for privacy protection on the Internet, and respective responsibilities among governments, businesses, users and international organizations have been the focus of recent debates.

Anonymity as a mechanism for negotiating social relationships, especially between individuals and external power institutions, has been developed and defined in various ways. The traditional concept of anonymity is often against public and private institutions with ability and power. The main focus was the restriction of access to an individual, which was expected to mitigate the power imbalance between these institutions and individuals. With the development of new technologies that broaden and diversify the collectors and users of personal information, there have been attempts to negotiate the individual's relationship with the external environment by providing the individual with control over information about himself or herself. But in the interactive network, users' anonymity cannot be dealt with effectively by current legal and technological measures. In such a situation, what would constitute a factor that could ensure an individual's self-autonomy and self-governance in relationship with external forces? The greatest difficulty for individuals who become the objects of surveillance in the current technological environment is that users' identities have become increasingly exposed, while the subjects of surveillance and their activities have become less identifiable. Therefore, the major impetus for the power imbalance between the subjects and objects of surveillance in the network is their differences in identifiability. The right not to be identified should be the most important component of privacy on the Internet and that, by not being blatantly identified, individuals can protect themselves from the potential risk and threat of not easily identifiable entities of surveillance and their activities. This right not to be identified seems to reflect accurately the sentiment of individual users in the networked environment. The sentiment seems to be a more complex or confusing one than wanting to be left unidentified, which may be expressed as "please do contact me and give me benefits, but I still do not want to fully give up my control (but I do not know how to have that control)". Thus, the issue here is less one of restricting immediate access to the individuals than of the welcoming permission of the access combined with a hope for the restriction of some unknown, unidentifiable, future use of their information and identity. As such, with the new characteristics of interactive network media, the elements that are needed to ensure self-autonomy and self-governance also change. The right to be left unidentified was critical in maintaining one's autonomy, dignity and self-governance in the context of powerful governments and new communications media such as print. But the networked environment and subsequent sociocultural changes have influenced the relative importance between being left unidentified and actively seeking control. Therefore, the concept of anonymity changes dramatically from maintaining passive liberty and freedom from an external institution's interference to allowing limited access without identification of the users when desired.

A network user is often faced with a choice between giving up the benefits and services of the site and providing at least some kind of information, because the use of many sites or services is not allowed unless various personal information is given. Choosing between providing personal information and giving up the information and services that an individual wants from the network is particularly difficult in the current technological environment because, in many cases, it is not known what will happen to the personal information once it is out on the network. Individual users, governments, data-using industries and all other potential users of information are uncertain about whether and how personal information will be used in the future. So even if people do voluntarily provide personal information and make conscious decisions, this decision making process tends to be based on incomplete information and uncertainty. Incomplete information is the reason why network users hesitate to provide personal information, but at the same time do not want to give up their activities on the network because of that unknown, potential risk. When people are required to provide or reveal their information, they hesitate, but if the calculated benefits are greater than potential risks, they give in. Many people later have regrets, especially when their mailboxes are flooded with unsolicited emails or they receive notice of a summons based on some of their activities on the network. Now they realize that not having anonymity on the network is a risky business, and they may begin to conduct self-censorship. Network anonymity becomes an essential part of maintaining the autonomy of network activities. Anonymity has long been discussed as an important element comprising privacy, but network anonymity in particular has become a widely discussed topic recently. The emergence of anonymous remailers that conceal a sender's identity and location has sparked so much controversy that sometimes laws are enacted to prohibit anonymous messages. Many argue against anonymous communication on the network, focusing on extreme cases such as anonymous threats and libellous messages. However, Froomkin [38] conducted an analysis of the costs and benefits of anonymity, acknowledging that anonymity has both valuable and harmful consequences. The most often cited cost of allowing anonymous communication is the difficulty in detecting illegal and immoral activities [38]. One of the primary reasons for monitoring Internet users is to prohibit infringement of intellectual property rights or to prevent cybercrime. Even some software products contain secret links to servers that allow them to pass along a variety of information regarding when consumers use the software, where, how long and the like, often without their knowledge. It is also possible that the manufacturer could command and control the software or even remotely disable the software if it seems to be working on the "wrong machine". In such an environment, network anonymity is completely compromised in the name of the often cited justification of piracy control. It has been argued that in cyberspace, the right to read anonymously that is protected in real space would be totally lost by copyright management systems and fee-based approaches to online activities.

What is often missing in the data about network anonymity is its advantages, as Froomkin [38] suggests. Important for considerations of free speech and democracy, anonymity may be the only way for ordinary individuals to protect themselves from governments' and private corporations' active use and profiling of their personal information in the networked environment [38]. Under the current conditions, the only way for network users to be ensured a minimum amount of privacy on the internet would be to conceal their identity or give a false one. Concealing an individual's information has been discussed, as well as practised and allowed, relatively more than disguising his or her identity. But if individuals do not want to identify themselves on the network while still being free to pursue all their activities, a logically possible solution is to provide false information. Concealing one's identity on the internet can be achieved by providing incorrect registration information or using a false identity. Many people do conceal their identity and many commercial books have been published on how to conceal identity on the internet. To have a right to protect themselves from revealing their personal information, consumers should be assisted by the right to lie. But will this right to lie be acknowledged by society or the law? Opinions vary, but those with authority and commercial power tend to say no at present. A number of statutory and regulatory restrictions on anonymous or pseudonymous communication in the United States exist and the constitutional protection of anonymous or pseudonymous communication is not clear, especially in non-political speech [39]. The difficulty and costs of concealing and disguising one's identity on the network also surpass the legal realm. ISPs and websites require correct registration information and if registrants or users are found to have provided a false identity or information, they are at a clear legal, social and cultural disadvantage when damages or disputes occur. Because of these disadvantages resulting from providing false personal information, a right to conceal and disguise one's identity is not yet widely recognized in a practical sense on the network. This may pose a serious risk to individual privacy because it might be the most effective and sometimes the only practically available way of ensuring privacy and anonymity on the network.

The ways in which people interact with the information environment are changing. The development of telecommunications technology and its convergence with computer technology has generated dramatic changes in the ways in which information can be collected and managed. Understanding the changes in the information environment and what it means to people's lives and experiences is critical in formulating a new conception of privacy as a changed social condition and proceeding with policymaking endeavors. In the current technological and regulatory scheme, individual privacy in terms of anonymity is less protected on the Internet than in real space. For example, in real space, people usually have a right not to be listed in the telephone directory or to read without always revealing their identity. But on the network, anonymity cannot be ensured without a practical option to disguise user identity and conceal personal information. In addition, given the voluntary nature of revealing and providing personal information, to apply traditional policy measures that attempt to "provide" privacy "for" individuals by limiting identifiable data users' information activities to the network environment is ineffective and futile. Users' self-solutions, enabled by their right to secrecy and deception on the network, are a logical and practical approach to ensure the least amount of network anonymity and privacy needed for personal autonomy. The most pertinent method to achieve this purpose seems to be providing individual network users with some right to engage in Internet activities without being visibly identified and allowing for an active search for network anonymity both legally and technically. Therefore, policy measures for network privacy should focus on ensuring individual users' searches for anonymity by recognizing the right to be silent about their identities and the right to disguise their identities rather than providing restrictions on easily identifiable external forces and institutions.

It is not difficult to imagine that the solution suggested here would face challenge and opposition. However, many of the concerns are based on social and cultural reflections rather than on legal or logical foundations. Our society seems to favour disclosure over secrecy and speech over silence. The sentiment that concealing data is a bad thing and more than less information is better seems to be a deeply-held social value. Therefore, privacy as a tool to give the right to prevent personal information-sharing may have a natural and inherent disadvantage that can be compared to the obvious distinction between "sunlight" and "shadow". A close review of society's customs and practices suggests that secrets and lies are essential elements of society's function. Every society tolerates, and even respects, some forms of untruth. People tell lies about themselves and their motives and actions, a reality reflected in many cases of secrecy exercised in government and the news media. Wikileaks lists the occasions of government secrecy, including military relations, diplomacy, juvenile proceedings and the identity of information sources, as examples of such sanctioned secrecy. There are many circumstances in which attaining knowledge is considered undesirable and these circumstances are supported by various justifications such as national interest and protection from foreign entities. Ironically, in the case of undercover operations, deception is used legitimately to uncover other deception and secrets. Therefore, deception can be good or bad, much as we distinguish between white and black lies, or between small and big lies. The basis for such distinctions, in the case of government secrets and undercover operations, is that when the benefits outweigh potential harm and risk, secrecy and deception seem to be justified. Also, good purpose and good intention seem to be other justifications for this kind of deception. Thus, the clearly negative connotations associated with deception, disguise, dishonesty and concealment may have a rather relative meaning when applied to specific circumstances. Concealing and deceiving identity to gain anonymity on the current network environment is a tool for protection from unknown harm or invasion and for the maintenance of individual control over private space. This kind of "defensive lying" has clear benefits and a positive purpose and often is permitted in society. It is argued here that, similarly, activities with the purpose of gaining anonymity on the network deserve social permission.

Furthermore, transparency and certainty are always sought by those who want order and discipline in a society. There is a close connection between deceit and power, as deception is often used by people to seek power or avoid its exertion on them. Lies may function to protect the weak from the strong. In that sense, the right to conceal and disguise one's identity on the network is a very important tool to influence the distribution of social and political power. In the interactive network, anonymity is the most important element for individuals to have a mechanism of counterbalance against powerful invaders and unknown risks. Network anonymity works as a critical device for mitigating power relations. Therefore, the right to actively seek one's anonymity so as not to be easily identified, rather than the right to be left alone, deserves to be the centre of the privacy concept on the network. The question that confronts us is this: are we ready and willing to allow a right to lie for the sake of a right to privacy? In this new networked environment, perhaps we cannot have one without the other. Are we willing to sacrifice transparency and bureaucratic efficiency for the sake of network privacy? In the networked environment, we cannot have both. Thus, it would be futile to discuss technical and social methods to achieve privacy when we have not decided whether we are ready to change our fundamental moral concept to achieve it. It is one thing to claim that privacy is an important right, but it is quite another to actually sacrifice other important values for it. Only after we answer these questions can we approach the greater issue of privacy and self-autonomy, which has significant financial, social and human consequences for the future.

In summary, worrying about their privacy and anonymity and taking measures to protect them is a right of the users of network communication although it is sometimes negotiable. At the 2000 RSA Security Conference, privacy law expert Stewart Baker observed that there are four basic rules of privacy and anonymity opinion and behavior today:

- Each individual firmly believes that he or she has a right to complete anonymity in all situations.

- Each individual also firmly believes that other people do not have that right. Messages or letters from anonymous callers are always seen as suspicious, if not outright threatening. Individuals are also concerned that while they would never do so, others might employ anonymity to commit crimes.

- If an individual chooses to give up some private personal information, that information cannot be recovered.

- Most individuals choose to give up private information in exchange for trivial things, such as access to a web site or to register a new purchase.

While disheartening, these attitudes do not constitute a reason to abandon privacy and anonymity research. Rather, it is due to the lack of good alternatives that these rules have evolved.

1.2   When We Need to Be Anonymous

Usage of Tor, one of the most famous anonymous networks, is investigated and analysed in [23]. The investigation provides a deep analysis of the Tor network in the wild, by setting several exit nodes and distributing them worldwide. Taking special cautionary measures to comply with the legal and ethical aspects of users' privacy, it performed an analysis of the application usage of the Tor network through a deep packet inspection (as opposite to a simple port-based classification), and show that most of the traffic exchanged through Tor is undesirable BitTorrent traffic. The study also observed an important fraction of "unknown" traffic. It reveals that the vast majority of this traffic is actually encrypted BitTorrent traffic. The analysis shows then that the BitTorrent traffic on top of Tor accounts for much more traffic size than commonly believed. It also studied the HTTP and BitTorrent usage over Tor and compared Tor user behaviors to those of typical Internet users.

As explained in [23] and will be detailed later, Tor is a circuit-based low-latency anonymous communication service. Its main design goals are to prevent attackers from linking communication partners and from linking multiple communications to or from a single user. Tor relies on a distributed overlay network and onion routing to anonymize TCP-based applications like web browsing, secure shell, or peer-to-peer communications. When a client wants to communicate with a server via Tor, he selects n nodes of the Tor system and builds a circuit using those selected nodes. Messages are then encrypted n times using the following onion encryption scheme: messages are first encrypted with the key shared with the last node (called the exit node of the circuit) and from $node_{n-1}$ to $node1_n$. As a result of this onion routing, each intermediate node only knows its predecessor and successor, but no other nodes of the circuit. In addition, the onion encryption ensures that only the last node is able to recover the original message. A Tor client typically uses multiple simultaneous circuits. As a result, all the streams of a user are multiplexed over these circuits. For example, a BitTorrent user can use one of the circuits for his connections to the tracker and other circuits for his connections to the peers. Finally, some ISP may block access to Tor network by filtering the IP addresses of Tor nodes. To circumvent this censorship, the Tor project has created the so-called bridges. These are new types of Tor routers that are not listed in the main Tor directory, and hence cannot be blocked. Tor restricts access to this list and gives a small subset (3 bridges IP addresses) per unique requester IP for a fixed period of time.

Tor has gained in popularity through the years, and its related traffic has certainly evolved. So it is interesting to analyse its traffic through deep packet inspection, and not through a simple port-based classification. This provides more accurate classification of the traffic that is exchanged through the Tor network. In this way, a clear picture can be obtained about what applications are typically used on top of Tor. The statistics in [23] show that among all the Tor traffic, HTTP takes 34.3%, BitTorrent takes 25.3%, SSL takes 1%, other P2P/file-sharing than BitTorrent take 0.26%, insecure services like ftp, telnet and email take 1.3%, instant massaging takes 1.2%, other recognised protocols take 3.4%, and 29% packets are not recognised.

It is noticed in [23] that a significant part of the traffic is still unclassified. It represents more than 25% of the entire volume. This behavior suggests that such traffic likely belongs to any of the P2P protocols. To verify this, Chaabouni analyzed the distribution of destination ports for those unclassified connections. They observed that destination ports were uniformly distributed, which can lead to a belief that such traffic is BitTorrent traffic. In fact, to avoid port-based detection, BitTorrent clients choose a random port at installation time. This results in uniformly distributed ports. Although these proofs suggest BitTorrent to be responsible for this traffic, the analysis does not recognize it. This is most likely because this traffic is encrypted and thus unrecognizable. A step further is then to compute the entropy of sample data. The computed high entropy value confirmed that this data is either encrypted or compressed.

So most traffic in anonymous communciation on Tor networks belongs to BitTorrent. A torrent is a set of peers sharing the same content. To join a torrent, a user sends an announce message to the tracker that maintains the list of all peers in that torrent. The announcement is an HTTP GET message containing the identifier of the requested torrent. Such identifier is known as the *infohash* of the torrent and is unique. Once the tracker receives the announce message for a specific torrent identified by the infohash, it selects a random subset of peers in that torrent and returns the endpoints (the IP and port of a peer) of those peers. Then, the user establishes a TCP connection and sends a handshake message to each peer. Finally, popular BitTorrent clients, e.g., νTorrent and Vuze, configure SOCKS proxies and give the option to use the proxies for connections to the tracker, to the peers, or both. Therefore, a BitTorrent client can use Tor, configuring the Tor interface as a SOCKS proxy, for communication to the tracker or the peers independently. The user can then decide to connect to the tracker via Tor, but have a direct connection to peers in order not to have performance penalty.

HTTP protocols take a large part of the anonymous traffic as well. The analysis in [23] shows that the HTTP protocol carries a wide spectrum of data going from simple text to rich media such as images and video. Furthermore, a large variety of applications are embedded into browsers to enrich the end user environment. Analyzing this data allows the readers to have a more comprehensive view of how the web is used on top of Tor. More precisely, among all the packets transported on Tor networks, 31.7% are for pictures, 27.9% are for text/html, 18% are for applications,

11.1% are for flashes, and 8.9% are for other services. The most significant content is, as expected, images and text/html. Surprisingly, applications (e.g., rar and zip) content represents a significant proportion of the observed traffic. In addition, it is noticed that 6% of the entire traffic is originating from Direct Download Link (DDL). This can be explained by the fact that some users may have switched from P2P networks known to be heavily monitored to DDL-based content, much harder to control. This behaviour switching has already been noticed in residential broadband Internet. On the other hand, flash and video usage representing 13.5% of the observed content, shows that the latency induced by the Tor relaying is not an actual brake for browsing Web 2.0.

An interesting question is which webs are most frequently visited through Tor. The analysis in [23] shows that 14.45% are search engines or portals, 11.50% are pornography webs, 11.45% are computers/Internet webs, 9.52% are social networking webs, 2.26% are blogs/web communication sites, 1.82% are streaming-media/MP3 webs, 1.66% are webs providing software downloading, 0.3% are hacking webs, 0.18% are political webs, 0.15% are illegal/questionable webs, and 0.06% are illegal-drug webs. Another interesting question is who uses Tor. The analysis in [23] shows that more than 70% of the clients were originating from only 10 countries. Germany and U.S represent more than a quarter of the clients. Such a high ratio may be explained by Internet demographics (especially the high Internet penetration in these countries) on one hand, and also by the increase and strengthening of anti-piracy and copyright laws during the past few years. The concentration of Tor clients among this small subset of countries and in particular, the absence of politically-sensitive countries among the top countries of the observed clients coupled with the announcements of the Tor project that bridges are still in their infancy and not yet often used by clients may be good indicators of the common usage of Tor. Eastern European nations (Poland, Romania and Russia) represent nearly 20% of the Tor clients and Chinese clients correspond to 5.8% of overall clients.

1.3   The Current Situation and Where We Start

In practice, achieving anonymity in network communication is not an easy task. According to [66], the challenge of private information may be simply stated: you can restrict it totally or you give it all:

- If privacy was guaranteed then every individual would have the capability to act anonymously in the virtual world. Therefore, the individuals could use the great power of the information processing systems for their own benefits. The danger here is that everyone, including criminals and terrorists, could use that power for their activities.

- If law enforcement agencies are given the capabilities to undo anonymity, then they can undo it for all people and have this great power to observe everyone in greatest detail.

- There are also "complete non-anonymity" proponents. In his "Transparent Society" [18], Brin imagines a world in which all aspects of everyone's public life are subject to viewing by web cameras. He then proposed two variants: one with the government and law enforcement being the only ones who can view the images from the omnipresent cameras, and another where everyone, individuals as well as government, will have full, immediate access to any of the images via the Internet.

There may be no general solution to this all-or-nothing problem that satisfies everyone. Even so, we should begin to address this problem now. We suggest that initially focusing on application-specific anonymity techniques may help. For instance, not all people should have the same ability to use anonymity techniques, just as not all people have access to prescription drugs (restriction to some persons). Similarly, absolute anonymity should be guaranteed in electronic elections (restriction of application). Thus, we have the real challenge of how to achieve practical privacy through anonymity, i.e., while maintaining acceptable network performance. The rest of this chapter will address this technical question and will present the important results of the last twenty-plus years of research in this area.

The first attempt was made by Pfitzmann, whose definition and classification of privacy and anonymity from a technical angle in German were translated by Kesdogana and Palme [66] as follows.

- Anonymity is the state of being not identifiable within a set of subjects, known as the anonymity set. Anonymity in communications can be further distinguished as sender and recipient anonymity.

- Unobservability is the state of an item of interest being indistinguishable from any other item of interest.

- Unlinkability of two or more items or actions means that these items are no more and no less related than they were previously (attacker gains no information).

Unobservability can be reduced to a set of data items, senders or receivers. For example, a concrete requirement for messages is that each message cannot be linked to any potential sender or receiver from the set. At a higher level, relationship unobservability requires that it is not discernable whether anything is sent from a set of potential senders to a set of potential recipients. A definition of anonymity is incomplete if an attacker model (opponent model) is not specified. The attacker model describes the demands placed on the anonymity techniques and is also for the evaluation and comparison of proposed solutions. In general, a direct relation exists between the strength of the attacker model and the quality of the protection provided by a given solution. To guarantee formal and reliable anonymity, it is needed to assume that anonymity is to be provided in the presence of a powerful attacker. Thus, the capabilities of an attacker A may vary. For the sake of simplicity, it is assumed here that the cryptography used is unbreakable. However, it is good to keep in mind that it is inappropriate to provide or demand more anonymity protection than the underlying cryptography can provide. Attackers may be classified as follows according to [66].

A1 Passive attacker. Attacker can observe all communication links.

A2 Passive attacker with sending capabilities. The A2 attacker is not much stronger than A1, yet the A2 attacker poses a bigger threat than A3 because it is by definition undetectable. Attacker may take part in the anonymity technique (i.e., attacker can send messages) if participation has not been explicitly forbidden for him.

A3 Active attacker. Attacker can control all communication links, switches, etc. and can attack all messages with delete, replay, and send, or delay actions.

By choosing the powerful attacker model it follows that a single transmission by a single person can be neither anonymous nor unobservable. The omnipresent attacker can observe the sender of a message (the sending act) and follow the message to the receiver, thereby detecting the communication relation without needing to read the content of the message. Hence, it is straightforward to notice that anonymity techniques require additional traffic, called cover traffic. Having the additional traffic, it is feasible to employ an embedding function for the subject traffic in order to confuse the adversary and conceal the particular sender, recipient, and their communication relationship. The following results are needed.

- Group function (cover traffic). Since single transmissions are observable in the network, additional traffic is organized by the group function. It is essential that the attacker not be able to gain control over this additional traffic.

- Embedding function. The traffic generated by a particular user must be efficiently and untraceably embedded into the cover traffic.

If the attacker can control the cover traffic, all anonymity is lost. To avoid this and other attacks wherein the attacker exerts some control over the cover traffic, the CUVE requirements must be met as explained in [99].

- Completeness. All users can verify that their messages have been correctly sent, received, or transmitted.

- Un-reusability. Within any given session, 55A is the transmission of a packet using an embedding function and sent in the presence of cover traffic. No user can participate more than an allowed number of times.

- Verifiability. An adversary cannot change another user's message without being discovered by the system.

- Eligibility. Only authorized users can participate in a given session.

The embedding function has to be applied in an environment. The only exception to this statement is in the case of recipient anonymity for broadcasted messages. where there is no room for any attackers. This simplifying assumption is needed in order to focus only on the anonymity techniques. This is similar to the case of encryption, wherein the application of the encryption algorithm has to be performed in a trusted environment. Otherwise, security cannot be guaranteed, since the attacker will have full knowledge of the process. However, unlike encryption, the users depend on other assumptions. In general, encryption is a unilateral function and anonymity a multilateral function, i.e., a user can encrypt his electronic diary on his machine but to act anonymously he always needs additional users (due to the requirement of cover traffic). Thus, while the security point of view recommends having the embedding function applied only within the trusted domains of the sender and receiver (the end-to-end solution), from a practical point of view it may be preferable for the group function to use central Trusted Third Parties (TTPs).

The desired goal of anonymity is only achievable if at least two honest participants work together. In general, it is always appropriate to assume that $n > 1$ users participate in the application of a given anonymity technique. A typical circumstance is where the network itself is unsecure and the trusted domains of the users are secure. TTPs sit between these two trusted end points and must fulfill some special trust requirements:

- A single point of outside trust should be avoided; the trust has to be distributed equally over all used N TTPs.

- TTPs should be as transparent to the user as possible, i.e., the correct functionality of the environment should be controlled by the user.

- TTPs should be independently designed and produced and have independent operators.

If $(n - 1)$ of the users providing the cover traffic are dishonest, then obviously the technique cannot provide any protection. Many of the previous works in anonymity neglect to consider the corrupt user, and make the assumption that all participating users are honest. Certainly in open environments like the Internet, the attacker could be an alliance of $(n - 1)$ dishonest persons. Unfortunately, there is no technical means to test the honesty of people and, thus, no way of providing perfect protection. Note that using one-time pad cryptography can provide perfect security in the technical sense.

Anonymity protocols belong to the family of group communication protocols. Typically, networks (e.g., the Internet) are not designed to handle the huge amount of traffic produced by these protocols. In general, the situation is even worse for anonymity techniques since they depend upon dummy messages. To evaluate the performance of anonymity techniques, it may be necessary to abstract from a concrete network structure and consider it as a black box. In this network model, it is appropriate to assume that the cost of sending a message without an anonymity-providing technique is one and the transmission time is also one.

Since anonymity techniques need cover traffic in order to provide unobservable communication, it is important to maximize the number of real messages sent in a session. Consider a technique with a group function that handles $n > 1$ messages from n distinct users. Suppose k of the messages are real and m are dummy ($m = n - k$). With anonymity, something more (bits or energy) has to be provided to meet the goal. So system effectiveness can be defined as k/n. It is always less than 1, since there cannot be more real messages sent than all of the messages sent. If the message is sent via several TTPs, then these additional reroutings count as re-sending all of the messages again.

Clearly, it is desirable to have an anonymity technique with high system effectiveness approximately equal to one. Assuming that such a technique exists, it would mean that there exists n people who want to send n real messages. Since there are not always n people who want to send real messages within a given time period, the technique has to wait for enough real messages before beginning. The waiting time interval could be chosen with high probability that n people will want to send something. Thus, the people may have to wait until the specified time interval has elapsed. This time cost can be measured as time efficiency t. Additionally, if the message is sent over several TTPs, that time has to be counted as well.

Chapter 2

Mix Networks

Mix networks are anonymous communication channels widely employed in popular private network applications like e-voting [63, 70, 35] and e-auctions [92]. They consist of multiple routing nodes that shuffle a batch of encrypted messages in turn. The shuffling operation of each routing node re-orders (using a random permutation) and randomizes (e.g. re-encrypts) the encrypted messages. The output of every routing node is shuffled by the next routing node. In this way, the encrypted messages are repeatedly shuffled in succession by all the routing nodes in the mix network. If at least one routing node conceals this permutation, the repeatedly shuffled encrypted messages cannot be traced. The most popular application of mix network is electronic voting, which employs a mix network to shuffle sealed votes before they are opened.

Security of a mix network depends on the underlying shuffling operations. To convincingly show that a mix network works properly, each routing node in it needs to publicly prove that it does not deviate from the shuffling protocol. This is a basic security requirement for shuffling. When it is not satisfied, the mix network may go wrong. Of course, each routing node cannot reveal its permutation in the proof of validity of shuffling. Proof and verification of validity of shuffling create the bottleneck of computation in a mix network. High cost for validity verification is not only a heavy burden for the users and routing nodes, but also intolerable for an observer who is interested to check that the mix network works well.

In this chapter, mix networks are introduced and the current mix networks are classified. As proof and verification of validity of shuffling are the most important and costly operations in mix networks, the first step to study mix network in this chapter is to classify it according to its verification operations into two categories: mix network with general verification and mix network with separate verification. Then various methods to prove and verify validity of shuffling efficiently are discussed in both categories. When the number of shuffled messages is very large and the overhead is very heavy, messages are

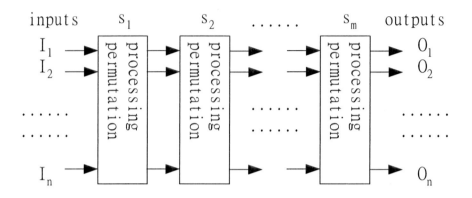

Figure 2.1: Mix Network

grouped and then shuffling is carried out in the groups such that each instance of shuffling is not too costly. Special techniques are introduced to improve efficiency in the grouped shuffling mechanism. Finally, the mix network schemes are surveyed and analysed such that their concerns in security and efficiency are addressed and their inappropriately functioning security and efficiency properties are corrected. As a result security properties and efficiency of the existing mix network schemes are precisely assessed and their application in practice can be realistic.

2.1   Definition of Mix Network

The first mix network scheme was proposed by Chaum [25] to implement anonymous email. After that, various mix networks have been proposed. Although they are differently designed, they share some common properties. In a mix network, there are several servers. A number of users of the mix network submit their inputs anonymously. Each of them submits an encrypted input to the mix network. One by one, those servers shuffle the inputs. The shuffling operation of each server on its inputs includes two steps. The first step is to process the inputs, which may use re-encryption or partial decryption, which will be detailed in Section 2.2. The second step is to reorder the processed ciphertexts. Finally, after the repeatedly shuffled ciphertexts are completely decrypted a set of outputs unlinkable to the users is produced, which forms a permutation of the plaintexts of the inputs. A typical mix network is illustrated in Figure 2.1. Usually, the following five properties must be satisfied in a mix network.

1. Correctness: if all the participants are honest and do not deviate from the mix network protocol, the outputs must be a permutation of the plaintexts of the inputs.

2. Privacy: if at least one server conceals his shuffling, the permutation between the inputs and the outputs is unknown, so that the users cannot be linked to their outputs.

3. Public verifiability: honesty of the participants can be verified publicly.

4. Soundness: passing the public verification guarantees that the output is a permutation of the plaintexts of the inputs.

5. Robustness: the mix network can still work properly in abnormal situations, such as failure of one or more servers.

2.2 Classification of Mix Networks

Numerous mix network schemes have been proposed so far. Performance, efficiency and application areas vary. Different standards can be employed to classify them.

2.2.1 Decryption Chain or Re-encryption

It is well known that mix networks can be classified into those employing decryption chain and those employing re-encryption according to the way each server shuffles its inputs [48]. In a DMN (decryption chain mix network), the shuffling of a server is composed of decryption and permutation. Its characterisation is as follows.

- Each input is encrypted with every server's public key in sequence.

- Each server removes one layer of encryption on all his inputs by decrypting them using his private key. After that the system permutes them to its outputs.

DMN is illustrated in Figure 2.2.

In a RMN (re-encryption mix network), the shuffling of a server is composed of re-encryption and permutation. Its characterisation is as follows.

- Each input is encrypted only once with a public encryption key while the corresponding private key is shared by several decrypting authorities.

- Each server re-encrypts all its inputs. After that it permutes them to its outputs.

- In the end, the decrypting authorities (e.g., may be the servers) cooperate to decrypt the final encrypted outputs.

RMN is illustrated in Figure 2.3

A widely recognized drawback of DMN is lack of robustness. If a server refuses to decrypt its inputs properly, the whole mix network fails and must be

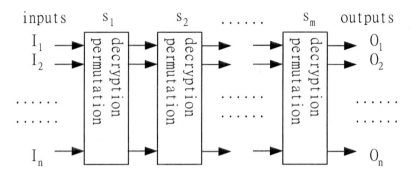

Figure 2.2: Decryption-chain Mix Network

re-run. A method to overcome this problem is to share every server's private key in a threshold way among the other servers. So when a server fails to decrypt its inputs correctly, a number of other servers over the threshold can cooperate to perform the decryption. This method is denoted as PKS (private key sharing). However, this countermeasure sacrifices some privacy as a collusion involving a number of servers over the threshold can breach privacy of the mix network. Therefore, robustness is repaired at the cost that privacy is weakened.

A not fully realized drawback of DMN is the expansion of ciphertext length as a few layers of encryption are exerted on every input to the mix network. Park et al. [84] proposed a special method to apply El Gamal encryption to multi-layer encryption, such that the length of the ciphertext does not increase. However, in their scheme after each server performs its decryption, it has to re-encrypt each of its outputs to keep privacy. Therefore, decryption chain and re-encryption must both be applied. This method is not worthwhile as it loses the advantages of RMN by adding decryption and keeps all disadvantages of RMN. A pure RMN can do better.

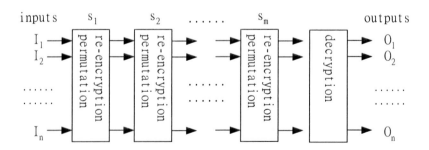

Figure 2.3: Re-encryption Mix Network

The only circumstance where DMN is necessary is when hybrid encryption is applied to shuffle long messages efficiently [81, 62]. As the inputs are encrypted actually with symmetric encryption algorithms, which are not randomised and thus do not support re-encryption, decryption chain must be employed.

Ogata et al. [80], introduced a basic structure for re-encryption mix networks, which was further developed in many later papers. Suppose the El Gamal encryption scheme is employed with private key x and public key $(g, y = g^x)$. Several decrypting authorities share x by t-out-of-m threshold verifiable secret sharing. The m servers A_j for $j = 1, 2, \ldots, m$ form a mix network to shuffle n encrypted inputs c_i for $i = 1, 2, \ldots, n$. Inputs to A_j are $c_{j-1,i}$ for $i = 1, 2, \ldots, n$ while $c_{0,i} = c_i$ for $i = 1, 2, \ldots, n$. Outputs of A_j are $c_{j,i}$ for $i = 1, 2, \ldots, n$. On server A_j, input $c_{j-1,i} = (a_{j-1,i}, b_{j-1,i})$ is permuted to $c_{j,\pi_j(i)} = (a_{j,\pi_j(i)}, b_{j,\pi_j(i)}) = (g^{r_{j,i}} a_{j-1,i}, y^{r_{j,i}} b_{j-1,i})$ where $r_{j,i}$ is randomly chosen and π_j is a secret random permutation from $\{1, 2, \ldots, n\}$ to $\{1, 2, \ldots, n\}$. The outputs of the mix network are $c'_i = c_{m,i}$ for $i = 1, 2, \ldots, n$. The shuffling from n inputs to n outputs on every server is denoted as $PN(n)$, correctness of which must be verified. Finally, the decrypting authorities (e.g., the servers themselves) cooperate to decrypt c'_i for $i = 1, 2, \ldots, n$.

2.2.2 General or Separate Verification

According to how correctness is verified, mix networks can be classified into GMN (general verification) and SMN (separate verification).

GMN does not provide a verification of correct shuffling by each server separately. Instead, correctness of the shuffling by the whole mix network is verified after the outputs are produced in plaintext. GMN [25, 84, 48, 92] is illustrated in Figure 2.4.

An advantage of GMN is that schemes in this category are usually very efficient as only one final verification for shuffling validity is needed. A key

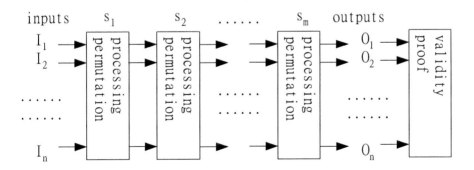

Figure 2.4: General Verification Mix Network

drawback of this category is that a malicious server and its invalid shuffling cannot be found instantly. This leads to the following problems.

1. The shuffling of the mix network goes on after a malicious server does his shuffling incorrectly. Time and resources are wasted unnecessarily.

2. A costly function must be employed to identify the cheating server when the shuffling is found to be invalid.

3. In most GMN schemes, it is suggested that a SMN is employed to perform the mixing again if incorrect shuffling is found in GMN. That means GMN cannot exist independently without support from SMN always ready.

4. As correctness of the mix network must be publicly verifiable, some outputs are revealed in plaintext when the mix network fails due to invalid shuffling by a malicious server. Revealing of the outputs in this case results in the following concerns.

   • As some outputs are revealed, the users must not regenerate their inputs in the following re-mixing. For example, if the mix network is used to implement a selection, re-voting when some votes are revealed is not fair as the voters may be affected by others' selections. That means DMN without PKS cannot be used.

   • The mix network may be vulnerable to certain types of attacks as pointed out in [48]. In these attacks, some server(s) (e.g., the first server) may shuffle a certain user's input incorrectly in a special way (e.g., adding a value to it). In this way the user's output can be traced as an incorrectly shuffled output is distinguishable from the correctly shuffled outputs and is in plaintext. The attacker can recover the user's original input in plaintext from the identified incorrect output by undoing his change on the input. Additional functions must be applied to overcome these attacks. For example, double encryption is applied in [48] as a countermeasure.

In SMN, each server proves that his shuffling is correct. Whenever incorrect shuffling is performed, it is detected and the mixing stops instantly. Therefore no plaintext is obtained if the mixing is not correct. SMN is illustrated in Figure 2.5 The most serious problem in this approach is inefficiency. Some schemes use a partial proof of correctness on each server to improve efficiency [60, 15]. However, that means some correctness is only achieved with a probability and privacy is weakened (in [60] the probability is not big enough for many applications and in [15], privacy is weakened to a dangerous level if correctness is strong enough for most applications). Many other mechanisms are applied to various mix network schemes [5, 6, 42, 74, 75, 52, 93, 90, 41, 51, 50, 86] to improve efficiency of complete

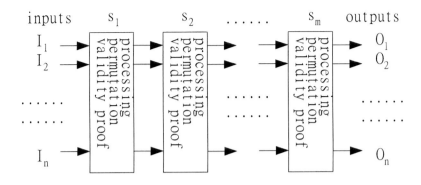

Figure 2.5: Separate Verification Mix Network

proof of correctness in SMN. Abe [5, 6] uses several switching gates to construct the mix network, so that a costly verification of the shuffling by a server can be replaced by verification of validity of each of the server's gates. In [42, 41] verification of a special property of a matrix is employed to verify validity of shuffling. Neff [74, 75] applies *zero knowledge proof of equality of products of exponents* to verify correct shuffling by every server. The most efficient SMN mix network schemes with complete proof of correctness are [52, 93, 90, 51, 50, 86]. They achieve high efficiency, strong correctness and acceptable privacy compared to others in this category.

There are very few (actually only one is known so far [81]) mix networks without any verification of correctness of the servers' operations. In [81] the shuffling is correct if most servers are trusted to be honest. This type is denoted as NMN (non-verified mix network).

2.2.3 Tag Attached to Input

In most mix networks, the function verifying the shuffling of a server or a group of servers (all the servers in GMN) only take the inputs (ciphertexts of the shuffled messages) and outputs (re-encryption or decryption of the inputs) of the server(s) as its inputs. This type of mix network is denoted as WTMN (without a tag).

In some mix networks, a special tag is attached to the messages or inputs and acts as an input to the verification function. A tag to a message or input can only be produced by its owning user and may be a signature [25, 84] or a MAC [62]. This type of mix network is denoted as TMN (with tag). While the tags may be helpful for efficient verification of shuffling validity, there are two concerns in TMN.

1. Distribution of the keys for signature or MAC causes additional computation and communication.

Table 2.1: Classification of mix networks

	GMN	SMN	NMN
DMN	*[25]* *[84]*	*[62]*	[81]
RMN	*[48]* [92]	[60] [15] [80] [96] [5, 6] [42, 41] [74, 75] [52, 51] [93] [50] [90, 86]	

2. A user can change its message after the shuffling starts. With conspiracy of some server, this change cannot be detected. This is especially dangerous when the mix network is used in auction. To solve this problem, one more round of shuffling of the commitments of the messages is needed.

2.2.4   Summary

The classification is summarized in Table 2.1 where italic means TMN. From the analysis and this table, the following conclusions can be drawn.

1. Re-encryption mix networks are more popular and suitable to more applications.

2. Most mix networks apply separate verification as it achieves the desired properties better.

3. Efficiency improvement in SMN is still needed in large-scale applications.

4. Mix networks employing general verification may be suitable for some special applications because of their high efficiency, although incorrect shuffling may cause some trouble.

2.3   Efficient and Secure GMN: a Simple and Efficient Solution

In some applications, the mix network employed to implement the anonymous channel must be very efficient, so a mix network employing general verification of shuffling validity should be chosen. Among the mix network schemes in this category, Chaum's mix network [25] was the original scheme, which was then improved by Park et al. [84]. In [48], each encrypted input to the mix network is attached with its hash function. Each server has to re-encrypt and permute the inputs together with the attachments. Each server does not need to prove that its shuffling is correct; instead it proves the product of the attachments does not change after shuffling. This is a very efficient proof (costing $O(1)$ exponentiations) but not sufficient for the verification of validity of shuffling. Actually, it is also proved in [48] that the product of the inputs does not change. However this extra proof is meaningless as even with it the validity of shuffling is not guaranteed without a final general verification. After all the inputs and their attachments are shuffled and decrypted to plaintext, a final check verifies that each output attachment is really the hash function of the corresponding output. Golle et al. [48] were aware that an attack by a malicious server against the privacy of a user is possible. The server can change two or more users' inputs, so that the hash relation between the input and attachment becomes incorrect for those users while the product of the inputs and attachments is not changed. The invalidity of shuffling can be found in the final verification and the cheating server can be identified. But the attacked user's output can be traced as it is incorrectly shuffled and distinguishable from other outputs. In other words, the malicious user breaks the attacked user's privacy at the cost of being identified as a cheater. To overcome this attack, Golle et al. employ double-encryption in their mix network. When the final verification is performed, only one layer of encryption is removed. If incorrect shuffling is found, the second layer of encryption is not removed and a SMN is employed to perform the mixing again. Correctness of this mix network is dependent on an unusual assumption: if $H()$ is a one-way and collision-resistant hash function, it is infeasible to find $\prod_{i=1}^{n} H(x_i) = \prod_{i=1}^{n} H(y_i)$ where $\{x_i | i = 1, 2, \ldots, n\} \neq \{y_i | i = 1, 2, \ldots, n\}$. Moreover, a flaw in privacy was found in [48] by Abe and Imai in [8].

Park et al. [84] proposed a decryption-chain mix network that employs two rounds of shuffling. In the first round, the users choose their short-term private keys and public keys and send the short-term public keys to be shuffled. The servers do not prove correctness of their shuffling in the first round. At the end of the first round, each user checks that his short-term public key is among the published results of the first round. Any user can protest if the check fails. In the second round, the users' inputs signed by their short-term private keys are shuffled and the outputs are published in plaintext. Again the servers do not prove correctness of their shuffling, which can be verified by anyone using signature verification. If any output cannot be verified to be correctly signed with one public key published in the first round, the second round of shuffling is known to be wrong. As in [48], revealing of outputs in plaintext while the shuffling is not correct is a concern. In this scheme, a cut-and-choose mechanism is used to divide every input into several pieces, which are shuffled in the second round. In the end, all pieces of the output are decrypted and verified one by one and the decryption stops whenever the verification fails. The probability that outputs are revealed when a malicious server performs an invalid shuffling is low. As mentioned in Section 2.2, a decryption chain mix network cannot achieve a good trade-off between robustness and strong privacy, so a re-encryption mix network is preferred in practice.

Both schemes in [84] and [48] are efficient although an unproved assumption is used in [48] and cut-and-choose causes more computational cost in [84]. However, neither scheme supports unconditional fairness in practical applications like e-auction. In an auction scheme, the users are bidders and they submit their bids as the inputs. The auctioneer can act as the server in the mix network and share the decryption key using a threshold secret sharing. The auctioneers can conspire with a bidder. The bidder waits for other bidders to bid and the auctioneers decrypt the submitted bids. After knowing the other bids from the colluding auctioneers, the colluding bidder chooses his own bid (e.g., just a little higher than the other bids). That means confidentiality and fairness of the auction depend on the auctioneers. Unlike bid privacy, confidentiality and fairness are compulsory properties and should be achieved without trust. The two current GMNs are not suitable for auction applications.

2.3.1   The GMN in [92]

A mix network [92] is proposed to optimise the previous GMN schemes [84, 48]. It is composed of two rounds. Each user commits to his inputs first and the commitments are mixed in the first round. Any user can easily verify that his commitment is shuffled correctly or protest if the verification fails. Any protest can be publicly verified and the malicious server can be identified and removed. The inputs are mixed in the second round. After the outputs are produced, they can be verified publicly against the commitments published in the first round. Both decryption chain and re-encryption can be applied to implement the shuffling. In the following, the protocol is described in detail in the case of shuffling by re-encryption. The employed encryption algorithm can be any semantically secure encryption algorithm like El Gamal or Paillier.

1. The private key of the encryption function is shared among some decryption authorities.

2. Each user P_i chooses an input b_i and commits to it as $c_i = H(b_i, v_i)$ where $H()$ is a one-way and collision-resistant hash function and v_i is a random integer.

3. Commitments c_i for $i = 1, 2, \ldots, n$ are encrypted to e_i for $i = 1, 2, \ldots, n$, which are signed by the corresponding users and submitted to the mix network.

4. Each server in the network re-encrypts and permutes e_i for $i = 1, 2, \ldots, n$ in sequence. The servers do not need to prove correctness of their shuffling.

5. Let e'_i for $i = 1, 2, \ldots, n$ denote the shuffled outputs of the last server. The decryption authorities cooperate to decrypt e'_i for $i = 1, 2, \ldots, n$ to c'_i for $i = 1, 2, \ldots, n$ and publish them.

6. Each user P_i verifies that his commitment c_i is among the published shuffled commitments. Any user can complain if he cannot find his commitment in the published outputs. Any dispute is solved as follows.

   (a) The protesting user P_i publishes e_i and his signature on e_i.

   (b) Each server (from the first one to the last one) has to prove his shuffling of e_i is correct by publishing his output for e_i and the random value used in the re-encryption. If any server has performed an incorrect shuffling, it will be discovered and the next step is skipped. Otherwise, some e'_j will be revealed, which is A_m's output for e_i.

   (c) Each server has to prove that it decrypted e'_j correctly using a proof of correct decryption. Any incorrect decryption can be found.

   (d) If any server fails to prove his innocence, he is removed (or replaced if necessary) and the mixing is performed again. If all the servers prove their innocence, the protesting user is identified as a cheater and removed.

7. The pair of input (b_i, v_i) is encrypted to the ciphertext pair $(e1_i, e2_i)$ and signed by P_i for $i = 1, 2, \ldots, n$.

8. The encrypted inputs $(e1_i, e2_i)$ for $i = 1, 2, \ldots, n$ are submitted to the servers that perform the second round of mixing to mix them. As in the first round, shuffling in the second round is also composed of re-encryption and permutation and not proved by the servers to be valid. Ciphertext pairs $(e1_i, e2_i)$ for $i = 1, 2, \ldots, n$ are shuffled to $(e1'_i, e2'_i)$ for $i = 1, 2, \ldots, n$.

9. The decryption authorities cooperate to decrypt the shuffled outputs $(e1'_i, e2'_i)$ for $i = 1, 2, \ldots, n$ and publish the result (b'_i, v'_i) for $i = 1, 2, \ldots, n$.

10. Anyone can publicly verify that every published output is correctly committed to a different commitment. If an output (b'_i, v'_i) of the second round cannot be matched to any published commitments c'_j for $j = 1, 2, \ldots, n$, the problem is solved as follows.

    (a) Each server has to prove that its decryption to (b'_i, v'_i) is correct using a proof of correct decryption (proof of equality of logarithms if El Gamal encryption is employed). If an incorrect decryption is found, the server performing it is identified as a cheater and the next step is skipped. Otherwise, $(e1'_j, e2'_j)$, the ciphertext corresponding to (b'_i, v'_i) is revealed.

(b) Each server (from the last one to the first one) has to prove its shuffling leading to $(e1'_j, e2'_j)$ is correct by publishing the input for $(e1'_j, e2'_j)$ and the random value used to re-encrypt the input to $(e1'_j, e2'_j)$. If any server has performed an incorrect shuffling, he will be discovered.

(c) If any server fails to prove innocence, it is removed (or replaced if necessary) and the mixing is performed again. If all the servers prove their innocence, the output in dispute has been traced back to an input of the mix network. The user submitting the input in dispute is identified as a cheater and removed.

2.3.2   Analysis and Summary

The achieved properties of the GMN in [92] are as follows.

1. Correctness:
   As the users do not want tampering of their input, they can supervise that the first round of mixing is correct, namely the commitments to their inputs are correctly mixed. As the hash function is one-way and collision-resistant, incorrect shuffling by any malicious server in the second round of mixing can be detected publicly by anyone.

2. Privacy:
   As threshold trust is assumed, no inputs can be decrypted before they are mixed and at least one server conceals its shuffling. The permutation in the mix network is secret and privacy is achieved.

3. Robustness:
   As demonstrated in Section 2.21, dishonest servers or users can be identified. As re-encryption is employed in this mix network, the identified malicious parties can be removed while the mix can continue without them.

Although correctness of the first round mix is not publicly verifiable, any incorrect mixing of an input in the first round can be found by a user submitting the input and the dispute can be solved publicly. As a user usually does not want to be abused and is eager to protect his rights, any incorrect mixing in the first round can still be found and verified publicly. Moreover, the method is highly efficient as general verification is employed. The computational cost of NGMN in the normal case is as follows where El Gamal re-encryption is employed and there are m servers in the mix network.

- Re-encryption: $6\ nm$ exponentiations (on every server, two exponentiations for each El Gamal re-encryption while each input requires three re-encryptions, one for the input, one for a random value and one for their hash function).

- Decryption: 3 mn exponentiations (one exponentiation per server for each El Gamal decryption while each input requires three decryptions, one for the input, one for a random value and one for their hash function).

A special property —independence of input— is also realized in this mix network. Independence of input means that a user cannot choose or change his inputs according to the other inputs. This property is necessary to implement strict fairness in application like e-voting and e-auction. In this mix network, every user's commitment is published (anonymously) before any other user's input is submitted to the mix network. Even though a malicious user can collude with a server to change its input (violating correctness) without being detected, this change is restricted as follows.

- During the first round of shuffling, the malicious user can collude with a server to change its commitment, thus actually changing its committed input. However, during the first round of shuffling, even if he can get collusion from all the servers the malicious user has no information about the other users' inputs if the hash function is one-way.

- During the second round of shuffling, the malicious user may get some information about the other users' inputs if he gets collusion of some parties processing the decryption key(s) of the mix network. However, if the hash function is collision-resistant he cannot change his input during the second round as his commitment has been published in the first round.

Therefore, a malicious user cannot change his input according to some other users' inputs if those users do not collude with him and the hash function is one-way and collision-resistant. This is the advantage over the other schemes [25, 84, 48]. This advantage makes NGMN especially suitable for applications like e-voting and e-auction, as fairness can be guaranteed without any trust.

Comparison with the practical GMNs is presented in Table 2.2 where 10000 inputs are mixed. It is demonstrated in this table that the new mix network is secure and efficient.

2.4 Efficient and Secure SMN: the Most Important Mix Network

SMN is the most useful solution to mix network as it guarantees reliable correctness and strong flexibility. SMN is usually based on re-encryption as it needs to support formal and strict privacy in proof of validity of shuffling. Among the existing SMN schemes, the schemes in [62, 60, 15] are not secure enough. The mix network in [62] is not publicly verifiable; while the mix network schemes in [60, 15] only provide incomplete verification of validity of

Table 2.2: Comparison of GMN

Schemes	Privacy			Computation		Communi-cation
	Extent of Correctness	Diffusion of single input	Diffusion of all inputs	Cost of proof on server	Cost of verifica-tion on server	
Park 93	high	1 among 10000	10000! permutations	proof not needed	10000	2 rounds
Golle 02	high	1 among 10000	10000! permutations	proof not needed	10000 hash functions	1 round
[92]	high	1 among 10000	10000! permutations	proof not needed	10000 hash functions	2 rounds

shuffling. The first completely verifiable mix network was proposed by Abe [5]. In [5], correctness of every gate is still verified naively (zero knowledge proof of 1-out-of-2 equality of logarithms). However, correctness proof and verification in each gate are efficient (12 exponentiations and 16 exponentiations respectively) and Abe claimed $n \log_2 n - n + 1$ binary gates are needed to realize a $PN(n)$. So the computational costs for each server's correctness proof and verification become $12(n \log_2 n - n + 1)$ and $16(n \log_2 n - n + 1)$ exponentiations. However, efficiency improvement on correctness verification is achieved at the cost that re-encryption becomes less efficient. In [5], the cost of re-encryption for each server is $4(n \log_2 n - n + 1)$ exponentiations while in most mix network this cost is $2n$ exponentiations. However, in general, acceptable efficiency is achieved in Abe's scheme when the number of users is not large. Despite its improved efficiency, Abe's scheme has the following drawbacks.

1. The precise extent of correctness of the mix network is not provided. It is not specified exactly how difficult it is for an incorrect shuffling to pass the verification.

2. The scheme is still not as efficient as desirable for some applications.

Later Abe modified his scheme with Hoshino [6]. They pointed out that in the original scheme all the possible permutations are not equally likely. In their new scheme, all the $n!$ possible permutations are equally likely in the mix network if the number of dishonest servers is no more than t. However, the two drawbacks above were not overcome in [6].

Although naive verification using proof of partial knowledge [28] can explicitly guarantee the correctness of A_j's shuffling, it is too inefficient to be practical. A more efficient verification technique uses the following equation.

$$
\begin{aligned}
\log_g (a_{j,1}/a_{j-1,i}) &= \log_y (b_{j,1}/b_{j-1,i}) \vee \\
\log_g (a_{j,2}/a_{j-1,i}) &= \log_y (b_{j,2}/b_{j-1,i}) \vee \ldots \\
\vee \log_g (a_{j,n}/a_{j-1,i}) &= \log_y (b_{j,n}/b_{j-1,i}) \text{ for } i = 1, 2, \ldots n
\end{aligned}
\tag{2.1}
$$

For simplicity and without losing generality, suppose $\log_g (a_{j,1}/a_{j-1,i}) = \log_y (b_{j,1}/b_{j-1,i})$ and $x_1 = \log_g (a_{j,1}/a_{j-1,i})$ is known to A_j. Then $\log_g (a_{j,1}/a_{j-1,i}) = \log_y (b_{j,1}/b_{j-1,i}) \vee \log_g (a_{j,2}/a_{j-1,i}) = \log_y (b_{j,2}/b_{j-1,i}) \vee \ldots \vee \log_g (a_{j,n}/a_{j-1,i}) = \log_y (b_{j,n}/b_{j-1,i})$ can be proved as follows.

1. The prover chooses r_1 from $Z_{[G]}$ randomly and calculates $a_1 = h^{r_1}$, $b_1 = g^{r_1}$. The prover chooses w_k and c_k for $k = 2, 3, \ldots, n$ from $Z_{[G]}$ randomly and calculates $a_k = g^{w_k}(a_{j,k}/a_{j-1,i})^{c_k}$, $b_k = y^{w_k}(b_{j,k}/b_{j-1,i})^{c_k}$ for $k = 2, 3, \ldots, n$. He sends a_i and b_i for $k = 1, 2, \ldots, n$ to the verifier.

2. The verifier chooses a random challenge c from $Z_{[G]}$ and sends it to the prover.

3. The prover calculates $c_1 = c - \sum_{k=2}^{n} c_k \bmod [G]$ and $w_1 = r_1 - c_1 x_1 \bmod [G]$. Then he sends c_k and w_k for $k = 1, 2, \ldots, n$ to the verifier.

4. The verifier checks $c = \sum_{k=1}^{i} c_k$, $a_k = g^{w_k}(a_{j,k}/a_{j-1,i})^{c_k}$ and $b_k = y^{w_k}(b_{j,k}/b_{j-1,i})^{c_k}$ for $k = 1, 2, \ldots, n$.

This is an interactive proof. If a hash function imitating a random oracle is used to generate the challenge, it can be transferred into a non-interactive proof. The non-interactive protocol is denoted as *CV (correctness verification)* in the rest of this thesis. The computational cost of proof and verification of *CV* is $n(4n - 2)$ and $4n^2$ exponentiations respectively.[1] It is proved in Theorem 1 that *CV* is enough for the correctness verification.

Definition 1 $A_j(c_{j-1,\mu}, c_{j,\nu}) = 1$ means A_j can efficiently calculate $r_{j,\nu}$ satisfying $a_{j,\nu} = g^{r_{j,\nu}} a_{j-1,\mu}$ and $b_{j,\nu} = y^{r_{j,\nu}} b_{j-1,\mu}$.

Theorem 1 *If the shuffling by A_j is incorrect, CV can be satisfied with a probability no more than $1/q$ without collusion of all the previous $j-1$ servers and at least two users, assuming DL problem is intractable.*

To prove Theorem 1, the following lemma is used.

Lemma 1 *If the shuffling by A_j is incorrect and for every $c_{j-1,\mu}$ with $1 \leq \mu \leq n$ there exists some $c_{j,\nu}$ with $1 \leq \nu \leq n$ such that $A_j(c_{j-1,\mu}, c_{j,\nu}) = 1$, A_j can efficiently calculate $\log_g a_{j-1,i'} - \log_g a_{j-1,i''}$ where $1 \leq i' < i'' \leq n$.*

Proof: If the shuffling is incorrect and for every $c_{j-1,\mu}$ for $\mu = 1, 2, \ldots, n$, there exists a $c_{j,\nu}$ with $1 \leq \nu \leq n$ satisfying $A_j(c_{j-1,\mu}, c_{j,\nu}) = 1$, there must be two inputs $c_{j-1,\mu 1}$ and $c_{j-1,\mu 2}$ satisfying $A_j(c_{j-1,\mu 1}, c_{j,\tau}) = 1$ and $A_j(c_{j-1,\mu 2}, c_{j,\tau}) = 1$ with $1 \leq \tau \leq n$. Otherwise there exists a permutation PM between the inputs and outputs such that $c_{j,\nu} = PM(c_{j-1,\mu})$ if $A_j(c_{j-1,\mu}, c_{j,\nu})$, which is contradictory to the assumption that the shuffling is incorrect.

$A_j(c_{j-1,\mu 1}, c_{j,\tau}) = 1$ and $A_j(c_{j-1,\mu 2}, c_{j,\tau}) = 1$ means A_j can efficiently calculate λ_1 and λ_2, so that $a_{j,\tau} = g^{\lambda_1} a_{j-1,\mu 1}$, $b_{j,\tau} = y^{\lambda_1} b_{j-1,\mu 1}$, $a_{j,\tau} = g^{\lambda_2} a_{j-1,\mu 2}$ and $b_{j,\tau} = y^{\lambda_2} b_{j-1,\mu 2}$. Therefore A_j can efficiently calculate $\log_g a_{j-1,\mu 1} - \log_g a_{j-1,\mu 2} = (\log_g a_{j,\tau} - \lambda_1) - (\log_g a_{j,\tau} - \lambda_2) = \lambda_2 - \lambda_1$
$\square$

Proof of Theorem 1: As A_j cannot get collusion of all the previous $j-1$ servers and at least two users and the *DL* problem is intractable, the inputs to A_j are encrypted independently of each other in viewpoint of A_j and A_j can

---

[1] There are n instances of batch proof and verification. Each instance of proof is composed of proof of n equations and costs $4n - 2$ exponentiations, where four exponentiations for each of the $n - 1$ incorrect equations and two exponentiations for the correct equation. Every instance of verification is composed of verification of n equations, each of which costs four exponentiations.

efficiently calculate $\log_g a_{j-1,i}$ for at most one $c_{j-1,i} = (a_{j-1,i}, b_{j-1,i})$ where $1 \leq i \leq n$. This fact is denoted as *limitation of a server's knowledge*. As a result of this fact, if the shuffling by A_j is incorrect, there exists $c_{j-1,\mu}$, so that $A_j(c_{j-1,\mu}, c_{j,\nu}) \neq 1$ for $\nu = 1, 2, \ldots, n$. Otherwise according to Lemma 1 A_j can efficiently calculate $\log_g a_{j-1,i'} - \log_g a_{j-1,i''}$ where $1 \leq i' < i'' \leq n$, which is contradictory to *limitation of a server's knowledge*. So

$$
\begin{aligned}
\log_g (a_{j,1}/a_{j-1,\mu}) &= \log_y (b_{j,1}/b_{j-1,\mu}) \vee \\
\log_g (a_{j,2}/a_{j-1,\mu}) &= \log_y (b_{j,2}/b_{j-1,\mu}) \vee \ldots \\
\vee \log_g (a_{j,n}/a_{j-1,\mu}) &= \log_y (b_{j,n}/b_{j-1,i})
\end{aligned}
$$

can be proved in CV with a probability no more than $1/q$ as proof of equality of logarithms in CV implies knowledge of logarithm (without knowledge of the logarithm, A_j can only guess the challenge and the success probability of the guess is $1/q$).

Therefore, CV can be satisfied with a probability no more than $1/q$. $\quad\square$

Even when A_j colludes with all previous $j-1$ servers and at least two users, invalid shuffling of the honest users' inputs will still be discovered in CV with an overwhelmingly large probability. This conclusion is straightforward from the proof of Lemma 1. In proof of Lemma 1, it is illustrated that the only possible attack against correctness is for a malicious server to collude with two or more malicious users and all the previous servers to tamper with any of these malicious users' inputs. Since an honest user will not conspire with the malicious server and will conceal the randomising factor in his encrypted input, the attack against the integrity of his input can only succeed with a negligible probability if the DL problem is intractable.

Among the efficient SMN schemes proposed in recent years [52, 93, 90, 41, 102, 51, 50, 86], the most efficient solution in computation is the scheme in [93]. However, unlike all the other shuffling protocols it only allows a shuffling node to choose a permutation from a small fraction of all the possible permutations. So it is not a complete shuffling and is weak in privacy. The techniques in [52, 90, 41, 102, 51, 50, 86] are usually employed to implement efficient and secure mix networks. Suppose input ciphertexts $c_1, c_2, \ldots, c_n$ are shuffled to output ciphertexts $c'_1, c'_2, \ldots, c'_n$. Most of them [52, 90, 102, 51, 86, 50, 86] employ the same main idea: if

$$
RE(\textstyle\prod_{i=1}^{n} c_i^{t_i}) = \prod_{i=1}^{n} c'_i{}^{t'_i} \tag{2.2}
$$

and t_i for $i = 1, 2, \ldots, n$ are random integers and $t'_1, t'_2, \ldots, t'_n$ is a permutation of $t_1, t_2, \ldots, t_n$ then $D(c'_1), D(c'_2), \ldots, D(c'_n)$ is a permutation of

$D(c_1), D(c_2), \ldots, D(c_n)$ with an overwhelmingly large probability where $RE()$ and $D()$ denote re-encryption function[2] and decryption respectively.

In the mix network schemes depending on (2.2) [52, 90, 102, 51, 86, 50, 86], several encryption algorithms may be employed. They can be classified into two types: additive homomorphic encryption algorithms and multiplicative homomorphic encryption algorithms. An additive homomorphic encryption algorithm with decryption function $D()$ requires that $D(c_1 c_2) = D(c_1) + D(c_2)$ for any ciphertexts c_1 and c_2. A typical example of additive homomorphic encryption algorithm is Paillier encryption [83]. A multiplicative homomorphic encryption algorithm with decryption function $D()$ requires that $D(c_1 c_2) = D(c_1)D(c_2)$ for any ciphertexts c_1 and c_2. A typical example of multiplicative homomorphic encryption algorithm is El Gamal encryption.

2.4.1 SMN Employing Multiplicative Homomorphic Encryption Algorithm

Let's recall the parameter setting of El Gamal encryption in mix networks.

- G_1 is a cyclic group with order q and multiplication modulus p where $p - 1 = 2q$ and p, q are large primes. More generally, $p - 1$ is a multiple of q and $(p - 1)/q$ may be larger than 2. For simplicity and without losing generality, the most usual setting in shuffling with El Gamal encryption is adopted: $p - 1 = 2q$.

- Let g_1 be a generator of G_1. Private key x is chosen (usually generated and shared by multiple parties) from Z_q and public key $y = g_1^x$ is published.

- The message space is G_1. A message m is encrypted into $E(m) = (g_1^r, my^r)$ where r is randomly chosen from Z_q.

- A ciphertext $c = (a, b)$ can be re-encrypted into $RE(c) = (ag_1^r, by^r)$ where r is randomly chosen from Z_q.

- A ciphertext $c = (a, b)$ is decrypted into b/a^x.

- Product of two ciphertexts $c_1 = (a_1, b_1)$ and $c_2 = (a_2, b_2)$ is $c_1 c_2 = (a_1 a_2, b_1 b_2)$.

Suppose the input ciphertexts are $c_i = (a_i, b_i)$ for $i = 1, 2, \ldots, n$ and they are shuffled to $c_i' = RE(c_{\pi(i)}) = (a_i', b_i')$ for $i = 1, 2, \ldots, n$ where $\pi()$ is a random permutation of $\{1, 2, \ldots, n\}$. Random L-bit integers t_i for $i = 1, 2, \ldots, n$ are chosen (e.g., by a verifier or multiple verifiers) where L is a

---

[2]Re-encryption is a probabilistic operation on a ciphertext and outputs another ciphertext containing the same message. It is supported by various probabilistic encryption algorithms like El Gamal encryption and Paillier encryption. More details can be found in descriptions of those encryption algorithms.

---

1. Anyone can publicly calculate Legendre symbols of $a'_1, b_1, a'_2, b'_2, \ldots, a'_n, b'_n$ to check validity of the output ciphertexts.

2. c'_i is valid iff both a'_i and b'_i have Legendre symbols 1 as they are only valid when they are quadratic residues.

3. Any invalid ciphertext c'_i is adjusted to $-c'_i$.

Figure 2.6: Checking and Adjusting Output Ciphertexts

security parameter and $2^L < q$. The shuffling node proves satisfaction of (2.2).

Note that the setting requiring that the p is prime $p - 1 = 2q$ message space is G_1 and $2^L < q$ is a little more strict than in some shuffling schemes. Theorem 2 and a special check-and-adjustment mechanism[3] in Figure 2.6 demonstrate that such a setting helps to guarantee soundness of shuffling and is suggested to be adopted by the mix network schemes depending on (2.2). If message G_1 is not suitable for an application (e.g., requiring a message space in the form of Z_ρ), it is suggested to employ an additive homomorphic encryption algorithm and use the technique in Section 2.4.2.

Theorem 2 *When $a'_1, b_1, a'_2, b'_2, \ldots, a'_n, b'_n$ are in G_1, the probability that (2.2) is successfully proved and verified but $D(c'_1), D(c'_2), \ldots, D(c'_n)$ is not a permutation of $D(c_1), D(c_2), \ldots, D(c_n)$ is a negligible concrete probability.*

To prove Theorem 2, a lemma is proved first.

Lemma 2 *Suppose $y_i, z_i \in G_1$ for $i = 1, 2, \ldots, n$. Let t_i for $i = 1, 2, \ldots, n$ be random integers such that $t_i < 2^L$. If $Pr\,[\,t_1, t_2, \ldots, t_n \in \{0, 1, \ldots, 2^L - 1\}\,|\,\log_{g_1} \prod_{i=1}^n y_i^{t_i} = \log_y \prod_{i=1}^n z_i^{t_i}\,] > 2^{-L}$, then $\log_{g_1} y_i = \log_y z_i$ for $i = 1, 2, \ldots, n$.*

Proof: $Pr\,[\,t_1, t_2, \ldots, t_n \in \{0, 1, \ldots, 2^L - 1\}\,|\,\log_{g_1} \prod_{i=1}^n y_i^{t_i} = \log_y \prod_{i=1}^n z_i^{t_i}\,] > 2^{-L}$ implies that for any given integer v in $\{1, 2, \ldots, n\}$ there must exist integers $t_1, t_2, \ldots, t_n$ and t'_v in $\{0, 1, \ldots, 2^L - 1\}$ such that

$$\log_{g_1} \prod_{i=1}^n y_i^{t_i} = \log_y \prod_{i=1}^n z_i^{t_i} \tag{2.3}$$

$$\log_{g_1} ((\prod_{i=1}^{v-1} y_i^{t_i}) y_v^{t'_v} \prod_{i=v+1}^n y_i^{t_i}) = \log_y ((\prod_{i=1}^{v-1} z_i^{t_i}) z_v^{t'_v} \prod_{i=v+1}^n z_i^{t_i}) \tag{2.4}$$

Otherwise, for any $(t_1, t_2, \ldots, t_{v-1}, t_{v+1}, \ldots, t_n)$, there is at most one t_v to satisfy $\log_{g_1} \prod_{i=1}^n y_i^{t_i} = \log_y \prod_{i=1}^n z_i^{t_i}$. This implies that among the 2^{nL} possible choices for $(t_1, t_2, \ldots, t_n)$ (combination of $2^{(n-1)L}$ possible choices for $(t_1, t_2, \ldots, t_{v-1}, t_{v+1}, \ldots, t_n)$ and 2^L possible choices for t_v), there are at

---

[3]This check-and-adjustment mechanism is necessary for soundness of shuffling although it is sometimes ignored (e.g., in [52]).

most $2^{(n-1)L}$ choices to satisfy $\log_{g_1} \prod_{i=1}^{n} y_i^{t_i} = \log_y \prod_{i=1}^{n} z_i^{t_i}$, which is a contradiction to the assumption that $Pr\ [\ t_1, t_2, \ldots, t_n \in \{0, 1, \ldots, 2^L - 1\}\ |\ \log_{g_1} \prod_{i=1}^{n} y_i^{t_i} = \log_y \prod_{i=1}^{n} z_i^{t_i}\ ] > 2^{-L}.$

Equation (2.3) divided by (2.4) yields

$$log_{g_1} y_v^{t_v - t_v'} = log_y z_v^{t_v - t_v'}$$

Namely

$$(t_v - t_v')log_{g_1} y_v = (t_v - t_v')log_y z_v \bmod q$$

Note that $t_v \neq t_v'$ and $t_v, t_v' < 2^L < q$. So $t_v - t_v' \neq 0 \bmod q$ and

$$log_{g_1} y_v = log_y z_v$$

Therefore, $\log_{g_1} y_i = \log_y z_i$ for $i = 1, 2, \ldots, n$ as v can be any integer in $\{1, 2, \ldots, n\}$. □

Proof of Theorem 2: Let A_1 be the event that $D(c_1'), D(c_2'), \ldots, D(c_n')$ is a permutation of $D(c_1), D(c_2), \ldots, D(c_n)$; A_2 be the event that (2.2) is correct; A_3 be the event that the shuffling passes the verification of (2.2); and $P(A)$ denote the probability of event A.

$$P(A_3/\bar{A}_1) = P((A_3 \wedge A_2)/\bar{A}_1) + P((A_3 \wedge \bar{A}_2)/\bar{A}_1)$$
$$= P(A_3 \wedge A_2 \wedge \bar{A}_1)/P(\bar{A}_1) + P(A_3 \wedge \bar{A}_2 \wedge \bar{A}_1)/P(\bar{A}_1)$$
$$= P(\bar{A}_1 \wedge A_2)P(A_3/\bar{A}_1 \wedge A_2)/P(\bar{A}_1) +$$
$$P(A_3 \wedge \bar{A}_2 \wedge \bar{A}_1)P(\bar{A}_2 \wedge \bar{A}_1)/(P(\bar{A}_1)P(\bar{A}_2 \wedge \bar{A}_1))$$
$$= P(A_2/\bar{A}_1)P(A_3/\bar{A}_1 \wedge A_2) +$$
$$P(\bar{A}_2/\bar{A}_1)P(A_3 \wedge \bar{A}_2 \wedge \bar{A}_1)/P(\bar{A}_2 \wedge \bar{A}_1)$$
$$= P(A_2/\bar{A}_1)P(A_3/\bar{A}_1 \wedge A_2) +$$
$$P(\bar{A}_2/\bar{A}_1)P(A_3 \wedge \bar{A}_2 \wedge \bar{A}_1)/(P(\bar{A}_2)P(\bar{A}_1/\bar{A}_2))$$

$P(\bar{A}_1/\bar{A}_2) = 1$ as $P(A_2/A_1) = 1$. So

$$P(A_3/\bar{A}_1) = P(A_2/\bar{A}_1)P(A_3/\bar{A}_1 \wedge A_2) +$$
$$P(\bar{A}_2/\bar{A}_1)P(A_3 \wedge \bar{A}_2 \wedge \bar{A}_1)/P(\bar{A}_2)$$
$$\leq P(A_2/\bar{A}_1)P(A_3/\bar{A}_1 \wedge A_2) + P(\bar{A}_2/\bar{A}_1)P(A_3 \wedge \bar{A}_2)/P(\bar{A}_2)$$
$$\leq P(A_2/\bar{A}_1)P(A_3/\bar{A}_1 \wedge A_2) + P(\bar{A}_2/\bar{A}_1)P(A_3/\bar{A}_2)$$
$$\leq P(A_2/\bar{A}_1)P(A_3/\bar{A}_1 \wedge A_2) + P(A_3/\bar{A}_2)$$

If $P(A_2/\bar{A}_1) > 2^{-L}$, then when $\bar{A}_1$ happens the probability that (2.2) is correct is larger than 2^{-L}. Namely, when $\bar{A}_1$ happens,

$$RE(\prod_{i=1}^{n} c_i^{t_i}) = \prod_{i=1}^{n} c_i'^{t_{\pi(i)}'}$$

with a probability larger than 2^{-L} where $\pi()$ is a permutation of $\{1, 2, \ldots, n\}$. Namely, when $\bar{A}_1$ happens,

$$RE(\prod_{i=1}^{n} c_i^{t_i}) = \prod_{i=1}^{n} c'^{t_i}_{\pi^{-1}(i)}$$

with a probability larger than 2^{-L} .

According to multiplicative homomorphism of the employed encryption algorithm, when $\bar{A}_1$ happens,

$$\prod_{i=1}^{n} (c_i/c'_{\pi^{-1}(i)})^{t_i} = E(1)$$

with a probability larger than 2^{-L}. Namely, when $\bar{A}_1$ happens

$$\log_{g_1} \prod_{i=1}^{n} (a_i/a'_{\pi^{-1}(i)})^{t_i} = \log_y \prod_{i=1}^{n} (b_i/b'_{\pi^{-1}(i)})^{t_i}$$

with a probability larger than 2^{-L}.

So, according to Lemma 2, when $\bar{A}_1$ happens,

$$\log_{g_1} (a_i/a'_{\pi^{-1}(i)}) = \log_y (b_i/b'_{\pi^{-1}(i)}) \text{ for } i = 1, 2, \ldots, n$$

and thus $D(c'_1), D(c'_2), \ldots, D(c'_n)$ is a permutation of $D(c_1), D(c_2), \ldots, D(c_n)$, which is a contradiction. So $P(A_2/\bar{A}_1) \leq 2^{-L}$ must be true to avoid the contradiction.

As with multiplicative homomorphic encryption, algorithm (2.2) is proved using a standard Chaum-Pedersen proof of equality of discrete logarithms [27], $P(A_3/\bar{A}_1 \wedge A_2) = 1$ and $P(A_3/\bar{A}_2) < 2^{-L'}$ where L' is the bit length of the challenge in the Chaum-Pedersen proof of equality of logarithms. Therefore,

$$P(A_3/\bar{A}_1) \leq P(A_2/\bar{A}_1) + P(A_3/\bar{A}_2) = 2^{-L} + 2^{-L'}$$

$\square$

2.4.2 SMN Employing Additive Homomorphic Encryption Algorithm

Let's recall the parameter setting of Paillier encryption in mix networks. Other factorization-based homomorphic encryption algorithms like [82] can be employed in the same way. Suppose Paillier encryption [83] or Paillier encryption with distributed decryption [37] is employed. The latter may be more suitable as in shuffling applications like e-voting and it is usually desired that the private key is shared by multiple parties.

- The multiplication modulus is N^2 where $N = p'q'$ and p', q' are large primes.

- A message m is encrypted into $c = g^m r^N$ where g is a public integer generated by the key generation algorithm (see [37] for more details) and r is randomly chosen from Z_N^*.

- A ciphertext c is re-encrypted into $c' = RE(c) = cr^N$ where r is randomly chosen from Z_N^*.

Suppose the input ciphertexts are c_i for $i = 1, 2, \ldots, n$ and they are shuffled to $c'_i = RE(c_{\pi(i)})$ for $i = 1, 2, \ldots, n$ where $\pi()$ is a random permutation of $\{1, 2, \ldots, n\}$. Random L-bit integers t_i for $i = 1, 2, \ldots, n$ are chosen (e.g., by a verifier or multiple verifiers) where L is a security parameter and $2^L < min(p', q')$. The shuffling node proves satisfaction of (2.2). Theorem 3 formally and precisely guarantees soundness of mix network with Paillier encryption.

Theorem 3 *With Paillier encryption, the probability that (2.2) is successfully proved and verified but $D(c'_1), D(c'_2), \ldots, D(c'_n)$ is not a permutation of $D(c_1), D(c_2), \ldots, D(c_n)$ is a negligible concrete probability.*

To prove Theorem 3, a lemma is proved first.

Lemma 3 *If $\prod_{i=1}^{n} y_i^{t_i}$ is an Nth residue with a probability larger than 2^{-L} where $t_1, t_2, \ldots, t_n$ are randomly chosen from $\{0, 1, \ldots, 2^L - 1\}$, then $y_1, y_2, \ldots, y_n$ are N^{th} residues.*

Proof: $\prod_{i=1}^{n} y_i^{t_i}$ is an Nth residue with a probability larger than 2^{-L} implies that for any given integer v in $\{1, 2, \ldots, n\}$ there must exist integers $t_1, t_2, \ldots, t_n$ and t'_v in $\{0, 1, \ldots, 2^L - 1\}$, x and x' such that

$$\prod_{i=1}^{n} y_i^{t_i} = x^N \tag{2.5}$$

$$(\prod_{i=1}^{v-1} y_i^{t_i})y_v^{t'_v} \prod_{i=v+1}^{n} y_i^{t_i} = x'^N \tag{2.6}$$

Otherwise, for any $(t_1, t_2, \ldots, t_{v-1}, t_{v+1}, \ldots, t_n)$ in $\{0, 1, \ldots, 2^L - 1\}^{n-1}$, there are at most one t_v in $\{1, 2, \ldots, 2^L - 1\}$ such that $\prod_{i=1}^{n} y_i^{t_i}$ is an Nth residue. This implies that among the 2^{nL} possible choices for $(t_1, t_2, \ldots, t_n)$ (combination of $2^{(n-1)L}$ possible choices for $(t_1, t_2, \ldots, t_{v-1}, t_{v+1}, \ldots, t_n)$ and 2^L possible choices for t_v) there are at most $2^{(n-1)L}$ choices to construct N^{th} residue $\prod_{i=1}^{n} y_i^{t_i}$, which is a contradiction to the assumption that $\prod_{i=1}^{n} y_i^{t_i}$ is an Nth residue with a probability larger than 2^{-L}.

Equations (2.5) and (2.6) imply $y_v^{t_v - \hat{t}_v}$ is an Nth residue. According to Euclidean algorithm there exist integers α and β to satisfy $\beta(t_v - \hat{t}_v) = \alpha N + GCD(N, t_v - \hat{t}_v)$. $GCD(N, t_v - \hat{t}_v) = 1$ as $t_v, \hat{t}_v < 2^L < min(p', q')$. So $y_v^{\beta(t_v - \hat{t}_v)} = y_v^{\alpha N} y_v$. Thus,

$$y_v = y_v^{\beta(t_v - \hat{t}_v)}/y_v^{\alpha N} = (y_v^{(t_v - \hat{t}_v)})^{\beta}/y_v^{\alpha N} = (x/x')^{N\beta}/(y_v^{\alpha})^N = ((x/x')^{\beta}/y_v^{\alpha})^N$$

So y_v is an Nth residue. Therefore, $y_1, y_2, \ldots, y_n$ are N^{th} residues as v can be any integer in $\{1, 2, \ldots, n\}$. □

Proof of Theorem 3: Let A_1 be the event that $D(c'_1), D(c'_2), \ldots, D(c'_n)$ is a permutation of $D(c_1), D(c_2), \ldots, D(c_n)$; A_2 be the event that (2.2) is correct;

A_3 be the event that the shuffling node successfully proves (2.2); and $P(A)$ denote the probability of event A.

$$P(A_3/\bar{A}_1) = P((A_3 \wedge A_2)/\bar{A}_1) + P((A_3 \wedge \bar{A}_2)/\bar{A}_1)$$
$$= P(A_3 \wedge A_2 \wedge \bar{A}_1)/P(\bar{A}_1) + P(A_3 \wedge \bar{A}_2 \wedge \bar{A}_1)/P(\bar{A}_1)$$
$$= P(\bar{A}_1 \wedge A_2)P(A_3/\bar{A}_1 \wedge A_2)/P(\bar{A}_1) +$$
$$P(A_3 \wedge \bar{A}_2 \wedge \bar{A}_1)P(\bar{A}_2 \wedge \bar{A}_1)/(P(\bar{A}_1)P(\bar{A}_2 \wedge \bar{A}_1))$$
$$= P(A_2/\bar{A}_1)P(A_3/\bar{A}_1 \wedge A_2) +$$
$$P(\bar{A}_2/\bar{A}_1)P(A_3 \wedge \bar{A}_2 \wedge \bar{A}_1)/P(\bar{A}_2 \wedge \bar{A}_1)$$
$$= P(A_2/\bar{A}_1)P(A_3/\bar{A}_1 \wedge A_2) +$$
$$P(\bar{A}_2/\bar{A}_1)P(A_3 \wedge \bar{A}_2 \wedge \bar{A}_1)/(P(\bar{A}_2)P(\bar{A}_1/\bar{A}_2))$$

$P(\bar{A}_1/\bar{A}_2) = 1$ as $P(A_2/A_1) = 1$. So

$$P(A_3/\bar{A}_1) = P(A_2/\bar{A}_1)P(A_3/\bar{A}_1 \wedge A_2) +$$
$$P(\bar{A}_2/\bar{A}_1)P(A_3 \wedge \bar{A}_2 \wedge \bar{A}_1)/P(\bar{A}_2)$$
$$\leq P(A_2/\bar{A}_1)P(A_3/\bar{A}_1 \wedge A_2) +$$
$$P(\bar{A}_2/\bar{A}_1)P(A_3 \wedge \bar{A}_2)/P(\bar{A}_2)$$
$$\leq P(A_2/\bar{A}_1)P(A_3/\bar{A}_1 \wedge A_2) + P(\bar{A}_2/\bar{A}_1)P(A_3/\bar{A}_2)$$
$$\leq P(A_2/\bar{A}_1)P(A_3/\bar{A}_1 \wedge A_2) + P(A_3/\bar{A}_2)$$

If $P(A_2/\bar{A}_1) > 2^{-L}$, then when $\bar{A}_1$ happens the probability that (2.2) is correct is larger than 2^{-L}. Namely, when $\bar{A}_1$ happens,

$$RE(\prod_{i=1}^{n} c_i^{t_i}) = \prod_{i=1}^{n} c'_i{}^{t_{\pi(i)}}$$

with a probability larger than 2^{-L} where $\pi()$ is a permutation of $\{1, 2, \ldots, n\}$. Namely, when $\bar{A}_1$ happens,

$$RE(\prod_{i=1}^{n} c_i^{t_i}) = \prod_{i=1}^{n} c'_{\pi^{-1}(i)}{}^{t_i}$$

with a probability larger than 2^{-L}.

According to additive homomorphism of the employed encryption algorithm, when $\bar{A}_1$ happens,

$$\prod_{i=1}^{n} (c_i/c'_{\pi^{-1}(i)})^{t_i} = E(0)$$

with a probability larger than 2^{-L}. Namely, when $\bar{A}_1$ happens, $\prod_{i=1}^{n}(c_i/c'_{\pi^{-1}(i)})^{t_i}$ is an Nth residue with a probability larger than 2^{-L}.

So, according to Lemma 3, when $\bar{A}_1$ happens $c_i/c'_{\pi^{-1}(i)}$ is an Nth residue for $i = 1, 2, \ldots, n$, and thus $D(c'_1), D(c'_2), \ldots, D(c'_n)$ is a permutation of $D(c_1), D(c_2), \ldots, D(c_n)$, which is a contradiction. $P(A_2/\bar{A}_1) \leq 2^{-L}$ must be true to avoid the contradiction.

As with Paillier encryption, (2.2) is proved using a standard proof of knowledge of root [53], $P(A_3/\bar{A}_1 \wedge A_2) = 1$ and $P(A_3/\bar{A}_2) < 2^{-L'}$ where L' is the bit length of the challenge in the proof of knowledge of root. Therefore,

$$P(A_3/\bar{A}_1) \leq P(A_2/\bar{A}_1) + P(A_3/\bar{A}_2) = 2^{-L} + 2^{-L'}$$

$\square$

With help of Lemma 3, we can prove that the probability that $D(c'_1), D(c'_2), \ldots, D(c'_n)$ is not a permutation of $D(c_1), D(c_2), \ldots, D(c_n)$ but knowledge of $(\prod_{i=1}^{n} c'^{t_{\pi(i)}}_i / \prod_{i=1}^{n} c^{t_i}_i)^{1/N}$ is no more than $2^{-L} + 2^{-L'}$ where L' is the bit length of challenge in the ZK proof in [53]. Theorem 3 guarantees that if the shuffling verification is passed, the plaintexts encrypted in the output ciphertexts are permutations of the plaintexts encrypted in the input ciphertexts with an non-negligible probability.

2.5   Grouped Shuffling: a Trade-off to Improve Efficiency of Mix Networks

Grouped shuffling is a mechanism to improve efficiency of mix networks without compromising its security in practice. Let us start discussing it by recalling the work by Abe. When the server A_j in a mix network performs El Gamal re-encryption and permutation π_j and Equation (2.1) is employed to verify the correctness of shuffling, the following properties are achieved.

1. A dishonest server A_j can prove its incorrect shuffling to be correct with probability no more than $1/q$ without collusion of all the previous $j - 1$ servers and at least two users. Even when A_j colludes with all the previous $j - 1$ servers and at least two users, invalid shuffling of honest users' inputs will still be discovered in CV with an overwhelmingly large probability.

2. Identified incorrect shuffling can be removed and the mix network can recover efficiently.

3. Computational costs for the prover and verifier of the correctness verification of a server's shuffling are $n(4n - 2)$ and $4n^2$ exponentiations respectively.

4. If at least one server is honest, all the $n!$ permutation are equally possible in the mix network and if the number of malicious decrypting authorities is no more than t, privacy is achieved.

This mix network is denoted as S-Mix-1 in [93]. However there are still some drawbacks of this solution:

- When two users conspire with the first server, correctness is not guaranteed.

- When n is large, $O(n^2)$ exponentiation is still a high cost.

To solve these problems, an idea of Abe [5, 6] is used: divide a $PN(n)$ into a few smaller shufflings, verification of whose correctness is efficient. However, switching gate $PN(2)$ is not applied to avoid complex construction of gate circuits. Instead, a simpler grouped shuffling technique is employed in [93] to improve efficiency.

2.5.1 Group Shuffling in [93]

On each server the n inputs are divided into groups with same size k, while re-encryption and random permutation are applied to each group. For simplicity, suppose $n = k^u$. There are $z = k^{u-1}$ groups. Usually $m \leq u$ as the number of servers is often small. The grouping function on every server is specially designed according to a general rule: if an input to the mix network is able to be permuted to a certain set of outputs after the shuffling of the first j servers, any two of these outputs (inputs to the $j+1^{th}$ server) cannot be divided into a same group on the $j+1^{th}$ server. This rule can provide the greatest diffusion, and thus as strong privacy as possible.

Before the shuffling, each server A_j randomly generates $v_{j,i} \in G$ for $i = 1, 2, \ldots, n$. Inputs to the mix network c_i for $i = 1, 2, \ldots, n$ are sorted to $c_{0,i} = (a_{0,i}, b_{0,i})$ for $i = 1, 2, \ldots, n$, so that $a_{0,i} + \sum_{j=1}^{m} v_{j,i} \bmod p$ increases as i increases. On server A_j, the shuffling is as follows (refer to Figure 2.7 for the details of the grouping where $k = 3$).

1. Grouping

    - Under this grouping mechanism, diffusion of the mix network increases server after server. After the jth server's shuffling, a complete mixing is realized for every k^j successive inputs, which is called a shuffling range. In other words, the wth shuffling range in the inputs is mixed to the wth shuffling range in the outputs where any input in the wth shuffling range may be shuffled to any output in the wth shuffling range with a uniform probability distribution. Before the work of the first server, the size of the shuffling range is 1. After its shuffling, the size of the shuffling range is k. Then the outputs are regrouped so that the second server can use its shuffling to extend the size of the shuffling range to k^2.

    - A_j get inputs $c_{j-1,i}$ for $i = 1, 2, \ldots, n$ from A_{j-1}. So far $c_{0,k^{j-1}w+1}$, $c_{0,k^{j-1}w+2}$, $\cdots c_{0,k^{j-1}w+k^{j-1}}$ have been shuffled to $c_{j-1,k^{j-1}w+1}$, $c_{j-1,k^{j-1}w+2}$, $\cdots c_{j-1,k^{j-1}w+k^{j-1}}$ for $w = 0, 1, \ldots, k^{u-j+1} - 1$. Denote $c_{j-1,k^{j-1}w+1}$, $c_{j-1,k^{j-1}w+2}$, $\cdots c_{j-1,k^{j-1}w+k^{j-1}}$ as shuffling range $R_{j-1,w+1}$, then A_j in fact receives k^{u-j+1} shuffling ranges $R_{j-1,1}$, $R_{j-1,2}$, $\ldots$, $R_{j-1,k^{u-j+1}}$.

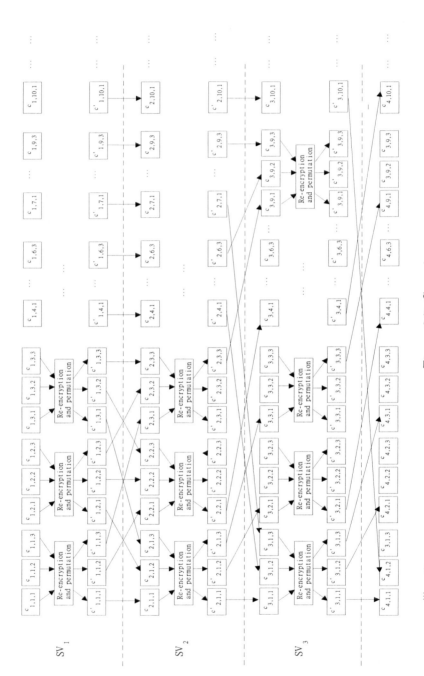

Figure 2.7: Grouping

- A_j regroups in every k successive shuffling ranges. The k inputs in the xth position in each shuffling range of the yth k successive shuffling ranges are regrouped into the xth group in the yth k successive shuffling ranges in the outputs. Namely, input $c_{j-1,i}$ is mapped to $c_{j,\alpha,\beta}$, which is the βth element in Group α, where $\alpha = ((i-1)/k^j)k^{j-1} + ((i-1) \bmod k^{j-1}) + 1$ and $\beta = ((i-1) \bmod k^j)/k^{j-1} + 1$.

2. Re-encryption and permutation
   $c_{j,\alpha,\beta} = (a_{j,\alpha,\beta}, b_{j,\alpha,\beta})$ is permuted to

   $$c'_{j,\alpha,\pi_{j,\alpha}(\beta)} = (a'_{j,\alpha,\pi_{j,\alpha}(\beta)}, b'_{j,\alpha,\pi_{j,\alpha}(\beta)}) = (g^{r_{j,\alpha,\beta}} a_{j,\alpha,\beta}, y^{r_{j,\alpha,\beta}} b_{j,\alpha,\beta})$$

   for $\alpha = 1, 2, \ldots, z$ and $\beta = 1, 2, \ldots, k$ where $r_{j,\alpha,\beta}$ is randomly chosen and $\pi_{j,\alpha}$ for $\alpha = 1, 2, \ldots, z$ are random secret permutations from $\{1, 2, \ldots, k\}$ to $\{1, 2, \ldots, k\}$.

3. De-grouping
   $c_{j,i} = c'_{j,\alpha,\beta}$ where $i = k(\alpha - 1) + \beta$

Shuffling of A_j is verified by A_{j+1} before it starts its own shuffling using the following equation.

$$\log_g (a'_{j,\alpha,1}/a_{j,\alpha,\beta}) = \log_y (b'_{j,\alpha,1}/b_{j,\alpha,\beta})$$

$$\vee \ \log_g (a'_{j,\alpha,2}/a_{j,\alpha,\beta}) = \log_y (b'_{j,\alpha,2}/b_{j,\alpha,\beta})$$

$$\vee \ \ldots \ \vee \ \log_g (a'_{j,\alpha,k}/a_{j,\alpha,\beta}) = \log_y (b'_{j,\alpha,k}/b_{j,\alpha,\beta})$$

$$\text{for } \alpha = 1, 2, \ldots, z \text{ and } \beta = 1, 2, \ldots, k \qquad (2.7)$$

Realization of verification of Equation (2.7) using existing zero knowledge proof techniques is denoted as *GCV (grouped correctness verification)*. If the verification fails, A_{j+1} gets the outputs of A_{j-1}, verifies them, and uses them as its inputs if they are valid. If A_{j-1}'s outputs are invalid too, it gets the outputs of the previous server until it finds a set of valid outputs as its inputs. After the shuffling of the last server, the outputs are decrypted as in S-Mix-1. This mix network applying grouped shuffling is denoted as S-Mix-2 in [93]. Theorem 4 is presented here for soundness of verification by Equation (2.7).

Theorem 4 *If the group shuffling by A_j is incorrect, Equation (2.7) can be satisfied with a probability no more than $1/q$ without collusion of all the previous $j - 1$ servers and at least two users in a same group on A_j, assuming DL problem is intractable.*

Proof: According to Theorem 1, if the shuffling in the αth group by A_j is incorrect, the probability that

$$\log_g (a'_{j,\alpha,1}/a_{j,\alpha,\beta}) = \log_y (b'_{j,\alpha,1}/b_{j,\alpha,\beta})$$

$$\lor \ \log_g \left(a'_{j,\alpha,2}/a_{j,\alpha,\beta}\right) = \log_y \left(b'_{j,\alpha,2}/b_{j,\alpha,\beta}\right)$$

$$\lor \ \ldots \ \lor \ \log_g \left(a'_{j,\alpha,k}/a_{j,\alpha,\beta}\right) = \log_y \left(b'_{j,\alpha,k}/b_{j,\alpha,\beta}\right)$$

$$\text{for } \beta = 1, 2, \ldots, k$$

is satisfied is no more than $1/q$ without collusion of all the previous $j - 1$ servers and at least two users in a same group on A_j, assuming DL problem is intractable. $\qquad\square$

When a conspiracy of all the previous servers and at least two malicious users is available, attack against correctness is more difficult than in S-Mix-1. As the grouping function is dependent on $v_{j,i}$ for $j = 1, 2, \ldots m$ and $i = 1, 2, \ldots, n$, if at least one server is trusted to generate them randomly, the grouping on any server is random. So if only static attack (all colluding users and servers are chosen before the attack starts) is considered and at least one server A_j is honest to choose $v_{j,i}$ for $i = 1, 2, \ldots, n$ randomly, the probability that the colluding users are in the same group on any server is low. For example, even if A_1 colludes with two users, they happen to fall in a same group with a probability $1/z$. That means although attacks involving more than one user and the first few servers against correctness are still possible, they succeed with a low probability.[4] As in S-Mix-1, the probability to tamper with an honest user's input successfully is negligible if DL is intractable. Therefore, correctness property is improved.

The computational cost to produce the proof is $n(4k - 2)$ exponentiations. The computational cost to verify the proof is $4nk$ exponentiations.[5] Better efficiency is achieved compared to S-Mix-1.

Privacy of S-Mix-2 is achieved if the number of malicious decrypting authorities is no more than t. The extent of privacy is measured by two factors: diffusion of any single input and diffusion of the inputs as a whole. As stated before, in normal applications $m < u$. So, if a dishonest server reveals its shuffling, it makes no difference to the situation where this server performs re-encryption without permutation. Therefore, the only impact of this attack on the privacy of the shuffling of the whole mix network is to degrade the mix network to a mix network containing one fewer server. The shuffling of the other servers is not affected and can still provide strong privacy protection.

- Diffusion of any single input: each input may be permuted to any of a set of k^ϵ outputs with an equal probability, where ϵ is the number of honest servers.

---

[4] As k is usually small, z is large when n is large and the probability is very low when n is very large as in a large-scale voting.

[5] There are n instances of batch proof and verification. Each instance of proof is composed of proof of k equations and costs $4k - 2$ exponentiations, where four exponentiations for each of the $k - 1$ incorrect equations and two exponentiations for the correct equation. Every instance of verification is composed of verification of k equations, each of which costs four exponentiations.

- Diffusion of the inputs as a whole: $(k!)^{z\epsilon}$ possible permutations from the inputs of the mix network to its outputs are equally likely.

If $m \geq u$, greater privacy is possible.

- When $\epsilon = u$, diffusion of single input may be as great as that in S-Mix-1 (any input to n equally likely outputs).

- When $\epsilon > u$, diffusion of the inputs as a whole may be as great as that in S-Mix-1 (all $n!$ possible permutations are equally likely).

However, it depends on the distribution of the honest servers.

Efficiency of correctness verification of S-Mix-2 is better compared to that of S-Mix-1. However it is still costly when n is large. Batch verification technique can be employed to improve the efficiency further. If every server A_j uses a unique permutation π_j to replace $\pi_{j,\alpha}$ for $\alpha = 1, 2, \ldots, z$ and the concept of correctness is slightly changed in Definition 2, according to Theorem 3, Equation (2.7) can be batched to Equation (2.8).

Definition 2 *In S-Mix-3, group shuffling by A_j is correct if for any $1 \leq \alpha \leq z$, the same permutation exists between $|D(c_{j,\alpha,\beta})|$ for $\beta = 1, 2, \ldots, k$ and $|D(c'_{j,\alpha,\beta})|$ for $\beta = 1, 2, \ldots, k$ where $D()$ denotes decryption.*

$$
\begin{aligned}
& \log_g \prod_{\alpha=1}^{z} (a'_{j,\alpha,1}/a_{j,\alpha,\beta})^{t_{j,\alpha}} = \log_y \prod_{\alpha=1}^{z} (b'_{j,\alpha,1}/b_{j,\alpha,\beta})^{t_{j,\alpha}} \\
\vee \ & \log_g \prod_{\alpha=1}^{z} (a'_{j,\alpha,2}/a_{j,\alpha,\beta})^{t_{j,\alpha}} = \log_y \prod_{\alpha=1}^{z} (b'_{j,\alpha,2}/b_{j,\alpha,\beta})^{t_{j,\alpha}} \quad (2.8) \\
\vee \ \ldots \ \vee \ & \log_g \prod_{\alpha=1}^{z} (a'_{j,\alpha,k}/a_{j,\alpha,\beta})^{t_{j,\alpha}} = \log_y \prod_{\alpha=1}^{z} (b'_{j,\alpha,k}/b_{j,\alpha,\beta})^{t_{j,\alpha}} \\
& \hspace{6cm} \text{for } \beta = 1, 2, \ldots, k
\end{aligned}
$$

To reduce the number of full-length exponentiations (a division is assumed to have the same cost of a full-length exponentiation), Equation (2.8) is simplified to Equation (2.9).

$$
\begin{aligned}
& \log_g \left(\prod_{\alpha=1}^{z} a'^{t_{j,\alpha}}_{j,\alpha,1} / \prod_{\alpha=1}^{z} a^{t_{j,\alpha}}_{j,\alpha,\beta} \right) = \log_y \left(\prod_{\alpha=1}^{z} b'^{t_{j,\alpha}}_{j,\alpha,1} / \prod_{\alpha=1}^{z} b^{t_{j,\alpha}}_{j,\alpha,\beta} \right) \\
\vee \ & \log_g \left(\prod_{\alpha=1}^{z} a'^{t_{j,\alpha}}_{j,\alpha,2} / \prod_{\alpha=1}^{z} a^{t_{j,\alpha}}_{j,\alpha,\beta} \right) = \log_y \left(\prod_{\alpha=1}^{z} b'^{t_{j,\alpha}}_{j,\alpha,2} / \prod_{\alpha=1}^{z} b^{t_{j,\alpha}}_{j,\alpha,\beta} \right) \quad (2.9) \\
\vee \ \ldots \ \vee \ & \log_g \left(\prod_{\alpha=1}^{z} a'^{t_{j,\alpha}}_{j,\alpha,k} / \prod_{\alpha=1}^{z} a^{t_{j,\alpha}}_{j,\alpha,\beta} \right) = \log_y \left(\prod_{\alpha=1}^{z} b'^{t_{j,\alpha}}_{j,\alpha,k} / \prod_{\alpha=1}^{z} b^{t_{j,\alpha}}_{j,\alpha,\beta} \right) \\
& \hspace{6cm} \text{for } \beta = 1, 2, \ldots, k
\end{aligned}
$$

where $t_{j,\alpha}$ for $\alpha = 1, 2, \ldots, z$ are random integers with length l. The verification in Equation (2.9) for any β by employing existing zero knowledge proof techniques is denoted as $BGCV_{j,\beta}$. If $BGCV_{j,\beta}$ holds for $\beta = 1, 2, \ldots, k$, it is denoted as $BGCV(j - 1 \to j)$, which means the correction verification for A_j is passed. $BGCV(j - 1 \to j)$ is checked for $j = 1, 2, \ldots, m$ to ensure the correctness of the mix network.

This mix network is denoted as S-Mix-3 in [93].

To apply Equation (2.9), the construction of the mix network must be changed slightly as follows. After the shuffling of all the servers, the outputs of the mix network are decrypted. Every decrypted message M_i for $i = 1, 2, \ldots, n$ is checked to be in G by testing whether $M_i^q = 1$. If $M_i^q \neq 1$, an additional computation is performed: $M_i = -M_i = g_0^q M_i$.

2.5.2   Another Grouped Shuffling Protocol to Support Efficient SMN

The grouped shuffling mechanism in [93] suggests use of very small groups and thus cannot achieve very strong privacy. To guarantee stronger privacy the group size must be larger, especially when the number of shuffled ciphertexts is large. This idea is adopted in [86] to support strong privacy in grouped shuffling-based mix networks. When multiple instances of grouped shuffling employ the same permutation, their validity can be proved in a batch to improve efficiency. More precisely, in [86] the ciphertexts to be shuffled are divided into multiple groups and the same permutation is employed to shuffle the ciphertexts in each group, such that it is feasible to prove and verify validity of shuffling in all the groups in a batch. After being shuffled, we know which group each output ciphertext is from, but every output ciphertext is computationally indistinguishable from the other output ciphertexts in the same group. The mix network in [86] is designed for applications with a large number of inputs, so that strong privacy can be achieved. Unlike in [93], large group size is supported at a low cost in [86], such that strong privacy can be efficiently achieved.

An additive homomorphic semantically secure encryption algorithm (e.g., Paillier encryption [83] or modified El Gamal encryption [67, 68]) with re-encryption function $RE()$ and decryption function $D()$ is employed for encryption in [86]. Private key of the encryption algorithm is kept secret (e.g., shared by multiple parties). The shuffling node receives ciphertexts $c_1, c_2, \ldots, c_n$ and shuffles them into $c_1', c_2', \ldots, c_n'$ as follows.

1. Group size k is chosen, which is large enough for privacy requirement. For simplicity of description assume that k is a divider of n.

2. $c_1, c_2, \ldots, c_n$ are randomly divided into n/k groups $G_1, G_2, \ldots, G_{n/k}$ where G_j contains k ciphertexts $c_{j,1}, c_{j,2}, \ldots, c_{j,k}$.

3. An additional group of ciphertexts, G_0, is generated and contains $c_{0,1}, c_{0,2}, \ldots, c_{0,k}$ where $c_{0,i} = H(c_{1,i}, c_{2,i}, \ldots, c_{n/k,i})$ and $H()$ is a pseudorandom function (e.g., implemented through a hash function).

4. The shuffling node chooses $\pi()$, a permutation of $\{1, 2, \ldots, k\}$, and outputs

$$c'_{j,i} = RE(c_{j,\pi(i)}, r_{j,i}) \text{ for } j = 0, 1, \ldots, n/k \text{ and } i = 1, 2, \ldots, k \quad (2.10)$$

as its shuffling result where $r_{j,i}$ is randomly chosen from Q.

5. A challenger (e.g., trusted parties, independent observers or a pseudorandom function) randomly chooses L-bit integers s_i and s'_i for $i = 1, 2, \ldots k$.

6. The shuffling node proves that the challenger can find integers t_i and t'_i for $i = 1, 2, \ldots k$ in polynomial time, such that

$$\sum_{i=1}^{k} s_i D(c_{0,i}) = \sum_{i=1}^{k} t_i D(c'_{0,i}) \quad (2.11)$$

$$\sum_{i=1}^{k} s'_i D(c_{0,i}) = \sum_{i=1}^{k} t'_i D(c'_{0,i}) \quad (2.12)$$

$$\sum_{i=1}^{k} s_i s'_i D(c_{0,i}) = \sum_{i=1}^{k} t_i t'_i D(c'_{0,i}) \quad (2.13)$$

$$\sum_{i=1}^{k} s_i D(c_{j,i}) = \sum_{i=1}^{k} t_i D(c'_{j,i}) \text{ for } j = 1, 2, \ldots, n/k \quad (2.14)$$

Note that an additional group of random ciphertexts, G_0, is shuffled using the same permutation and proved to be valid in the same batch. This additional group is necessary to satisfy a certain linear ignorance assumption. When $H()$ is regarded as a random oracle, linear ignorance assumption on the shuffling node with regard to $D(c_{0,1}), D(c_{0,2}), \ldots, D(c_{0,k})$ is automatically satisfied without any trust.

Suppose Paillier encryption with distributed decryption [37] is employed for encryption in [86]. Parameters and re-encryption function of the employed encryption function are as follows.

- Multiplication modulus is N^2 where $N = p'q'$ and p', q' are secret large primes.

- $RE(c) = cr^N \bmod N^2$ where r is randomly chosen from Z_N^*.

Re-encryption operation in (2.10) is implemented in [86] through

$$c'_{j,i} = c_{j,\pi(i)} r_{j,i}^N \bmod N^2 \text{ for } j = 0, 1, \ldots, n/k \text{ and } i = 1, 2, \ldots, k$$

where $r_{j,i}$ is randomly chosen from Z_N^* for $j = 0, 1, \ldots, n/k$ and $i = 1, 2, \ldots, k$. The shuffling node instantiates proof of (2.11), (2.12), (2.13) and (2.14) as follows.

1. The shuffling node chooses r'_i from Z_N^* for $i = 1, 2, \ldots k$ and publishes $c''_{0,i} = c'^{t_i}_{0,i} r'^N_i \bmod N^2$ for $i = 1, 2, \ldots k$.

2. The node then proves a knowledge statement:

$$ST\ (\ t_i, t'_i, r'_i \text{ for } i = 1, 2, \ldots k, R_1, R_2, R_3, R_4 \qquad (2.15)$$
$$\mid c''_{0,i} = c'^{t_i}_{0,i} r'^{N}_i \bmod N^2 \text{ for } i = 1, 2, \ldots k,$$
$$R^N_1 \prod^k_{i=1} c^{s_i}_{0,i} = \prod^k_{i=1} c''_{0,i} \bmod N^2,$$
$$R^N_2 \prod^k_{i=1} c^{s'_i}_{0,i} = \prod^k_{i=1} c'^{t'_i}_{0,i} \bmod N^2,$$
$$R^N_3 \prod^k_{i=1} c^{s_i s'_i}_{0,i} = \prod^k_{i=1} c''^{t'_i}_{0,i} \bmod N^2,$$
$$R^N_4 \prod^k_{i=1} c^{s_i}_{j,i} = \prod^k_{i=1} c'^{t_i}_{j,i} \bmod N^2 \text{ for } j = 1, 2, \ldots, n/k\ )$$

Knowledge statement (2.15) is proved in detail in Figure 2.8 where S denotes a shuffling node and V denotes a verifier. Note that unlike in [90] L can be long (e.g., a full length like 1024 bits) in the new scheme. The only restriction is $2^L < p'$ and $2^L < q'$. As p' and q' are full length integers, the challenges can be full length integers as well. With full length challenges, not only stronger soundness can be achieved, but also the proof protocol in Figure 2.8 can become non-interactive when necessary by generating the challenges through a hash function. It will be illustrated that efficiency improvement in the new shuffling scheme is so great that efficiency is still very high when full length challenges are employed.

It is straightforward that in [86] if the shuffling node is honest, the ciphertexts are correctly shuffled and the shuffling operations are successfully verified. Theorem 5 guarantees public verifiability and soundness of the shuffling protocol in [86].

Theorem 5 *If s_i and s'_i for $i = 1, 2, \ldots, n$ are randomly chosen from $\{0, 1, \ldots, 2^L - 1\}$ and the shuffling node can find t_i and t'_i in polynomial time to satisfy Equations (2.11), (2.12), (2.13) and (2.14) with a probability larger than 2^{-L}, then there is an identical permutation from $D(c_{j,1}), D(c_{j,2}), \ldots, D(c_{j,k})$ to $D(c'_{j,1}), D(c'_{j,2}), \ldots, D(c'_{j,k})$ for $j = 0, 1, \ldots, n/k$.*

To prove Theorem 5, Lemma 4, Lemma 5, Lemma 6 and Lemma 7 are needed. Lemma 4, Lemma 5, Lemma 6 in this paper are Lemma 1, Lemma 4, Lemma 5 respectively in [90] while Lemma 7 in this paper is Theorem 1 in [90]. Their proof is not repeated here.

Lemma 4 *If given random integers s_i from $\{0, 1, \ldots, 2^L - 1\}$ for $i = 1, 2, \ldots, k$, a party can calculate in polynomial time integers t_i for $i = 1, 2, \ldots, k$ with a probability larger than 2^{-L}, such that $\sum^k_{i=1} s_i m_i = \sum^k_{i=1} t_i m'_i$, then he can calculate in polynomial time a matrix M such that $(m'_1, m'_2, \ldots, m'_k)M = (m_1, m_2, \ldots, m_k)$.*

1. $S \longrightarrow V$:
$$a_i = c'^{v_i}_{0,i} x^N_i \bmod N^2 \text{ for } i = 1, 2, \ldots, k$$
$$f = W^N_1 \bmod N^2$$
$$a = (\textstyle\prod_{i=1}^k c'^{v'_i}_{0,i})/W^N_2 \bmod N^2$$
$$b = (\textstyle\prod_{i=1}^k c''^{v_i}_{0,i})/W^N_3 \bmod N^2$$
$$g_j = (\textstyle\prod_{i=1}^k c'^{v_i}_{j,i})/W^N_{4,j} \bmod N^2 \text{ for } j = 1, 2, \ldots, n/k$$

where $x_i \in_R Z^*_N$ for $i = 1, 2, \ldots, k$, W_1, W_2, $W_3 \in_R Z^*_N$, $W_{4,j} \in_R Z^*_N$ for $j = 1, 2, \ldots, n/k$, $v_i, v'_i \in_R \{0, 1, \ldots, 2^L - 1\}$ for $i = 1, 2, \ldots, k$.

2. $V \longrightarrow S$:
$$c \in_R Z_N$$

3. $S \longrightarrow V$:
$$\alpha_i = x_i r'^c_i \bmod N^2 \text{ for } i = 1, 2, \ldots, k$$
$$z_1 = W_1 R^c_1 \bmod N^2$$
$$z_2 = W_2 R^c_2 \bmod N^2$$
$$z_3 = W_3 R^c_3 \bmod N^2$$
$$z_{4,j} = W_{4,j} R^c_{4,j} \bmod N^2 \text{ for } j = 1, 2, \ldots, n/k$$
$$\gamma_i = ct_i + v_i \bmod N \text{ for } i = 1, 2, \ldots, k$$
$$\gamma'_i = ct'_i + v'_i \bmod N \text{ for } i = 1, 2, \ldots, k$$

where $R_1 = \prod_{i=1}^k (r^{t_i}_{0,i} r'_i) \bmod N^2$, $R_2 = \prod_{i=1}^k (r^{t'_i}_{0,i}) \bmod N^2$, $R_3 = \prod_{i=1}^k (r^{t_i t'_i}_{0,i} r'^{t_i}_i) \bmod N^2$, $R_{4,j} = \prod_{i=1}^k r^{t_i}_{j,i} \bmod N^2$ for $j = 1, 2, \ldots, n/k$, $t_i = s_{\pi(i)}$, $t'_i = s'_{\pi(i)}$ and $\pi()$ is the permutation used in the shuffling.

Anyone can verify
$$a_i c''^c_{0,i} = c'^{\gamma_i}_{0,i} \alpha^N_i \bmod N^2 \text{ for } i = 1, 2, \ldots, k$$
$$f C^c_1 = z^N_1 \bmod N^2$$
$$a C^c_2 z^N_2 = \textstyle\prod_{i=1}^k c'^{\gamma'_i}_{0,i} \bmod N^2$$
$$b C^c_3 z^N_3 = \textstyle\prod_{i=1}^k c''^{\gamma'_i}_{0,i} \bmod N^2$$
$$g_j C^c_{4,j} z^N_{4,j} = \textstyle\prod_{i=1}^k c'^{\gamma_i}_{j,i} \bmod N^2 \text{ for } j = 1, 2, \ldots, n/k$$

where $C_1 = \prod_{i=1}^k c''_{0,i}/\prod_{i=1}^k c^{s_i}_{0,i} \bmod N^2$, $C_2 = \prod_{i=1}^k c^{s'_i}_{0,i} \bmod N^2$, $C_3 = \prod_{i=1}^k c^{s_i s'_i}_{0,i} \bmod N^2$ and $C_{4,j} = \prod_{i=1}^k c^{s_i}_{j,i} \bmod N^2$ for $j = 1, 2, \ldots, n/k$.

Figure 2.8: Public Proof and Verification of (2.15) in [86]

Lemma 5 *If given random integers s_i from $\{0, 1, \ldots, 2^L - 1\}$ for $i = 1, 2, \ldots, k$, a party can calculate a $n \times n$ non-singular matrix M and integers t_i for $i = 1, 2, \ldots, k$ in polynomial time such that $(m_1, m_2, \ldots, m_k) = (m'_1, m'_2, \ldots, m'_k)M$ and $\sum_{i=1}^{k} s_i m_i = \sum_{i=1}^{k} t_i m'_i$ where $(m_1, m_2, \ldots, m_k)$ and $(m'_1, m'_2, \ldots, m'_k)$ are two vectors, then $(s_1, s_2, \ldots, s_k)M = (t_1, t_2, \ldots, t_k)$ under linear ignorance assumption on the party with regard to $m_1, m_2, \ldots, m_k$.*

Lemma 6 *If $\sum_{i=1}^{k} y_i s_i = 0$ with a probability larger than 2^{-L} for random integers $s_1, s_2, \ldots, s_k$ from $\{0, 1, 2, \ldots, 2^L - 1\}$, then $y_i = 0$ for $i = 1, 2, \ldots, k$.*

Lemma 7 *If s_i and s'_i are randomly chosen from $\{0, 1, \ldots, 2^L - 1\}$ for $i = 1, 2, \ldots, n$ and the shuffling node can find t_i and t'_i in polynomial time to satisfy Equations (2.16), (2.17) and (2.18) with a probability larger than 2^{-L}, there exists an $n \times n$ permutation matrix M such that $(D(c'_1), D(c'_2), \ldots, D(c'_n))M = (D(c_1), D(c_2), \ldots, D(c_n))$ under linear ignorance assumption on the shuffling node with regard to $D(c_1), D(c_2), \ldots, D(c_n)$.*

$$\sum_{i=1}^{n} s_i D(c_i) = \sum_{i=1}^{n} t_i D(c'_i) \tag{2.16}$$

$$\sum_{i=1}^{n} s'_i D(c_i) = \sum_{i=1}^{n} t'_i D(c'_i) \tag{2.17}$$

$$\sum_{i=1}^{n} s_i s'_i D(c_i) = \sum_{i=1}^{n} t_i t'_i D(c'_i) \tag{2.18}$$

Proof of Theorem 5:
If given random integers s_i and $s'_i \in \{0, 1, \ldots, 2^L - 1\}$ for $i = 1, 2, \ldots, k$, the shuffling node can calculate integers t_i and t'_i for $i = 1, 2, \ldots, k$ in polynomial time to satisfy Equations (2.11), (2.12), (2.13) and (2.14), then the following deductions can be made with the help of Lemma 7, Lemma 4 and a fact: linear ignorance assumption on any party with regard to $D(c_{0,1}), D(c_{0,2}), \ldots, D(c_{0,k})$ is automatically satisfied in the random oracle model without any trust assumption.

According to Lemma 7, Equations (2.11), (2.12) and (2.13) imply that there exists a permutation matrix M such that

$$(D(c'_{0,1}), D(c'_{0,2}), \ldots, D(c'_{0,k}))M = (D(c_{0,1}), D(c_{0,2}), \ldots, D(c_{0,k}))$$

According to Lemma 5,

$$(s_1, s_2, \ldots, s_k)M = (t_1, t_2, \ldots, t_k) \tag{2.19}$$

According to Lemma 4 and Lemma 5, Equation (2.14) implies that there exist matrices M_j such that

$$(D(c'_{j,1}), D(c'_{j,2}), \ldots, D(c'_{j,k}))M_j = (D(c_{j,1}), D(c_{j,2}), \ldots, D(c_{j,k}))$$
$$\text{for } j = 1, 2, \ldots, n/k$$

and

$$(s_1, s_2, \ldots, s_k)M_j = (t_1, t_2, \ldots, t_k) \text{ for } j = 1, 2, \ldots, n/k \tag{2.20}$$

Subtracting (2.20) from (2.19) yields

$$(s_1, s_2, \ldots, s_n)(M - M_j) = (0, 0, \ldots, 0) \text{ for } j = 1, 2, \ldots, n/k$$

According to Lemma 6, every column vector in matrix $M - M_j$ contains k zeros for $j = 1, 2, \ldots, n/k$. So $M = M_j$ for $j = 1, 2, \ldots, n/k$. Therefore there is an identical permutation (matrix) from $D(c_{j,1}), D(c_{j,2}), \ldots, D(c_{j,k})$ to $D(c'_{j,1}), D(c'_{j,2}), \ldots, D(c'_{j,k})$ for $j = 0, 1, \ldots, n/k$. □

As the encryption algorithm suitable for shuffling is at most semantically secure against a polynomial adversary, no stronger privacy can be achieved in any shuffling if every variable possible to reveal the permutation (including the output ciphertexts) is taken into account. Although some existing shuffling schemes claim stronger privacy (e.g., perfect ZK), they only cover incomplete shuffling transcripts and ignore some ciphertexts which reveal the permutation to an unlimited adversary. In the following, complete shuffling transcript including all the possible information-revealing variables is used to formally prove computational ZK of the new shuffling scheme.

Theorem 6 *The shuffling scheme in [86] is computational ZK.*

To prove Theorem 6, a lemma is proved first.

Lemma 8 *When $k = n$ and there are only two groups, the shuffling scheme in [86] is computational ZK.*

Proof of Theorem 6: Mathematical induction is used in this proof. When there are two groups, Lemma 8 illustrates that this theorem is correct.

If this theorem is correct when there are m groups, it is correct as well when there are $m + 1$ groups due to the follow deduction. If this theorem is incorrect when there are $m + 1$ groups, as it is correct when there are m groups, there must exist a certain group G_l such that $l \in \{1, 2, \ldots, m+1\}$, the proof in $G_0, \ldots G_{l-1}, G_{l+1}, \ldots, G_{m+1}$ is computational ZK, and the proof in G_l is not computational ZK. So the proof in G_0, G_l is not computational ZK. This is contradictory to Lemma 8. Therefore, this theorem is correct when there are $m + 1$ groups.

This theorem is proved when there are two groups and induction from m groups to $m + 1$ groups is proved. So this theorem is correct. □

2.6 Survey and Analysis of SMN

When employing the existing mix network schemes to implement anonymous communication in practice, we need to be aware that some of them have drawbacks and limitations. Especially, the SMN schemes often need to make some trade-offs in security to improve efficiency. More precisely, some of them can only work under some conditions; some of them have some security concerns; some of them may even fail in functionality. An appropriate mix network scheme for a certain application must be chosen very carefully.

2.6.1 The Assumptions Needed in the Mix Networks in [51] and [52]

Groth proposes a mix network scheme [52] and then cooperates with Lu to improve its efficiency in [51]. In [52], it is suggested to prove validity of the shuffling by showing

$$\prod_{i=1}^{n} D(c_i)^{t_i} = \prod_{i=1}^{n} D(c_i')^{t_{\pi(i)}} \tag{2.21}$$

where $\pi()$ is a permutation of $\{1, 2, \ldots, n\}$ and t_i for $i = 1, 2, \ldots, n$ are random integers. Unfortunately, Equation (2.21) cannot be proved or verified explicitly since the messages and $\pi()$ must be kept secret. Groth requires a homomorphic encryption algorithm like El Gamal encryption and proves satisfaction of Equation (2.21) by showing

$$\prod_{i=1}^{n} c_i^{t_i} = \prod_{i=1}^{n} c_i'^{t_{\pi(i)}}. \tag{2.22}$$

Then he proposed a technique to publicly compute $c = \prod_{i=1}^{n} c_i^{t_i}$ and $c' = \prod_{i=1}^{n} c_i'^{t_{\pi(i)}}$ without revealing $\pi()$. Finally $D(c'/c) = 1$ can be proved and verified. For simplicity, his prototype protocol instead of his final optimised protocol is described as follows since the latter only optimises some calculation details and both protocols share the same method.

1. El Gamal encryption is employed. Private key $\hat{X}$ is chosen from $Z_{\hat{q}}$ and public key $(\hat{g}_1, \hat{Y} = \hat{g}_1^{\hat{X}})$ is published. A message m in $\hat{G}$ is encrypted into $(\hat{g}_1^r, m\hat{Y}^r)$ where r is randomly chosen from $Z_{\hat{q}}$. Re-encryption function $RE(c, r')$ re-encrypts ciphertext $c = (a, b)$ to $c' = (a', b') = (\hat{g}_1^{r'} a, \hat{Y}^{r'} b)$ where r' is randomly chosen from $Z_{\hat{q}}$. A ciphertext $c = (a, b)$ is decrypted into $b/a^{\hat{X}}$.

2. The routing node publishes $s_i \in Z_{\hat{q}}$ and $S_i = \hat{g}_1^{s_{\pi(i)}} \hat{g}_2^{r_i}$ for $i = 1, 2, \ldots, n$ where $\pi()$ is a permutation of $\{1, 2, \ldots, n\}$ and r_i is randomly chosen from $Z_{\hat{q}}$. The node proves that s_i for $i = 1, 2, \ldots, n$ are permuted and committed in S_i for $i = 1, 2, \ldots, n$ where the permutation $\pi()$ is kept secret as detailed in [74, 52].

3. The routing node gets $c_i = (a_i, b_i)$ for $i = 1, 2, \ldots, n$ and shuffles them to $c_i' = RE(c_{\pi(i)}) = (a_i', b_i')$ for $i = 1, 2, \ldots, n$.

4. Random integers $t_i \in Z_{\hat{q}}$ for $i = 1, 2, \ldots, n$ are chosen by a verifier.

5. The routing node publishes $T_i = \hat{g}_1^{t_{\pi(i)}} \hat{g}_2^{r_i'}$ for $i = 1, 2, \ldots, n$ where r_i' is randomly chosen from $Z_{\hat{q}}$. It proves that the same permutation used to

shuffle and commit s_i for $i = 1, 2, \ldots, n$ in S_i for $i = 1, 2, \ldots, n$ is used to shuffle and commit t_i for $i = 1, 2, \ldots, n$ in T_i for $i = 1, 2, \ldots, n$ while the permutation $\pi()$ is kept secret as detailed in [74, 52].

6. The routing node calculates $a' = \hat{g}_1^\gamma \prod_{i=1}^n a'^{t_{\pi(i)}}_i$ and $b' = \hat{Y}^\gamma \prod_{i=1}^n b'^{t_{\pi(i)}}_i$ where γ is randomly chosen from $Z_{\hat{q}}$ and provides a ZK proof

$$ZP \ (\ \gamma, \ t_{\pi(1)}, t_{\pi(2)}, \ldots, t_{\pi(n)}, \ r'_1, r'_2, \ldots, r'_n$$
$$| \ a' = \hat{g}_1^\gamma \prod_{i=1}^n a'^{t_{\pi(i)}}_i, \ b' = \hat{Y}^\gamma \prod_{i=1}^n b'^{t_{\pi(i)}}_i,$$
$$T_i = \hat{g}_1^{t_{\pi(i)}} \hat{g}_2^{r'_i} \text{ for } i = 1, 2, \ldots, n \ )$$

which can be implemented using ZK proof of knowledge of logarithm [98] and ZK proof of equality of logarithms [27].

7. The routing node proves

$$\log_{\hat{g}_1} (a' / \prod_{i=1}^n a_i^{t_i}) = \log_{\hat{Y}} (b' / \prod_{i=1}^n b_i^{t_i}) \tag{2.23}$$

using the proof of equality of logarithms [27].

From the viewpoint of batch shuffling verification (see [93] for details), validity of shuffling in [52] actually depends on Hypothesis 1.

Hypothesis 1 *Suppose* $y_i \in Z_{\hat{p}}$, $z_i \in Z_{\hat{p}}$ *and* $t_i \in Z_{\hat{q}}$ *for* $i = 1, 2, \ldots, n$. *If* $\log_{\hat{g}_1} \prod_{i=1}^n y_i^{t_i} = \log_{\hat{Y}} \prod_{i=1}^n z_i^{t_i}$, *then* $\log_{\hat{g}_1} y_i = \log_{\hat{Y}} z_i$ *for* $i = 1, 2, \ldots, n$ *except for a negligible probability.*

However, in Hypothesis 1 there is an implicit assumption: y_i and z_i for $i = 1, 2, \ldots, n$ are in $\hat{G}$. When this assumption is satisfied, Hypothesis 1 is correct. When it is not satisfied, Hypothesis 1 may fail. For example, when $z_j \notin \hat{G}$, $\log_{\hat{g}_1} y_j = \log_{\hat{Y}} \hat{g}_0^{(\hat{p}-1)/2} z_j$ and $i \leq j \leq n$, the verification equation $\log_{\hat{g}_1} \prod_{i=1}^n y_i^{t_i} = \log_{\hat{Y}} \prod_{i=1}^n z_i^{t_i}$ can still be satisfied when t_j is even. As $(\hat{p}-1)/\hat{q}$ has at least one factor 2, this attack can work with a probability of at least 0.5. When $(\hat{p}-1)/\hat{q}$ has other factors than 2, the probability for Hypothesis 1 to fail under this attack is even larger.

Dependency of Hypothesis 1 on the assumption shows that security of the shuffling protocol in [52] depends on an assumption: (a_i, b_i) and (a'_i, b'_i) for $i = 1, 2, \ldots, n$ are valid ciphertexts in $\hat{G}^2$. As (a_i, b_i) for $i = 1, 2, \ldots, n$ are input ciphertexts in the shuffling, they may be from a trusted source and thus guaranteed to be in $\hat{G}^2$. However, there is no reason to take it for granted that (a'_i, b'_i) for $i = 1, 2, \ldots, n$ are in $\hat{G}^2$ without any verification as they are the output of the routing node, whose operations are not trusted and must be publicly verified in any shuffling scheme. When the output ciphertexts (a'_i, b'_i) for $i = 1, 2, \ldots, n$ are not verified to be valid ciphertexts in $\hat{G}^2$, a malicious routing node can break security of the shuffling protocol as follows.

- The routing node shuffles $c_{\pi(i)}$ to $c_i' = (a_i', \hat{g}_0^{(\hat{p}-1)/2}b_i')$ where $(a_i', b_i') = RE(c_{\pi(i)})$ for some i in $\{1, 2, \ldots, n\}$ while shuffling all the other input ciphertexts honestly. When $t_{\pi(i)}$ is even, Equation (2.23) is satisfied and this shuffling can pass Groth's verification.

- If the verifier always chooses odd t_i the dishonest server can still pass the verification by shuffling two inputs $c_{\pi(i)}$ and $c_{\pi(j)}$ to $c_i' = (a_i', \hat{g}_0^{(\hat{p}-1)/2}b_i')$ and $c_j' = (a_j', \hat{g}_0^{(\hat{p}-1)/2}b_j')$ and shuffling all the other input ciphertexts honestly where $(a_i', b_i') = RE(c_{\pi(i)})$ and $(a_j', b_j') = RE(c_{\pi(j)})$.

- All in all, this attack can always succeed with a probability no less than 0.5. When $(\hat{p} - 1)/\hat{q}$ has other factors than 2, the probability for its success is even larger.

The essence of the attack is that a ciphertext encrypting a message in $\hat{G}$ can be incorrectly shuffled to a ciphertext encrypting a message in $Z_{\hat{p}}^* - \hat{G}$ without being detected with a non-negligible probability. Obviously, if (a_i, b_i) and (a_i', b_i') for $i = 1, 2, \ldots, n$ are verified to be in $\hat{G}^2$, the attack can be prevented. However, membership test of the ciphertexts in $\hat{G}^2$ is not specified in the protocol description or counted in the cost estimation in [52]. Therefore, the shuffling protocol in [52] must specify the membership test and its efficiency estimation should be adjusted to include the additional cost.

In [51], the shuffling protocol is simplified into a three-move zero knowledge proof to illustrate validity of the shuffling. The commitment in the first move in the zero knowledge proof in [51] is a computationally binding commitment[6] of the secret permutation used in the shuffling. More precisely, the commitment function is $com(w_1, w_2, \ldots, w_k, r) = \prod_{i=1}^{k} g_i^{w_i} h^r$ where $g_1, g_2, \ldots, g_k, h$ are generators of a cyclic group and the secret permutation matrix used in the shuffling is committed to in multiple instances of this function. Security of the shuffling protocol in [51] is based on an assumption: the binding property of the commitment function is computationally unbreakable such that in the third move the prover is forced to use the unique set of secret integers committed in the first move to generate his response to the random challenge in the second move (see the two theorems in [51] for more details of this assumption). In [52, 102, 103] it is illustrated and emphasized that when batch proof (e.g., the proof in [51]) is used, security of shuffling fails if the prover can adjust the committed permutation after it receives the challenge.

When the cyclic group is large enough (e.g., containing 1024-bit integers) this assumption is sound. However, in [51] the cyclic group contains 240-bit integers for the sake of high efficiency. So an adversary can search for $\log_{g_i} g_j$ or $\log_{g_i} h$ in a space no larger than 2^{240} (e.g., using Pollard's lambda method) to break the binding property of the commitment function. Searching for discrete logarithm in a space with a size 2^{240} is not always difficult enough in

---

[6]A binding commitment cannot be opened in two different ways, so the message committed in it is unique.

the current standard of cryptography. Therefore, the assumption is not always unquestionable (especially when there is a powerful adversary) and security in the shuffling is not so strong as in other shuffling schemes, which employ much larger cyclic groups and have much stronger security. As a result, in some cases (e.g., with a critical security standard or powerful adversary) a dishonest routing node cannot be absolutely prevented from passing the verification with an invalid shuffling in [51]. In summary, [51] improves efficiency of a mix network but weakens its security. Our suggestion is that in applications with critical security requirements like mix networks for e-voting, a larger cyclic group should be employed in the shuffling scheme in [51] to strengthen its security. Although that means lower efficiency, sometimes security is more important.

2.6.2 Security Concerns in [90] and [102]

The mix network scheme in [90] employs some incorrect operations such that it may go wrong even if every participant is honest and strictly follows the protocol. In description of their shuffling scheme in Section 3 in [90], three equations they call (31), (32) and (33) in their paper are proved in a four-step protocol as follows where more details like complete parameter setting can be found in [90].

1. The shuffling party randomly chooses $W_1 \in Z_N^*$, $W_2 \in Z_N^*$, $W_3 \in Z_N^*$, $v_i \in Z_N$ for $i = 1, 2, \ldots, n$, $v_i' \in Z_N$ for $i = 1, 2, \ldots, n$ and $x_i \in Z_N^*$ for $i = 1, 2, \ldots, n$. He calculates

$$a_i = c'^{v_i}_i x_i^N \bmod N^2 \text{ for } i = 1, 2, \ldots, n$$
$$f = W_1^N \bmod N^2$$
$$a = (\prod_{i=1}^n c'^{v_i'}_i)/W_2^N \bmod N^2$$
$$b = (\prod_{i=1}^n (c''^{v_i'}_i))/W_3^N \bmod N^2$$

2. The shuffling party calculates $c = H(f, a, b, a_1, a_2, \ldots, a_n)$ where $H()$ is a random oracle query implemented by a hash function with a 128-bit output.

3. Integers

$$z_1 = W_1 R_1^c \bmod N^2$$
$$z_2 = W_2/R_2^c \bmod N^2$$
$$z_3 = W_3/R_3^c \bmod N^2$$
$$\alpha_i = x_i r_i'^c \bmod N^2 \text{ for } i = 1, 2, \ldots, n$$
$$\gamma_i = v_i + c t_i \bmod N \text{ for } i = 1, 2, \ldots, n \tag{2.24}$$
$$\gamma_i' = c t_i' - v_i' \bmod N \text{ for } i = 1, 2, \ldots, n \tag{2.25}$$

are calculated as responses to 128-bit challenge c where $v_i, v'_i \in Z_N$, $t_i, t'_i \in Z_{2^L}$ and Z_N is the message space of the employed Paillier encryption algorithm and L is a security parameter.

4. Equation

$$c = H(\ z_1^N / C_1^c,\ C_2^c / (z_2^N \textstyle\prod_{i=1}^n c'^{\gamma'_i}_i),$$
$$C_3^c / (z_3^N \textstyle\prod_{i=1}^n c''^{\gamma'_i}_i),$$
$$c'^{\gamma_i}_i \alpha_i^N / c''^c_i \text{ for } i = 1, 2, \ldots, n\ )$$

is verified.

As the orders of c'_i and c''_i are not N in [90], calculation of $c'^{\gamma'_i}_i$, $c''^{\gamma'_i}_i$ and $c'^{\gamma_i}_i$ in the verification raises bases to exponents calculated with a modulus unequal to their orders. So (2.24) and (2.25) use wrong moduli. Therefore, even if the prover is honest and strictly follows the protocol, the verification may fail, while the parameter setting of c, v_i, v'_i, t_i, t'_i decides that the probability of failure is non-negligible.

A similar mistake occurs in [102], which describes its shuffling protocol in a so-called Protocol 2. As Protocol 2 is a complex seven-step proof protocol, it is not recalled here in its complete form and interested readers can find its complete description in [102]. We only focus on its incorrect operations as follows where definition of all the involved integers can be found in [102].

- In Step 6 of Protocol 2 in [102], the prover calculates and publishes

$$e_i = ct_i + s_i \bmod 2^{K_2 + K_4 + 2K_5} \tag{2.26}$$
$$e'_i = ct'_i + s'_i \bmod 2^{K_2 + K_4 + 2K_5} \tag{2.27}$$
$$d_i = cp_{\pi(i)} + r_i \bmod 2^{K_3 + K_4 + K_5} \tag{2.28}$$
$$e = ct + s \bmod 2^{K_2 + NK_3 + K_4 + K_5 + \log_2 N} \tag{2.29}$$
$$e' = ct' + s' \bmod 2^{K_2 + K_5 + \log_2 N} \tag{2.30}$$

where K_2, K_3, K_4, K_5 are integers defined in [102] as security parameters.

- In Step 7 of Protocol 2 in [102], verifications are

$$\mathbf{b}_i^c \gamma_i = \mathbf{h}^{e_i} \mathbf{b}_{i-1}^{d_i} \tag{2.31}$$
$$\mathbf{b}'^c_i \gamma'_i) = \mathbf{h}^{e'_i} \mathbf{g}^{d_i} \tag{2.32}$$
$$(b_1^c \alpha_1,\ (V/b_2)^c \alpha_2,\ W^c \alpha_3) =$$
$$(g^{f_1} \textstyle\prod_{i=1}^N (u'_i)^{d_i},\ g^{-f_2} \textstyle\prod_{i=1}^N (v'_i)^{d_i}, \tag{2.33}$$
$$g^{f_{r'}} \textstyle\prod_{i=1}^N (g_i)^{d_i})$$
$$(\mathbf{b}_i^c \gamma_i,\ (\mathbf{b}'^c_i \gamma'_i) = (\mathbf{h}^{e_i} \mathbf{b}_{i-1}^{d_i},\ \mathbf{h}^{e'_i} \mathbf{g}^{d_i}) \tag{2.34}$$
$$(\mathbf{g}^{-\prod_{i=1}^N p_i} \mathbf{b}_N)^c \gamma = \mathbf{h}^e \tag{2.35}$$
$$(\mathbf{g}^{-\sum_{i=1}^N p_i} \textstyle\prod_{i=1}^N \mathbf{b}'_i)^c \gamma = \mathbf{h}^{e'} \tag{2.36}$$

Note that

- The order of $\mathbf{h}$ is $(\mathbf{p}-1)(\mathbf{q}-1)/2$ instead of $2^{K_2+K_4+2K_5}$ and $ct_i + s_i$, $ct'_i + s'_i$ distributes beyond $2^{K_2+K_4+2K_5}$

- The order of g_i is q as set in Section 2 of [102] instead of $2^{K_3+K_4+K_5}$ and $cp_{\pi(i)} + r_i$ distributes beyond $2^{K_3+K_4+K_5}$

- The parameter setting of the encryption algorithm in Section 4 of [102] implies that the order of u'_i is q instead of $2^{K_3+K_4+K_5}$ and $cp_{\pi(i)} + r_i$ distributes beyond $2^{K_3+K_4+K_5}$

- In Section 4.5 of [102], the author assumes $m_i \in G_q$, so the order of v'_i is q instead of $2^{K_3+K_4+K_5}$ and $cp_{\pi(i)} + r_i$ distributes beyond $2^{K_3+K_4+K_5}$

- The order of $\mathbf{h}$ is secret and not $2^{K_2+NK_3+K_4+K_5+\log_2 N}$ and $ct + s$ distributes beyond $2^{K_2+NK_3+K_4+K_5+\log_2 N}$

- The order of $\mathbf{h}$ is secret and not $2^{K_2+K_5+\log_2 N}$ and $ct' + s'$ distributes beyond $2^{K_2+K_5+\log_2 N}$

where $\mathbf{p}$, $\mathbf{q}$ and q are secret system parameters defined in [102] and cannot be used by the prover. So (2.31), (2.32), (2.33), (2.34), (2.35) and (2.36) may not be satisfied even if the prover is honest and strictly follows the protocol.

The security problem in [90] and [102] seldom occurs in secure protocols. Usually, secure protocols always run smoothly when all the participants are honest and strictly follow the protocols. Their failure is usually discussed in the case that some dishonest participant deviates from the protocols. The possibility of automatic failure of secure protocols when every operation is legal is usually not large, but needs to be understood.

2.6.3 Failure in Functionality of the Mix Network by Wikstrom

The shuffling protocol in [102] shows validity of shuffling by proving knowledge of secret integers $\rho_1, \rho_2, \ldots, \rho_n$ to satisfy

$$\prod_{i=1}^n c'^{\rho_i}_i = D(\prod_{i=1}^n c^{p_i}_i) \tag{2.37}$$

where $p_1, p_2, \ldots, p_n$ are primes randomly chosen from a range $[2^{K_3-1}, 2^{K_3} - 1]$ and $\rho_1, \rho_2, \ldots, \rho_n$ is a permutation of $p_1, p_2, \ldots, p_n$. To guarantee that $\rho_1, \rho_2, \ldots, \rho_n$ is a permutation of $p_1, p_2, \ldots, p_n$ without revealing the permutation (which is actually the permutation used in the shuffling), the following three conditions are explicitly required in [102] where the relation between K

and K_3 is not explained in [102].[7]

$$\prod_{i=1}^{n} p_i = \prod_{i=1}^{n} \rho_i; \tag{2.38}$$

$$\sum_{i=1}^{n} p_i = \sum_{i=1}^{n} \rho_i; \tag{2.39}$$

$$-2^K + 1 \leq \rho_i \leq 2^K - 1 \text{ for } i = 1, 2, \ldots, n$$

to guarantee that no ρ_i can be the product

of multiple p_is

However, in [102] only proof of satisfaction of the first two conditions are provided, while proof of satisfaction of the third condition is not specified in description of the shuffling protocol. It is interesting to note that it is easy and efficient to prove satisfaction of the first two conditions (using simple zero knowledge proof primitives like zero knowledge proof of equality of discrete logarithms [27]) while proof of satisfaction of the third condition, n instances of range proof, is a complex and costly technique. Boudot has explained in [17] that each range proof costs at least scores of exponentiations unless in a special case with a large expansion rate where an integer in a range is proved to be in another much larger range (at least trillions of times larger than the range the integer is actually in).[8] Although only needing a constant cost independent of the size of the range, the existing range proof techniques [17, 69, 87] cost quite a few exponentiations, not to mention [87] had not been proposed by the time [102] was published. According to the efficiency estimation and analysis in [87], at least 25 exponentiations are needed for one instance of range proof. As $\rho_1, \rho_2, \ldots, \rho_n$ is a permutation of $p_1, p_2, \ldots, p_n$ and thus the range proof of ρ_i in $\{-2^K + 1, -2^K + 2, \ldots, 2^K - 1\}$ is not the special case with a large expansion rate, proof of satisfaction of the third condition costs at least $25n$ exponentiations and has a great influence on efficiency of the shuffling protocol in [102]. So, if Wikstrom includes proof of satisfaction of the third condition in his shuffling protocol but omits its specification in his protocol description for the sake of simplicity, its existence can still be noticed in the cost estimation of the shuffling protocol in [102]. However, we are surprised to find that the shuffling protocol in [102] is claimed to cost only $3.5n$ exponentiations (exactly the cost for proof of satisfaction of the first two conditions) in its cost estimation, which implies that the n instances of range proof are not included! Therefore, there is an obvious contradiction: the n instances of range proof are explicitly required in the shuffling protocol in [102] but disappear from its protocol description and cost estimation. As a result, whether the third condition is necessary in proof of validity of shuffling in [102] becomes a mystery and a doubt is cast upon security of the shuffling protocol in [102].

---

[7]Obviously, choice of K depends on K_3, otherwise the third condition is not helpful to prevent any ρ_i from being a product of p_is and guarantee validity of shuffling. Actually we guess that it is probable $K = K_3$.

[8]In [17], expansion rate is used to describe this special case and measure by how many times the range is expanded. So the special case can be called range proof with a large expansion rate.

In [103], a different argument is proposed: satisfaction of (2.38) and (2.39) is enough to guarantee that $\rho_1, \rho_2, \ldots, \rho_n$ is a permutation of $p_1, p_2, \ldots, p_n$ and thus that the shuffling is valid, while the third condition (satisfaction of the n instances of range inclusion) is not needed. Instead of easing the doubt about security of the shuffling scheme in [102, 103], this new argument shows failure of its security, although it is attempted in [103] to prove correctness of the argument. The reason is simple: in existence of concrete counter-examples, any argument or proof is in vain. A simple counter-example against this argument is $n = 10$, $p_1 = p_2 = \cdots = p_{10} = 2$ while $\rho_1 = \rho_2 = \rho_3 = \rho_4 = 4$, $\rho_5 = \rho_6 = 2$, $\rho_7 = \rho_8 = 1$ and $\rho_9 = \rho_{10} = -1$. Another simple counter-example is $n = 10$, $p_1 = p_2 = 2$, $p_3 = p_4 = 3$, $p_5 = p_6 = 5$, $p_7 = p_8 = 7$, $p_9 = p_{10} = 11$ while $\rho_1 = \rho_2 = 22$, $\rho_3 = \rho_4 = 15$, $\rho_5 = \rho_6 = -7$, $\rho_7 = \rho_8 = \rho_9 = \rho_{10} = -1$. Readers can easily verify that these two examples can satisfy both Equation (2.38) and Equation (2.39) while $\rho_1, \rho_2, \ldots, \rho_n$ is NOT a permutation of $p_1, p_2, \ldots, p_n$. Interested readers can easily find more counter-examples.

Our counter examples show that the third condition is necessary to guarantee validity of shuffling in [102, 103] and proof of its satisfaction must be provided and taken into account in cost estimation. So the n instances of range proof are needed in the shuffling scheme in [102, 103]. Therefore, at least $25n$ additional exponentiations are inevitable although including them means its efficiency will be greatly deteriorated. As a result, to redeem its security, the shuffling scheme in [102, 103] will lose its claimed advantage in efficiency over the previous shuffling schemes and become one of the least efficient shuffling schemes.

2.7 Efficiency of SMN: Claim and Reality

The mix network schemes in [52, 93, 90, 102, 51] claim much higher efficiency than the other SMN schemes and are usually regarded as efficient solutions to anonymous communication. For example, the shuffling proof in [51] is scores of times more efficient than that in [42, 41]. However, when carefully studying the principles and operations of their shuffling proof, we find that the shuffling proof mechanisms of the recent shuffling schemes are not much simpler than those of their predecessors, and some of the recent shuffling schemes are even more complex. For example, the shuffling schemes in [52] and [90] are developments of that in [74] using the same principle, the shuffling scheme in [102] needs additional range proofs, and the shuffling in [51] slightly modifies that in [42, 41] and extends it to a more complicated proof. How do the recent shuffling schemes achieve much higher efficiency without evolutionary breakthrough in shuffling proof? The reason partially lies in unfair claims and comparisons in efficiency. Some recent shuffling schemes employ much shorter exponents than usual in many computations, while assuming the previous shuffling schemes still employ exponents with normal length. Some recent shuffling scheme employs an efficiency improvement technique, which is appliable to the previous shuffling schemes as well but assumed not to apply to them. Some recent shuffling scheme even ignores its own very costly operations in efficiency claim and comparison. Those unfair factors in their efficiency claim and comparison will be detailed in this section.

2.7.1   Unfair Usage of Short Exponents

In public key cryptology, exponentiations are much more costly than multiplications and other basic computations, so they represent the dominant part of the computational cost of cryptographic protocols like shuffling. The cost of an exponentiation is approximately linear in the length of its exponent. In public key cryptographic applications, the bases of exponentiation computations are usually large integers in a large cyclic group. So a straightforward way to improve efficiency of the exponentiation computations is to shorten their exponents.

The first attempt to improve efficiency of shuffling schemes using this method is made in [93, 90]. In the shuffling schemes in [93, 90], after the ciphertexts are shuffled, some random integers are generated as challenges to the prover, who should respond to the challenges to carry on his proof of validity of his shuffling. Obviously, the longer the challenges are, the larger range they are randomly chosen from and the more difficult it is for an invalid shuffling to pass the following verification. As the challenges act as exponents in many exponentiation computations and greatly affect efficiency of the shuffling schemes, there is a conflict between soundness and efficiency. Long challenges support strong soundness but cause higher cost; short challenges improve efficiency but weaken soundness. In [93, 90], very short challenges (e.g., 20 bits long challenges) are used to achieve high efficiency, while soundness is weakened as a trade-off. Although this trade-off is acceptable for [93, 90] in some applications, an efficiency comparison with the previous shuffling schemes is unfair: it is assumed that the previous shuffling schemes use 1024-bit full-length challenges in their shuffling proof. Moreover, the sacrifice in soundness as a result of short challenges is not mentioned in [93, 90]. Obviously, if the previous shuffling schemes make the same sacrifice and employ challenges as short as 20 bits in their shuffling proof, their efficiency can be improved as well. To clearly and fairly show exactly how much efficiency improvement is achieved by the more advanced shuffling proof technique in [93, 90] over the previous shuffling schemes, the same security standard should be adopted and the same length should be chosen for their challenges. Therefore, the claim and comparison of efficiency in [93, 90] are unfair.

The same efficiency improvement mechanism using short challenges in shuffling proof is employed in [102] to improve efficiency. Again it assumes that the shuffling schemes before [93] employ full-length challenges. In [51], not only the challenges in shuffling proof but also the random exponents used in commitments are shortened where secret messages $m_1, m_2, \ldots, m_k$ are committed in $com(m_1, m_2, \ldots, m_k, r) = \prod_{i=1}^{k} g_i^{m_i} h^r$ and r is a random integer. It is not mentioned in [51] that short r weakens bindingness[9] of the commitment algorithm *com*() and thus soundness of the shuffling scheme and other shuffling schemes can employ the same mechanism to achieve higher efficiency. As in [93, 90] and [102], it is assumed in [51] that the shuffling schemes before [93] employ full-length exponents. Therefore, the claim and comparison of efficiency in [102] and [51] are unfair as well.

2.7.2 Other Unfair Factors in Efficiency Claim and Comparison

Besides short exponents, there are some other unfair factors in efficiency claim and comparison in the recent shuffling schemes. In [51], multiple secrets are committed in one commitment using only one random exponent to improve efficiency. Although the same commitment function can be employed in [52, 42, 41] to improve their efficiency too, it is assumed in [51] that the shuffling schemes in [52, 42, 41] still must commit to each secret in a separate commitment using a separate random exponent. In Section 5 of [52], an efficiency improvement mechanism is applied solely to itself and not employed in the previous shuffling schemes although it is appliable to them as well.

2.7.3 Re-evaluating Efficiency

As the efficiency advantages of the recent mix network schemes [52, 93, 90, 102, 51] over the other mix network schemes are not so great as they claim, their costs have to be re-estimated and their claimed efficiency advantage needs to be re-evaluated. Re-evaluation of the mix network schemes and a comparison against the existing claim of efficiency and security are given in Table 2.3. When computational cost of the shuffling schemes is estimated, the exponentiations are counted. For simplicity, they are counted in terms of multiples of n. As the re-encryption operation is efficient and costs almost the same in all the shuffling schemes, as in most existing shuffling schemes, in this paper only the shuffling proof is taken into account of the evaluation and comparison. For fairness of comparison, all the shuffling schemes are treated equally, especially in employment of efficiency improvement mechanisms. As stated before, applying an efficiency improvement mechanism to some shuffling schemes and excluding it from other shuffling schemes is unfair as all the efficiency improvement mechanisms discussed in this paper are simple and general techniques applicable to other schemes. So, for the sake of fairness and to show exactly how advanced the shuffling proof is in every shuffling scheme, the efficiency improvement mechanisms are not employed in any shuffling scheme in the estimation in Table 2.3. More precisely,

---

[9]Bindingness of a commitment algorithm guarantees that the committed secret is unique and cannot be changed.

Table 2.3: Comparison of shuffling schemes

Shuffling	Claimed computational cost	Fixed computational cost
[5, 6]	$16n \log_2 n$	$16n \log_2 n$
[42]	$6n$	$6n$
[74, 75]	$10n$	$10n$
[41]	$7n$	$7n$
[52][1]	$6n + 3n/\kappa$	$12n$
[93]	$< n$	$24n$
[90]	$5n$	$13n$
[102]	$\leq 3.5n$	$35n$
[51]	$< n$	$8n$
[50][2]	not claimed	$35n$
[86]	$2n$	$4n$

[1]κ is a security parameter used in the efficiency improvement mechanism in Section 5 in [52].

[2]The shuffling scheme in [50] is very special in comparison with other shuffling schemes. While the other shuffling schemes focus on computation in efficiency analysis as their communicational cost is approximately linear in their computational cost; the shuffling scheme in [50] achieves high efficiency in communication by sacrificing computational efficiency. So although communicational efficiency is not the subject of this paper, for the sake of fairness, we have to mention that the shuffling scheme in [50] has an advantage in communicational efficiency.

- All the exponentiations are supposed to have exponents with the same length and counted equally.

- The efficiency improvement mechanism in Section 5 in [52] is not employed.

- Each secret integer is committed in a separate commitment.

Moreover, ignored but necessary operations are taken into account and we suppose that the existing most efficient range proof technique [17] is employed to implement the n instances of range proof in [102].

The result of the re-evaluation is somewhat surprising. The efficiency advantage of the recent shuffling schemes over their predecessors is trivial, not to mention two of them have incomplete correctness and need fixing and one of them has to weaken its privacy. The most efficient secure shuffling scheme [42] is a very early proposal.

2.8 Summary

In summary, mix networks shuffle a batch of encrypted messages though multiple mixing servers such that the messages are re-encrypted (or partially decrypted) and reordered randomly. They are not traceable if at least one server conceals its shuffling and thus anonymous communication is realized. There are a few existing solutions to mix networks and they can be classified into different categories, according to how they randomise the shuffled ciphertexts (by partial decryption or re-encryption), how they prove validity of shuffling, and whether tags are used.

Proof and verification of validity of shuffling is the key operation in mix networks and can be implemented through general verification or separate verification. The former is suitable for applications with stronger requirement for efficiency and weaker requirement for security and flexibility; the latter is suitable for applications with weaker requirement for efficiency and stronger requirement for security and flexibility. In large-scale mix networks, grouped shuffling can be employed to achieve a better trade-off between privacy and efficiency. Some of the mix network schemes are successful and some others present concerns and problems in security and efficiency. They are surveyed and re-assessed so that appropriate solutions can be recommended to different applications of anonymous communication.

Chapter 3

Application of Mix Network to E-Voting: a Case Study

It has been stated in Chapter 2 that an important application of mix networks is electronic voting. In this chapter, application of mix networks to e-voting is studied in details. This practical case study is carried out in four steps. Firstly, a practical mix network protocol especially suitable for e-voting is described. Secondly, mix network based e-voting is designed. Thirdly, practical security concerns about the design are investigated and a solution is given. Fourthly, off-line pre-computation is employed to improve efficiency of mix networks in e-voting.

3.1   Mix Network for E-Voting

The existing mix network schemes cannot provide ideal support to e-voting. Among the well known mix network schemes [5, 6, 74, 42, 52, 93, 90, 102, 51, 50, 89], the most recent of them [52, 93, 90, 102, 51, 50, 89] (initially proposed in the past decade) are more efficient where the scheme in [41] is an extended journal version of [42] and the scheme in [75] is a formal publication of [74]. In the recent mix network schemes, the shuffling protocol in [93] is very efficient. However, unlike all the other shuffling protocols it only allows the routing node to choose its permutation from a small fraction of all the possible permutations. So it is not a complete shuffling and is weak in privacy. The other recent mix network schemes employ the same idea: given random integers t_i for $i = 1, 2, \ldots, n$, if

$$RE(\prod_{i=1}^{n} c_i^{t_i}) = \prod_{i=1}^{n} c'^{t'_i}_i \tag{3.1}$$

and $t_1', t_2', \ldots, t_n'$ is a permutation of $t_1, t_2, \ldots, t_n$, then $D(c_1'), D(c_2'), \ldots, D(c_n')$ is a permutation of $D(c_1), D(c_2), \ldots, D(c_n)$ with an overwhelmingly large probability. This idea is simple and effective and actually will be employed in the new mix network as well. However, its usage by the recent mix network schemes has two drawbacks. Firstly, they do not give a formal proof for soundness of shuffling guaranteed by this approach. Secondly, their methods to prove that $t_1', t_2', \ldots, t_n'$ is a permutation of $t_1, t_2, \ldots, t_n$ in (3.1) are not efficient enough as explained in Section 3.1.1.

In this section, a new proof protocol is proposed to prove that $t_1', t_2', \ldots, t_n'$ is a permutation of $t_1, t_2, \ldots, t_n$ in (3.1). The new proof method is simpler and more efficient than the existing ones. Moreover, for the first time a formal soundness analysis is given in a proposed mix network to illustrate why its satisfaction of (3.1) guarantees soundness of shuffling when $t_1', t_2', \ldots, t_n'$ is a permutation of $t_1, t_2, \ldots, t_n$. Therefore, both drawbacks in the recent mix network schemes [52, 93, 90, 102, 51, 50, 89] are overcome. To show their advantages, a comparison is made between the new mix network with the recent mix network schemes. The comparison avoids the imprecision, exaggeration and unfairness in the existing comparisons and is more fair and objective. To show its practical value, extending the new mix network to flexible environments and applying it to e-voting are discussed.

3.1.1   The Recent Mix Network Schemes

As stated before, the current methods to prove that $t_1', t_2', \ldots, t_n'$ is a permutation of $t_1, t_2, \ldots, t_n$ in (3.1) is complex and inefficient. In the mix network based on [52], a routing node firstly commits to a permutation $\pi()$ and then permutes $t_1, t_2, \ldots, t_n$ using $\pi()$ and commits them in $T_1, T_2, \ldots, T_n$ using a commitment function $Com()$. Neff's proof technique [74] is then employed to prove that $t_1, t_2, \ldots, t_n$ are permuted and committed in $T_1, T_2, \ldots, T_n$ using the permutation committed in the first step. Finally, the routing node publishes $c = \prod_{i=1}^n c_i^{t_i}$, $c' = \prod_{i=1}^n c_i'^{t_{\pi(i)}'}$ and proves ZP ($t_1', t_2', \ldots, t_n' \mid c' = \prod_{i=1}^n c_i'^{t_i'}$, $T_i = Com(t_i')$ for $i = 1, 2, \ldots, n$) and that c' is a re-encryption of c where ZP ($x_1, x_2, \ldots, x_k \mid y_1, y_2, \ldots, y_l$) denotes ZK (zero knowledge) proof of knowledge of integers $x_1, x_2, \ldots, x_k$ to satisfy conditions $y_1, y_2, \ldots, y_l$.

In the mix network based on [90], given random integers t_i and t_i' for $i = 1, 2, \ldots n$, a routing node has to prove that it knows secret integers s_i and s_i' for $i = 1, 2, \ldots n$, such that

$$\sum_{i=1}^n t_i D(c_i) = \sum_{i=1}^n s_i D(c_i') \bmod q$$
$$\sum_{i=1}^n t_i' D(c_i) = \sum_{i=1}^n s_i' D(c_i') \bmod q$$
$$\sum_{i=1}^n t_i t_i' D(c_i) = \sum_{i=1}^n s_i s_i' D(c_i') \bmod q$$

where $s_1, s_2, \ldots, s_n$ and $s_1', s_2', \ldots, s_n'$ are permutations of $t_1, t_2, \ldots, t_n$ and $t_1', t_2', \ldots, t_n'$ respectively.

In the mix network based on [102], $t_1, t_2, \ldots, t_n$ (denoted as $p_1, p_2, \ldots, p_n$) are randomly chosen from a special range and $t'_1, t'_2, \ldots, t'_n$ (denoted as $p_1, p_2, \ldots, p_n$) is guaranteed to be a permutation of $t_1, t_2, \ldots, t_n$ by proving satisfaction of

$$\prod_{i=1}^{n} t_i = \prod_{i=1}^{n} t'_i \tag{3.2}$$

$$\sum_{i=1}^{n} t_i = \sum_{i=1}^{n} t'_i \tag{3.3}$$

and that $t'_1, t'_2, \ldots, t'_n$ are in the same range. Besides the complexity in proving satisfaction of (3.2) and (3.3), the proof that $t'_1, t'_2, \ldots, t'_n$ are in the same range is left unimplemented and its cost is not included in efficiency estimation in [102]. Although it is vaguely mentioned in [102] that "We then note that a standard proof of knowledge over a group of unknown order also gives an upper bound on the bit-size of the exponents, i.e., it implicitly proves that $p_i \in [-2^K + 1, 2^K - 1]$", there is no more efficient way to prove that a secret integer chosen from a range is in the same range than the proof protocol in [17][1], whose cost in n instances of proof is much higher than the claimed total cost of shuffling in [102].

The mix network in [52] is optimised into two schemes in [51] and [50], concentrating on computational efficiency and communicational efficiency respectively; while the mix network in [90] is optimised into a scheme in [89]. The mix network schemes in [51, 50] and [89] prove that $t'_1, t'_2, \ldots, t'_n$ is a permutation of $t_1, t_2, \ldots, t_n$ in (3.1) as well and their proof techniques follow the same principles in [52] and [90] respectively. In summary, the proof techniques in the recent mix network schemes are complex and costly. However, all of them claim high efficiency and the shuffling protocol in [51] even claim to prove validity of shuffling of n ciphertexts at a cost lower than n exponentiations. The reason for their claimed extraordinarily high efficiency is that the recent mix network schemes employ unfair estimations and comparisons to exaggerate their advantage in efficiency over the previous work. Most of them [93, 90, 102, 51, 50, 89] employ much shorter exponents than usual in many computations, while assuming the previous mix network schemes still employ exponents with normal length. In this way, they can count multiple exponentiations with short exponents as one exponentiation with a normal-length exponent. For example, the shuffling protocol in [51] counts multiple times of n exponentiations it needs to prove validity of shuffling as a number smaller than n. In Section 5 of [52], an efficiency improvement mechanism is applied solely to itself and not employed in the previous shuffling schemes although it is applicable to them as well. When those efficiency improvement mechanisms are employed in the previous mix network schemes, their efficiency can be dramatically improved as well. So the efficiency comparisons in the recent mix network schemes are not very fair and do not precisely measure efficiency of different mix network schemes.

---

[1] As shown in Section 3.1.2, although there is no more efficient method to prove that a secret integer chosen from a range is in the same range, a secret integer chosen from a range can be proved to be in another much larger range efficiently.

3.1.2   The New Mix Network

The main idea in the new mix network technique is that a simpler and more efficient proof is given to prove that $t'_1, t'_2, \ldots, t'_n$ is a permutation of $t_1, t_2, \ldots, t_n$ in (3.1). We find that satisfaction of $\sum_{i=1}^{n} t_i = \sum_{i=1}^{n} t'_i$ as proved in [102] is not helpful to guarantee validity of shuffling. Moreover, to limit $t'_1, t'_2, \ldots, t'_n$ in a certain range is essential in efficient proof of validity of shuffling. For example,[2] when $t_1, t_2, \ldots, t_n$ are primes, $\sum_{i=1}^{n} t_i = \sum_{i=1}^{n} t'_i$ and $\prod_{i=1}^{n} t_i = \prod_{i=1}^{n} t'_i$ but they are not limited in any range, $t'_1, t'_2, \ldots, t'_n$ may not be a permutation of $t_1, t_2, \ldots, t_n$. To guarantee that $t'_1, t'_2, \ldots, t'_n$ is a permutation of $t_1, t_2, \ldots, t_n$, we randomly choose primes $t_1, t_2, \ldots, t_n$ from a range $R = \{2^T, 2^T + 1, 2^{T+1} - 1\}$ and then prove that

$$\prod_{i=1}^{n} t_i = \prod_{i=1}^{n} t'_i \tag{3.4}$$

and $t'_1, t'_2, \ldots, t'_n$ are in R where T is a security parameter. Since the product of any integers in R is out of R and $t_1, t_2, \ldots, t_n, t'_1, t'_2, \ldots, t'_n$ are in R, satisfaction of $\prod_{i=1}^{n} t_i = \prod_{i=1}^{n} t'_i$ guarantees that $t'_1, t'_2, \ldots, t'_n$ is a permutation of $t_1, t_2, \ldots, t_n$. Depending on the concrete employed encryption algorithm, the concrete proof of satisfaction of (3.1) and (3.4) is different. In the new design, the proof is described based on a popular encryption algorithms in mix network, Paillier encryption. Moreover, a very efficient proof mechanism is employed to prove that $t'_1, t'_2, \ldots, t'_n$ are in R. It is different from the range proofs in [102] and so can be much more efficient than the normal range proof techniques like [17].

Proof of Satisfaction of Equations (3.1) and (3.4)

The message space of Paillier encryption is Z_N where N is a composite with large secret factors. The multiplicative modulus is N^2 and the public key is g, a large number with secret order modulo N^2. Encryption of a message m is $g^m r^N \bmod N^2$ where r is randomly chosen from Z_N^*. More details of it can be found in [83]. When Paillier encryption is employed, shuffling and proof of its validity in the new mix network is as follows where 2^{T+1} is smaller than the factors of N.

1. The routing node calculates and publishes $c'_i = c_{\pi(i)} r_i^N \bmod N^2$ where $\pi()$ is the permutation he chooses and r_i randomly chosen from Z_N^*.

2. Random primes $t_1, t_2, \ldots, t_n$ in R are chosen by some verifier(s) or generated by a (pseudo)random function.

3. The routing node calculates and publishes $C = r^N \prod_{i=1}^{n} c'^{t'_i}_i \bmod N^2$ where $t'_i = t_{\pi(i)}$ and r is randomly chosen from Z_N^*.

---

[2]A simple example is $N = 10$, $t_1 = t_2 = \cdots = t_{10} = 2$ while $t'_1 = t'_2 = t'_3 = t'_4 = 4$, $t'_5 = t'_6 = 2$, $t'_7 = t'_8 = 1$ and $t'_9 = t'_{10} = -1$. Another simple example is $N = 10$, $t_1 = t_2 = 2$, $t_3 = t_4 = 3$, $t_5 = t_6 = 5$, $t_7 = t_8 = 7$, $t_9 = t_{10} = 11$ while $t'_1 = t'_2 = 22$, $t'_3 = t'_4 = 15$, $t'_5 = t'_6 = -7$, $t'_7 = t'_8 = t'_9 = t'_{10} = -1$.

4. The routing node proves knowledge of a secret integer $R' = r \prod_{i=1}^{n} r_i'^{t_i'} \bmod N$ such that $R'^N \prod_{i=1}^{n} c_i^{t_i} = C \bmod N^2$ using ZK proof of knowledge of root [53].

5. The routing node calculates and publishes $e_i = e_{i-1}^{t_i'} h^{r_i'} \bmod N^2$ where $e_0 = g$, h is an integer in the same cyclic group of g, $\log_g h$ and $\log_h g$ are secret and r_i' is randomly chosen from a large subset in Z_N for $i = 1, 2, \ldots, n$.

6. The routing node proves ZP ($t_1', t_2', \ldots, t_n', r, r_1', r_2', \ldots, r_n' \mid C = r^N \prod_{i=1}^{n} c_i'^{t_i'} \bmod N^2$, $e_i = e_{i-1}^{t_i'} h^{r_i'} \bmod N^2$ for $i = 1, 2, \ldots, n$) as detailed in Figure 3.1. Note that although w_i and v_i are calculated in Z, the proof protocol in Figure 3.1 is statistically private once s_i is statistically much larger than ct_i' and u_i is statistically much larger than cr_i'.

7. The routing node proves knowledge of a secret integer $R'' = \sum_{i=1}^{n} (r'_i \sum_{j=i+1}^{n} t_j')$ such that $e_n = g^{\prod_{i=1}^{n} t_i} h^{R''} \bmod N^2$ using ZK proof of knowledge of discrete logarithm [98].

---

1. The routing node randomly chooses integers $s_1, s_2, \ldots, s_n, u_1, u_2, \ldots, u_n$ from Z_N and U from Z_N^*. It calculates and publishes

$$C' = U^N \prod_{i=1}^{n} c_i'^{s_i} \bmod N^2$$
$$e_i' = e_{i-1}^{s_i} h^{u_i} \bmod N^2 \text{ for } i = 1, 2, \ldots, n.$$

2. Some verifier(s) or a (pseudo)random function generate a random challenge

$$c \in Z_L$$

where L is a security parameter.

3. The routing node publishes

$$w_i = s_i - ct_i' \text{ in } Z \text{ for } i = 1, 2, \ldots, n$$
$$W = U/r^c \bmod N$$
$$v_i = u_i - cr_i' \text{ in } Z \text{ for } i = 1, 2, \ldots, n.$$

Public verification:

$$C' = C^c W^N \prod_{i=1}^{n} c_i'^{w_i} \bmod N^2 \tag{3.5}$$
$$e_i' = e_{i-1}^{w_i} h^{v_i} e_i^c \bmod N^2 \text{ for } i = 1, 2, \ldots, n. \tag{3.6}$$

Figure 3.1: ZK Proof Protocol Employed in Paillier-Based Shuffling

Security of the proof protocol to guarantee satisfaction of Equations (3.1) and (3.4) is illustrated in Theorem 7 and Theorem 10.

Theorem 7 *The routing node's proof in Steps 4, 6 and 7 of the proof protocol can successfully pass their verifications if the node is honest and strictly follows the shuffling protocol.*

Proof: If the routing node is honest and strictly follows the shuffling protocol, Equations (3.1) and (3.4) are satisfied and $t'_1, t'_2, \ldots, t'_n$ is a permutation of $t_1, t_2, \ldots, t_n$. Then

$$R'^N \prod_{i=1}^n c_i^{t_i} = (r \prod_{i=1}^n r_i^{t'_i})^N \prod_{i=1}^n c_i^{t_i} = r^N (\prod_{i=1}^n r_i^{t'_i})^N \prod_{i=1}^n c_i^{t_i}$$
$$= r^N (\prod_{i=1}^n r_i^{t'_i})^N \prod_{i=1}^n c_{\pi(i)}^{t_{\pi(i)}} = r^N (\prod_{i=1}^n r_i^{t'_i})^N \prod_{i=1}^n c_{\pi(i)}^{t'_i}$$
$$= r^N \prod_{i=1}^n (c_{\pi(i)} r_i^N)^{t'_i} = r^N \prod_{i=1}^n c'^{t'_i}_i = C \bmod N^2$$

and

$$e_n = e_{n-1}^{t'_n} h^{r'_n} = (e_{n-2}^{t'_{n-1}} h^{r'_{n-1}})^{t'_n} h^{r'_n} = \ldots \ldots$$
$$= g^{\prod_{i=1}^n t'_i} h^{\sum_{i=1}^n (r'_i \sum_{j=i+1}^n t'_j)} = g^{\prod_{i=1}^n t'_i} h^{R''} = g^{\prod_{i=1}^n t_i} h^{R''} \bmod N^2;$$

and in the proof in Figure 3.1

$$C^c W^N \prod_{i=1}^n c'^{w_i}_i = (r^N \prod_{i=1}^n c'^{t'_i}_i)^c (U/r^c)^N \prod_{i=1}^n c'^{s_i - ct'_i}_i$$
$$= U^N \prod_{i=1}^n c'^{s_i}_i = C' \bmod N^2;$$
$$e_{i-1}^{w_i} h^{v_i} e_i^c = e_{i-1}^{s_i - ct'_i} h^{u_i - cr'_i} (e_{i-1}^{t'_i} h^{r'_i})^c$$
$$= e_{i-1}^{s_i} h^{u_i} = e'_i \bmod N^2 \text{ for } i = 1, 2, \ldots, n$$

Therefore, the routing node's proof in Steps 4, 6 and 7 of the shuffling protocol successfully passes their verifications.   □

Theorem 8 *If the routing node's proof in Steps 4, 6 and 7 successfully passes their verifications, Equations (3.1) and (3.4) are satisfied.*

Proof: If the routing node's proof in Steps 4, 6 and 7 successfully passes their verifications, the routing node can calculate in polynomial time integers $t'_1, t'_2, \ldots, t'_n, r, R', R'', r'_1, r'_2, \ldots, r'_n$ such that the following equations hold as the ZK proof primitives in the three steps (including ZK proof of knowledge of root [53], ZK proof of knowledge of discrete logarithm [98] and ZK proof of equality of discrete logarithms [27]) are sound and passing their verifications guarantees their claimed knowledge and relation.

$$R'^N \prod_{i=1}^n c_i^{t_i} = C \bmod N^2 \tag{3.7}$$

$$C = r^N \prod_{i=1}^n c'^{t'_i}_i \bmod N^2 \tag{3.8}$$

$$e_i = e_{i-1}^{t'_i} h^{r'_i} \bmod N^2 \text{ for } i = 1, 2, \ldots, n \tag{3.9}$$

$$e_n = g^{\prod_{i=1}^n t_i} h^{R''} \bmod N^2 \tag{3.10}$$

(3.7) and (3.8) imply

$$R'^N \prod_{i=1}^n c_i^{t_i} = r^N \prod_{i=1}^n c'^{t'_i}_i \bmod N^2$$

and so

$$\prod_{i=1}^n c'^{t'_i}_i = (R'/r)^N \prod_{i=1}^n c_i^{t_i} \bmod N^2 = RE(\prod_{i=1}^n c_i^{t_i}).$$

(3.9) implies

$$e_n = e_{n-1}^{t'_n} h^{r'_n} = (e_{n-2}^{t'_{n-1}} h^{r'_{n-1}})^{t'_n} h^{r'_n} = \ldots \ldots$$
$$= g^{\prod_{i=1}^n t'_i} h^{\sum_{i=1}^n (r'_i \sum_{j=i+1}^n t'_j)} \bmod N^2 \tag{3.11}$$

So

$$g^{\prod_{i=1}^n t_i} h^{R''} = g^{\prod_{i=1}^n t'_i} h^{\sum_{i=1}^n (r'_i \sum_{j=i+1}^n t'_j)} \bmod N^2$$

and thus

$$g^{\prod_{i=1}^n t_i - \prod_{i=1}^n t'_i} = h^{\sum_{i=1}^n (r'_i \sum_{j=i+1}^n t'_j) - R''} \bmod N^2$$

As the routing node can calculate in polynomial time $\prod_{i=1}^n t'_i$ and $\log_g h$ and $\log_h g$ are secret and no information about the order of g is known, (3.10) and (3.11) imply

$$\prod_{i=1}^n t_i = \prod_{i=1}^n t'_i$$

due to the following reasons.

- If $\prod_{i=1}^n t_i \neq \prod_{i=1}^n t'_i$ and $\prod_{i=1}^n t_i - \prod_{i=1}^n t'_i$ is a multiple of the order of g, then the routing node can calculate in polynomial time a multiple of the order of g, which is a contradiction.

- If $\prod_{i=1}^n t_i \neq \prod_{i=1}^n t'_i$ and $\prod_{i=1}^n t_i - \prod_{i=1}^n t'_i$ is not a multiple of the order of g, then

$$\log_h g = (\sum_{i=1}^n (r'_i \sum_{j=i+1}^n t'_j) - R'') / (\prod_{i=1}^n t_i - \prod_{i=1}^n t'_i)$$

and given the order of g the routing node can calculate $\log_h g$ in polynomial time, which is contradictory to the widely accepted hardness of the discrete logarithm problem.

$\square$

Specification of Efficient Range Proof

In Section 3.1.2, proof of satisfaction of (3.1) and (3.4) has been specified. However, to guarantee that $t'_1, t'_2, \ldots, t'_n$ is a permutation of $t_1, t_2, \ldots, t_n$ and thus $D(c'_1), D(c'_2), \ldots, D(c'_n)$ is a permutation of $D(c_1), D(c_2), \ldots, D(c_n)$, we still need to prove that $t'_1, t'_2, \ldots, t'_n$ are in the range R. Namely, n instances of range proof are needed. The normal range proof techniques [17, 69, 49, 19, 23, 88, 87] are not efficient for mix networks. Even the most efficient two of them [17, 87] still cost scores of exponentiations for one instance of range proof. So we have to prove that $t'_1, t'_2, \ldots, t'_n$ are in R in a different and more efficient way.

Although there is no efficient method to prove that $t'_1, t'_2, \ldots, t'_n$ are in R when $t'_1, t'_2, \ldots, t'_n$ are chosen from the primes in R, $t'_1, t'_2, \ldots, t'_n$ can be proved to be in R if they are primes chosen from a much smaller range. This idea is not strange to the research community but to the best of our knowledge the condition for it to work and the guideline to set its parameters have never been formally discussed in detail. To use this idea, there are some additional requirements on parameter setting in the proof of satisfaction of (3.1) and (3.4) in Section 3.1.2 besides statistical privacy. Its parameter setting needs to be modified as follows. Firstly, $t_1, t_2, \ldots, t_n$ are chosen from the primes in a subset R_1 in the middle of R and thus $t'_1, t'_2, \ldots, t'_n$ are in R_1 as well. Then in Figure 3.1, s_i is randomly chosen from a large set S_1 and c is randomly chosen from a large set S_2. If $w_i + c(2^T + 2^{T-1})$ is in a range R_2, t'_i can be guaranteed to be in R. Namely, if t'_i is chosen in a small fraction of R near its middle point $2^T + 2^{T-1}$ and $s_i - c(t'_i - (2^T + 2^{T-1}))$ is in R_2, the absolute value of $t_i - (2^T + 2^{T-1})$ is guaranteed to be smaller than $2^T - 2^{T-1}$. In this way, range proof of secret integer t_i in R is implemented through a simple and public membership test of $w_i + c(2^T + 2^{T-1})$ in R_2. When R_1 is small enough and S_1, S_2 and R_2 are appropriately set, the range proof can achieve the soundness specified in Definition 3.

Definition 3 *(Soundness of range proof). If t'_i is not in R, the probability that the verification in the range proof is passed is no more than a negligible parameter denoted as δ.*

More precisely, the parameters should be chosen according to the following three rules

$$Max(S_1) + Max(R_1 \times S_2) \leq Max(R_2)$$
$$Min(S_1) + Min(R_1 \times S_2) \geq Min(R_2)$$
$$(MaxAbs(\hat{R}) + 1)(Max(S_2) - Min(S_2))\delta \geq |R_2| \qquad (3.12)$$

where the following denotations are employed.

- $\hat{R} = \{x \mid x + (2^T + 2^{T-1}) \in R\}$.

- $MaxAbs()$ denotes the integer with the largest absolute value in a set.

- $Max()$ denotes the largest integer in a set.

- $Min()$ denotes the smallest integer in a set.

- $|T|$ denotes the size of a set T.

- dT denotes a set $\{\mathbf{t} \mid \mathbf{t} = dt,\ t \in T\}$ where T is a set of integers and d is an integer.

The meaning of the first two rules is very clear: an honest routing node must pass the verification. The third rule in (3.12) aims to guarantee soundness of the range proof, which means that if the routing node passes the verification, t'_i is guaranteed to be in R with an overwhelmingly large probability. Its principle is illustrated in detail in Theorem 9.

Theorem 9 *Soundness of the range proof means that* $(MaxAbs(\hat{R}) + 1)(Max(S_2) - Min(S_2))\delta \geq |R_2|$ *should be satisfied.*

To Prove Theorem 9, Lemma 9 is proved first.

Lemma 9 *In the range proof, the number of elements falling in* $(MaxAbs(\hat{R}) + 1)S_2$ *should be no more than* $|S_2|\delta$ *in any range with a width* $|R_2|$.

Proof: If the number of elements in $(MaxAbs(\hat{R}) + 1)S_2$ is more than $|S_2|\delta$ in a range with a width $|R_2|$, then there are at least $\lfloor|S_2|\delta\rfloor + 1$ integers in both $(MaxAbs(\hat{R}) + 1)S_2$ and a range $\{t, t+1, \ldots, t+|R_2|-1\}$. Denote these integers as $b_1, b_2, \ldots, b_{\lfloor|S_2|\delta\rfloor+1}$. The routing node chooses $s_i = Min(R_2) - t$ and then we have

$$b_j + s_i = b_j + Min(R_2) - t \text{ for } j = 1, 2, \ldots, \lfloor|S_2|\delta\rfloor + 1$$

where $0 \leq b_j - t \leq |R_2| - 1$. As b_j is in $\{t, t+1, \ldots, t+|R_2|-1\}$

$$Min(R_2) \leq b_j + s_i \leq Min(R_2) + |R_2| - 1 = Max(R_2)$$
$$\text{for } j = 1, 2, \ldots, \lfloor|S_2|\delta\rfloor + 1$$

Namely, $b_j + s_i$ is in R_2 for $j = 1, 2, \ldots, \lfloor|S_2|\delta\rfloor + 1$. As $b_1, b_2, \ldots, b_{\lfloor|S_2|\delta\rfloor+1}$ are in $(MaxAbs(\hat{R}) + 1)S_2$, So $b_j + s_i$ is in $(MaxAbs(\hat{R}) + 1)S_2 + s_i$ for $j = 1, 2, \ldots, \lfloor|S_2|\delta\rfloor + 1$. So, $(MaxAbs(\hat{R}) + 1)S_2 + s_i \cap R_2$ at least contains $b_j + s_i$ for $j = 1, 2, \ldots, \lfloor|S_2|\delta\rfloor + 1$ and

$$|((MaxAbs(\hat{R}) + 1)S_2 + s_i) \cap R_2| \geq \lfloor|S_2|\delta\rfloor + 1$$

Namely, with $t'_i = MaxAbs(\hat{R}) + 1$, if the probability that the verification in the range proof is passed is denoted as **P**, then

$$\mathbf{P} \geq |(t'_i S_2 + s_i) \cap R_2|/|S_2| \geq (\lfloor|S_2|\delta\rfloor + 1)/|S_2| > \delta$$

which is contradictory to Definition 3. This contradiction shows that Lemma 9 must be correct.   □

Proof of Theorem 9:

Note that if the probability that a random element in any part of a set falls into a certain subset is no more than a certain value, then the probability that a random element in the set falls into the certain subset is no more than the certain value. According to Lemma 9, the average probability that an integer in $\{(MaxAbs(\hat{R}) + 1)Min(S_2), (MaxAbs(\hat{R}) + 1)Min(S_2) + 1, \ldots, (MaxAbs(\hat{R}) + 1)Max(S_2)\}$ falls into $(MaxAbs(\hat{R}) + 1)S_2$ is no more than $|S_2|\delta/|R_2|$ and the number of integers in $(MaxAbs(\hat{R}) + 1)S_2$ is no more than $((MaxAbs(\hat{R})+1)Max(S_2)-(MaxAbs(\hat{R})+1)Min(S_2))|S_2|\delta/|R_2|$. Therefore,

$$((MaxAbs(\hat{R}) + 1)Max(S_2) - (MaxAbs(\hat{R}) + 1)$$
$$Min(S_2))|S_2|\delta/|R_2| \geq |(MaxAbs(\hat{R}) + 1)S_2| = |S_2|$$

and thus

$$(MaxAbs(\hat{R}) + 1)(Max(S_2) - Min(S_2))\delta \geq |R_2|$$

□

The analysis above shows that the n instances of range proof can be efficiently implemented after the parameters are adjusted. For example, R_1 can be $\{2^{T-1}+2^T-l, 2^{T-1}+2^T-l+1, \ldots, 2^{T-1}+2^T+l\}$ where l is much smaller than 2^T. Of course, besides the three rules, l should be large enough so that it is difficult to guess which primes are chosen from R_1 as $t_1, t_2, \ldots, t_n$. Since T can be as large as several hundred, those requirements can be easily satisfied and there are many valid choices for R_2, S_1 and S_2. Together with satisfaction of Equation (3.4), the n instances of range proof guarantee that $t'_1, t'_2, \ldots, t'_n$ is a permutation of $t_1, t_2, \ldots, t_n$ as analysed in the beginning of Section 3.1.2. Then with Equation (3.1) satisfied as well, validity of shuffling is guaranteed as illustrated in Section 3.1.3.

3.1.3   Security and Efficiency Analysis

As mentioned before, although many mix network schemes guarantee validity of shuffling by proving satisfaction of (3.1) and $t'_1, t'_2, \ldots, t'_n$ is a permutation of $t_1, t_2, \ldots, t_n$, none of them gives a formal analysis of the guarantee. Theorem 10 formally illustrates why satisfaction of (3.1) guarantees validity of shuffling in the new mix network when $t'_1, t'_2, \ldots, t'_n$ is a permutation of $t_1, t_2, \ldots, t_n$.

Theorem 10 *In the new mix network, the probability that Equation (3.1) is satisfied and $t'_1, t'_2, \ldots, t'_n$ is a permutation of $t_1, t_2, \ldots, t_n$ but $D(c'_1), D(c'_2), \ldots, D(c'_n)$ is not a permutation of $D(c_1), D(c_2), \ldots, D(c_n)$ is negligible.*

To prove Theorem 10, a lemma is proved first.

Lemma 10 *If $\prod_{i=1}^{n} y_i^{z_i}$ is an Nth residue with a probability larger than $1/K$ where every z_i is randomly chosen from a set S, which contains K integers smaller than the factors of N, then $y_1, y_2, \ldots, y_n$ are N^{th} residues.*

Proof: $\prod_{i=1}^{n} y_i^{z_i}$ is an Nth residue with a probability larger than $1/K$ implies that for any given integer v in $\{1, 2, \ldots, n\}$ there must exist integers $z_1, z_2, \ldots, z_n$ and z_v' in S and two different integers x and x' in Z_N such that

$$\prod_{i=1}^{n} y_i^{z_i} = x^N \bmod N^2 \tag{3.13}$$

$$(\prod_{i=1}^{v-1} y_i^{z_i}) y_v^{z_v'} \prod_{i=v+1}^{n} y_i^{z_i} = x'^N \bmod N^2 \tag{3.14}$$

Otherwise, for any $(z_1, z_2, \ldots, z_{v-1}, z_{v+1}, \ldots, z_n)$ in S^{n-1}, there is at most one z_v in S such that $\prod_{i=1}^{n} y_i^{z_i} \bmod N^2$ is an Nth residue. This implies that among the K^n possible choices for $(z_1, z_2, \ldots, z_n)$ (combination of the K^{n-1} possible choices for $(z_1, z_2, \ldots, z_{v-1}, z_{v+1}, \ldots, z_n)$ and the K possible choices for z_v) there are at most K^{n-1} choices to construct an Nth residue in the form $\prod_{i=1}^{n} y_i^{z_i} \bmod N^2$, which is a contradiction to the assumption that $\prod_{i=1}^{n} y_i^{z_i}$ is an Nth residue with a probability larger than $1/K$.

Equations (3.13) and (3.14) imply $y_v^{z_v - z_v'}$ is an Nth residue. According to Euclidean algorithm there exist integers α and β to satisfy $\beta(z_v - z_v') = \alpha N + GCD(N, z_v - z_v')$. Note that $GCD(N, z_v - z_v') = 1$ as z_v, z_v' are in S and thus smaller than the factors of N. So $y_v^{\beta(z_v - z_v')} = y_v^{\alpha N} y_v \bmod N^2$. Namely,

$$y_v = y_v^{\beta(z_v - z_v')}/y_v^{\alpha N} = (y_v^{(z_v - z_v')})^\beta / y_v^{\alpha N}$$
$$= (x/x')^{N\beta}/(y_v^\alpha)^N = ((x/x')^\beta / y_v^\alpha)^N \bmod N^2$$

So y_v is an Nth residue. Therefore, $y_1, y_2, \ldots, y_n$ are N^{th} residues as v can be any integer in $\{1, 2, \ldots, n\}$. □

Proof of Theorem 10: Let A_1 be the event that $D(c_1'), D(c_2'), \ldots, D(c_n')$ is a permutation of $D(c_1), D(c_2), \ldots, D(c_n)$; A_2 be the event that Equation (3.1) is correct; A_3 be the event that the routing node successfully proves satisfaction of (3.1); and $P(A)$ denote the probability of event A.

$$P(A_3/\bar{A}_1) = P((A_3 \wedge A_2)/\bar{A}_1) + P((A_3 \wedge \bar{A}_2)/\bar{A}_1)$$
$$= P(A_3 \wedge A_2 \wedge \bar{A}_1)/P(\bar{A}_1) + P(A_3 \wedge \bar{A}_2 \wedge \bar{A}_1)/P(\bar{A}_1)$$
$$= P(\bar{A}_1 \wedge A_2)P(A_3/\bar{A}_1 \wedge A_2)/P(\bar{A}_1) +$$
$$P(A_3 \wedge \bar{A}_2 \wedge \bar{A}_1)P(\bar{A}_2 \wedge \bar{A}_1)/(P(\bar{A}_1)P(\bar{A}_2 \wedge \bar{A}_1))$$
$$= P(A_2/\bar{A}_1)P(A_3/\bar{A}_1 \wedge A_2) +$$
$$P(\bar{A}_2/\bar{A}_1)P(A_3 \wedge \bar{A}_2 \wedge \bar{A}_1)/P(\bar{A}_2 \wedge \bar{A}_1)$$
$$= P(A_2/\bar{A}_1)P(A_3/\bar{A}_1 \wedge A_2) +$$
$$P(\bar{A}_2/\bar{A}_1)P(A_3 \wedge \bar{A}_2 \wedge \bar{A}_1)/(P(\bar{A}_2)P(\bar{A}_1/\bar{A}_2))$$

$P(\bar{A}_1/\bar{A}_2) = 1$ as $P(A_2/A_1) = 1$. So

$$
\begin{aligned}
P(A_3/\bar{A}_1) &= P(A_2/\bar{A}_1)P(A_3/\bar{A}_1 \wedge A_2) + \\
&\quad P(\bar{A}_2/\bar{A}_1)P(A_3 \wedge \bar{A}_2 \wedge \bar{A}_1)/P(\bar{A}_2) \\
&\le P(A_2/\bar{A}_1)P(A_3/\bar{A}_1 \wedge A_2) + \\
&\quad P(\bar{A}_2/\bar{A}_1)P(A_3 \wedge \bar{A}_2)/P(\bar{A}_2) \\
&\le P(A_2/\bar{A}_1)P(A_3/\bar{A}_1 \wedge A_2) + P(\bar{A}_2/\bar{A}_1)P(A_3/\bar{A}_2) \\
&\le P(A_2/\bar{A}_1)P(A_3/\bar{A}_1 \wedge A_2) + P(A_3/\bar{A}_2)
\end{aligned}
$$

Suppose there are k primes in R_1. If $P(A_2/\bar{A}_1) > 1/k$, then when $\bar{A}_1$ happens the probability that (3.1) is correct is larger than $1/k$. Namely, when $\bar{A}_1$ happens,

$$
RE(\textstyle\prod_{i=1}^{n} c_i^{t_i}) = \textstyle\prod_{i=1}^{n} c_i^{\prime t_{\pi(i)}}
$$

with a probability larger than $1/k$ where $\pi()$ is a permutation of $\{1, 2, \ldots, n\}$. Namely, when $\bar{A}_1$ happens,

$$
RE(\textstyle\prod_{i=1}^{n} c_i^{t_i}) = \textstyle\prod_{i=1}^{n} c_{\pi^{-1}(i)}^{\prime t_i}
$$

with a probability larger than $1/k$.

According to additive homomorphism of Paillier encryption algorithm, when $\bar{A}_1$ happens,

$$
\textstyle\prod_{i=1}^{n} (c_i/c'_{\pi^{-1}(i)})^{t_i} = E(0)
$$

with a probability larger than $1/k$. Namely, when $\bar{A}_1$ happens, $\prod_{i=1}^{n}(c_i/c'_{\pi^{-1}(i)})^{t_i}$ is an Nth residue with a probability larger than $1/k$.

So, according to Lemma 10, when $\bar{A}_1$ happens $c_i/c'_{\pi^{-1}(i)}$ is an Nth residue for $i = 1, 2, \ldots, n$, and thus $D(c'_1), D(c'_2), \ldots, D(c'_n)$ is a permutation of $D(c_1), D(c_2), \ldots, D(c_n)$, which is a contradiction. $P(A_2/\bar{A}_1) \le 1/k$ must be true to avoid the contradiction.

As with Paillier encryption (3.1) is proved using a standard proof of knowledge of root [53], $P(A_3/\bar{A}_1 \wedge A_2) = 1$ and $P(A_3/\bar{A}_2) < 2^{-L'}$ where L' is the bit length of the challenge in the proof of knowledge of root. Therefore,

$$
P(A_3/\bar{A}_1) \le P(A_2/\bar{A}_1) + P(A_3/\bar{A}_2) = 1/k + 2^{-L'}
$$

$\square$

The new mix network is compared with the recent mix network schemes in Table 3.1. When computational cost of a routing node is estimated, the exponentiations are counted. For simplicity, they are counted in terms of multiples of n, the dominating part of the cost. As the re-encryption operation is efficient and costs almost the same in all the shuffling protocols, as in most existing mix network schemes, in this section only the cost of the proof of

Table 3.1: Comparison of mix network schemes

Mix network	Privacy	Formal analysis	Computational cost of proof of validity of shuffling	Other comment
[52]	strong	incomplete	$12n$	
[93]	weak[1]	complete	$12n$	
[90]	strong	incomplete	$13n$	
[102]	strong	incomplete	$15n$	n instances of range proofs unimplemented
[51]	strong	incomplete	$10n$	
[50][2]	strong	incomplete	$22n$	
New	strong	complete	$7n$	

Note: [1]As explained before, it only supports a very small fraction of all the possible permutations.

[2]The mix network scheme in [50] is very special in comparison to other mix network schemes. While the other mix network schemes focus on computation in efficiency analysis as their communicational cost is approximately linear in their computational cost, the mix network scheme in [50] achieves high efficiency in communication by sacrificing computational efficiency. Thus although communicational efficiency is not the subject of this section, for the sake of fairness, we have to mention that the mix network scheme in [50] has an advantage in communicational efficiency.

validity of shuffling is included in the comparison. As stated before, applying an efficiency improvement mechanism like a small exponent to the recent mix network schemes and excluding it from other mix network schemes is unfair as the efficiency improvement mechanisms are simple and general techniques appliable to all the mix network schemes. For example, in the new mix network scheme, $t_1, t_2, \ldots, t_n$ and $s_1, s_2, \ldots, s_n$ can be set to be small exponents to greatly improve efficiency as well. For the sake of fairness and to show exactly how advanced every mix network scheme is, the efficiency improvement mechanisms are not included in any mix network scheme in the cost estimation in Table 3.1 and every exponentiation is counted equally. As explained before, most recent mix network schemes do not provide a complete formal security analysis as they do not formally explain why shuffling is valid when (3.1) is satisfied and $t'_1, t'_2, \ldots, t'_n$ is a permutation of $t_1, t_2, \ldots, t_n$. Except in [50], communicational cost of mix networks is approximately in direct proportion to their computational cost, so communicational cost is not separately estimated in Table 3.1 as it is in the efficiency analysis of most mix network schemes.

3.1.4   Extension and Application

Other popular encryption algorithms in mix network like El Gamal encryption can be employed in the new mix network as well. A typical El Gamal encryption algorithm employs two large primes p and q where q is a factor of $p - 1$. Suppose g is a generator of the cyclic subgroup of order q in Z_p^* and the private key is an integer x in Z_q, and the public key is $y = g^x \bmod p$. Encryption of a message m is $(g^r \bmod p,\ my^r \bmod p)$ where r is randomly chosen from Z_q. When El Gamal encryption is employed, shuffling and proof of its validity in the new mix network is as follows where 2^{T+1} is smaller than q.

1. The routing node calculates and publishes $c_i' = (a_i', b_i')$ where $c_i = (a_i, b_i)$, $a_i' = a_{\pi(i)} g^{r_i} \bmod p$, $b_i' = b_{\pi(i)} y^{r_i} \bmod p$, $\pi()$ is the permutation selected and r_i is randomly chosen from Z_q.

2. Random primes $t_1, t_2, \ldots, t_n$ in R_1 are chosen by some verifier(s) or generated by a (pseudo)random function where R_1 is in the middle of R and much smaller than it.

3. The routing node calculates and publishes $A = g^r \prod_{i=1}^n a_i'^{t_i'} \bmod p$ and $B = y^r \prod_{i=1}^n b_i'^{t_i'} \bmod p$ where $t_i' = t_{\pi(i)}$ and r is randomly chosen from Z_q.

4. The routing node proves knowledge of a secret integer $R' = r + \sum_{i=1}^n r_i t_i' \bmod q$ such that $g^{R'} \prod_{i=1}^n a_i^{t_i} = A \bmod p$ and $y^{R'} \prod_{i=1}^n b_i^{t_i} = B \bmod p$ using ZK proof of knowledge of discrete logarithm [98].

5. The routing node calculates and publishes $e_i = e_{i-1}^{t_i'} h^{r_i'} \bmod N$ where N is a composite with large secret factors, f and h are generators of a large cyclic subgroup with secret order in Z_N^*, $\log_f h$ and $\log_h f$ are secret and r_i' is randomly chosen from a large subset in Z_N for $i = 1, 2, \ldots, n$.

6. The routing node proves ZP ($t_1', t_2', \ldots, t_n', r, r_1', r_2', \ldots, r_n'\ |\ A = g^r \prod_{i=1}^n a_i'^{t_i'} \bmod p$, $B = y^r \prod_{i=1}^n b_i'^{t_i'} \bmod p$, $e_i = e_{i-1}^{t_i'} h^{r_i'} \bmod N$ for $i = 1, 2, \ldots, n$) as detailed in Figure 3.2.

7. The routing node proves knowledge of a secret integer $R'' = \sum_{i=1}^n (r_i' \sum_{j=i+1}^n t_j')$ such that $e_n = g^{\prod_{i=1}^n t_i} h^{R''} \bmod N$ using ZK proof of knowledge of discrete logarithm [98].

8. It is publicly verified that $w_i + c(2^T + 2^{T-1})$ is in R_2 to guarantee that t_i' is in R where choice of R_1, R_2, S_1, S_2 must satisfy the three rules in (3.12), (3.12) and (3.12) and guarantee statistical privacy of the proof.

When the new mix network employs El Gamal encryption-based shuffling, formal analysis of its security is similar to the analysis of its Paillier encryption-based version. Due to space limit, the analysis is not repeated

---

1. The routing node randomly chooses integers $s_1, s_2, \ldots, s_n$ from a large set S_1, $u_1, u_2, \ldots, u_n$ from Z_N and U from Z_q and then calculates and publishes

$$A' = g^U \prod_{i=1}^{n} a'^{s_i}_i \bmod p$$
$$B' = y^U \prod_{i=1}^{n} b'^{s_i}_i \bmod p$$
$$e'_i = e^{s_i}_{i-1} h^{u_i} \bmod N \text{ for } i = 1, 2, \ldots, n.$$

2. Some verifier(s) or a (pseudo)random function generate a random challenge

$$c \in S_2$$

where S_2 is a large set.

3. The routing node publishes

$$w_i = s_i - c t'_i \text{ in } Z \text{ for } i = 1, 2, \ldots, n$$
$$W = U - cr \bmod q$$
$$v_i = u_i - c r'_i \text{ in } Z \text{ for } i = 1, 2, \ldots, n.$$

Public verification:

$$A' = A^c g^W \prod_{i=1}^{n} a'^{w_i}_i \bmod p$$
$$B' = B^c y^W \prod_{i=1}^{n} b'^{w_i}_i \bmod p$$
$$e'_i = e^{w_i}_{i-1} h^{v_i} e^c_i \bmod N \text{ for } i = 1, 2, \ldots, n.$$

Figure 3.2: ZK Proof Protocol Employed in El Gamal-based Shuffling

here. As mentioned before, the most important application of mix network is e-voting. A mix network-based e-voting design is described in the following to show importance of the new mix network in practical applications.

1. Some talliers share the private key of an encryption algorithm, which is employed to encrypt the votes in the election. The sharing mechanism guarantees that decryption is only feasible when enough talliers (e.g., over a threshold) cooperate. For example, the private key of Paillier encryption can be shared using the technique in [37].

2. The voters encrypt their votes and submit the ciphertexts to the talliers.

3. The talliers set up a mix network and each of them acts as a routing node.

4. The talliers take turns to shuffle the encrypted votes.

5. The talliers cooperate to decrypt the repeatedly shuffled ciphertexts and recover the votes. Each of them publicly proves validity of his part of decryption work as detailed in [37].

6. Any election rule can be applied to count the decrypted votes and determine the result of the election.

If at least one tallier conceals the permutation used in his shuffling, the decrypted votes cannot be traced back to the voters and thus privacy of e-voting is guaranteed. As the new mix network is publicly verifiable, the voters and independent observers can verify validity of the talliers' shuffling such that any cheating in tallying can be detected.

3.2   Mix Network-Based E-Voting

Electronic voting is a popular application of cryptographic and network techniques to e-government. An e-voting scheme should satisfy the following properties.

- Correctness: all the valid votes are counted without being tampered with.

- Privacy: no information about any voter's choice in the election is revealed.

- Robustness: any dishonest behaviour or abnormal situation can be detected and solved without revealing any vote.

- Verifiability: correctness of the election can be verified. It is classified into two types as follows.

    - Individual verifiability: each voter can verify that his vote is counted and not tampered with.

    - Public verifiability: anyone can verify that all the votes are counted and not tampered with according to public information.

- High efficiency: the voting operation and tallying operation should be efficient enough for practical elections including large scale elections.

A property sometimes desired in e-voting, receipt freeness (or called coercion resistance elsewhere), is not the focus of this section, so is not discussed in detail in this section. Either of the two existing solutions to receipt freeness, deniable encryption [22] and re-encryption with untransferable zero knowledge proof of correctness by a third party (in the form of a trusted authority or a tamper-resistent hardware) linked through untappable communication channel[3] [67], can be employed if required.

---

[3]The untappable communication channel is in the form of an internal channel-like bus or USB cable when tamper-resistant hardware is employed.

Most of the existing e-voting schemes can be classified into two categories: homomorphic voting and shuffling-based voting. In a homomorphic voting scheme [9, 73, 97, 55, 12, 64, 30, 54, 65, 67, 68, 91], an encryption algorithm with special homomorphic property (e.g. El Gamal encryption or Paillier encryption [83]) is employed to encrypt the votes such that the sum of the votes can be recovered without decrypting any single vote. An advantage of homomorphic voting is efficient tallying. Tallying in homomorphic voting only costs one single decryption operation for each candidate. However, homomorphic voting has the following drawbacks.

- Complex vote: a vote must contain a ciphertext for each candidate (or possible choice) in the election. Thus encryption cost for each voter is high. This drawback is especially serious when the number of candidates is large or in a preferential election, where the preferential order of all the candidates must be contained in a vote.

- High cost in vote validity check. In a valid vote, each ciphertext must be in a special format. Correctness of homomorphic voting depends on validity of the votes. An invalid vote can compromise correctness of a homomorphic voting scheme, so must be detected and deleted before the tallying phase. Unfortunately, vote validity check is very costly (both for the voters to prove validity of their votes and for a tallier (and other verifiers) to verify validity of the votes) and becomes an efficiency bottleneck in homomorphic e-voting.

These two drawbacks imply that the computational and communicational cost for every voter is high, especially when the election is complex. Note that although the talliers can be several authorities with high computational power and linked with a broadband communication channel, the voters are common people and some of them possibly have limited computational power and communication bandwidth, especially when mobile devices are used to cast the votes. Therefore, although homomorphic voting is suitable for a very simple (yes or no) election, it is impractical in more complicated circumstances.

Shuffling-based voting [84, 48, 6, 42, 74, 75, 52, 93, 41, 90] is more suitable for complex elections (e.g., with multiple candidates or votes containing complex information like preference of the candidates) as it has the following merits. No matter how complex a vote is, it is sealed in one ciphertext. Moreover, no vote validity check is needed. So the cost for a voter is low and low-capability devices and low-performance communication channels can be used to cast the votes. A shuffling-based voting scheme employs multiple instances of shuffling to repeatedly shuffle the encrypted votes before they are decrypted (opened) so that the opened votes cannot be traced back to the voters if at least the permutation in one shuffling instance is concealed. Secure shuffling-based e-voting applications should follow three rules to achieve critically high security requirements and otherwise may cause serious chaos and turbulence.

- The security requirements of e-voting like correctness, privacy, robustness and public verifiability must be completely and strictly satisfied.

- Validity of shuffling must be publicly and completely verified.

- Multiple shuffling operations are performed in sequence such that no opened vote can be traced back to its voter if at least one shuffling node conceals his permutation.

E-voting schemes like [60, 93, 47] do not strictly follow these three rules, have looser security standards and cannot completely satisfy the security requirements of e-voting, so are not satisfactory solutions.[4]

The main concerns in shuffling-based e-voting are inefficiency in public verification and weak robustness. There are two methods to implement public verification in shuffling-based e-voting. The first method is instant verification: each shuffling operation is publicly verified before the votes are sent to the next shuffling node such that any deviating operation in the shuffling is detected immediately and no vote is decrypted unless all the shuffling nodes strictly follow the shuffling protocol. A drawback of this method [5, 42, 74, 52, 75, 90, 6, 40, 41, 79] is low efficiency. The second method is to omit separate public verifications in all the shuffling operations and to make a final public check after the votes are shuffled and decrypted [84, 48]. If any shuffling operation deviates from the shuffling protocol, the final check fails and a identifying function can be used to identify the dishonest shuffling node. This method is more efficient in public verification, but has its own drawback: weak robustness.

The most serious drawback of the second verification method is that it is more vulnerable to attacks against privacy. The first verification method guarantees that any dishonest behaviour of any shuffling node is instantly detected, rewound and redone. So with the first verification method, the only concern is dishonest behaviour of the voters. With the second verification method, the e-voting procedure continues until the final decryption of the votes even if some malicious shuffling node has deviated from the protocol, and thus gives more chances for attacks. For example, the votes are still decrypted even if they are tampered with in the shuffling in [84], which is vulnerable to many "relation attacks" (see [94] for definition, detailed explanation and more references). The e-voting scheme in [48] takes two additional operations on the voters' side, double encryption and zero knowledge proof of knowledge of certain secrets committed in the ciphertexts, to counteract those attacks. However, it is pointed out in [8] that [48] is still vulnerable to attacks from dishonest talliers, not to mention the two additional operations counteract the

---

[4][60] cannot guarantee complete correctness, privacy, robustness or public verifiability of election. [93] only supports a small fraction of all the possible permutations and thus is weak in privacy. [47] has a loose requirement on privacy and causes concerns with public verifiability.

efficiency improvement gained through omitting instant verification and compromise the advantage of shuffling-based e-voting in efficiency on the voters' side. Finally, even if instant verification is performed, shuffling-based e-voting is still vulnerable to an active attack launched by a malicious voter proposed in (Section 5 of) [94].

The new shuffling protocol proposed in Section 3.1 employs the first verification method and can be employed to build a e-voting scheme as follows.

1. The voters choose their vote according to the election rule. Their vote can be in any format and can contain any content and so support any election application.

2. The voters encrypt their votes and submit the encrypted votes to the talliers. The public key used in the encryption is pubished by the talliers and the corresponding private key is shared among the talliers using a threshold secret sharing mechanism.

3. The talliers form a mix network act as the routers to shuffle the encrypted votes in term, while every tallier publicly proves validity of his shuffling.

4. A number of tallliers over the private key sharing threshold cooperate to decrypt the repeatedly shuffled ciphertexts and recover the votes.

5. The decrypted votes are counted to determine the election result.

3.3 Security Concerns and Suggested Solution in Practice

Although the new shuffling protocol in Section 3.1 satisfies the security requirement of shuffling, its application to e-voting does not necessarily produce a secure e-voting scheme. The active attacks against privacy in [94, 8] must be prevented. However, the existing countermeasures against those attacks are not efficient (and especially increase the cost of the voters and thus counteract the advantage of shuffling-based e-voting in efficiency on the voters' side) as they explicitly or implicitly require costly zero knowledge proof operations on the voters' side. In addition, even if either of these two measures is employed to prevent the voters from deviating from the voting protocol, the shuffling nodes can still actively cheat if instant and complete public proof and verification is not performed on each shuffling node. In this section, simpler and more efficient countermeasures against the attacks are designed. The voters must be prevented from deviating from the voting protocol and launching active attacks [94, 8] in the new e-voting scheme. The essence of these attacks from actively malicious voters is to insert specially designed information into certain votes such that the chance to break privacy is obtained when these votes are decrypted. To prevent these attacks, the parameter setting and decryption function are modified in the new e-voting scheme such that no other information than election-related content is revealed when the encrypted votes are decrypted no matter how strange some deliberately generated votes may be. Unlike the existing countermeasures, the modification not only does not require any additional computation but also improves efficiency. As a result, the new e-voting scheme is correct, private, robust and highly efficient. It is especially suitable for large-scale election applications.

Relation attacks are introduced by Pfitzmann [94] and further explored in [8, 100, 7]. As research goes deeper, more and more kinds of relation attacks are found. Detailed definition and classification of relation attacks will be given in Section 3.3.1. In summary, a relation attack generates some special relations between some output messages so that an adversary can recognise the relation and trace one of the messages to its corresponding input ciphertext.

Since Chaum proposed the first mix network [25], many mix networks have appeared. Some of them involve a complete mix network composed of multiple mixers [84, 80, 5, 6, 81, 62, 60, 15, 48, 93, 101, 102, 104] and other designers argue that all the mixers employ the same shuffling operation and thus focus on one mixer's work [42, 74, 52, 75, 41, 90, 79, 10]. As all of them employ malleable encryption algorithms and a ciphertext encrypting a message related to the message in a given ciphertext can be easily generated in them. So all of them are vulnerable to relation attacks unless a countermeasure is employed to prevent the exploitation of malleability of the employed encryption algorithms. Some mix networks [56, 48] are specially designed to avoid relation attacks without addressing the problem of malleability, but they fail as explained in Section 3.3.1.

Some countermeasures [100, 21, 57, 33, 8, 7] have been proposed to prevent relation attacks in a general circumstance. Unfortunately, all of them explicitly or implicitly employ costly mechanisms to break malleability of the employed encryption algorithms and are thus inefficient. Moreover, as explained in Section 3.3.1, they implicitly need support of other costly operations and cannot protect the mix networks from many relation attacks without the supporting operations. Special countermeasures can be designed to prevent certain relation attacks in certain circumstances, but they are usually inefficient too as explained in Section 3.3.1. Although there are a couple of relatively efficient special countermeasures, they can only handle very special relation attacks and are not very useful in general. There is a co-called semi-general countermeasure [96], which is more general than the special ones. However, as explained in Section 3.3.1, it is extremely inefficient.

In this section, a novel countermeasure against relation attacks is designed. It prevents any relation attack in mix networks when they are used in e-voting applications. Relation attacks in other applications are not taken into account. It is actually a general countermeasure against relation attacks in mix-network-based e-voting. As the main application of mix network is e-voting, such a semi-general countermeasure is very useful. As we focus on e-voting applications and the mixed messages in e-voting applications (used to stand for the possible choices in an election) are short enough to be encrypted into one single asymmetric ciphertext, we do not take hybrid mix networks into account, which employ both a symmetric cipher and an asymmetric cipher to shuffle long messages. Important advantages of this new countermeasure are simplicity and high efficiency. It does not employ the complex and costly operations in the existing countermeasures. Actually, it employs a new encryption algorithm with a limited output space and does not need any additional operation. So it is much more efficient than any existing countermeasure against relation attacks. The new countermeasure is specified and shown to work effectively. The concrete specifications illustrate that it is applicable to the existing mix-based e-voting schemes to protect them from any relation attack.

3.3.1 Various Relation Attacks and the Existing Countermeasures

The intended functionality of a mix network is to achieve anonymity, so privacy is a very important property in mix networks. Unfortunately, there are various attacks against privacy in mix networks. Those attacks threaten security of many mixing-based e-voting schemes. Well known examples of such attacks include the passive attack against privacy proposed by Pfitzmann [94], the third attack proposed by Wikstrom [100], and the attack proposed by Horster and Michels [72]. Apart from attacks against privacy of asymmetric cipher-based mix networks mentioned above, there are also attacks against hybrid mix networks like the one against [62] proposed by Abe [8, 7] and attacks against correctness of mix networks like the fifth attack by Wikstrom [100] against [48, 59].

In comparison with the attacks listed in the last paragraph, relation attacks affect more mix networks and are more difficult to prevent. While those attacks can be efficiently handled,[5] in general there is no efficient countermeasure against relation attacks.

As there are many kinds of relation attacks it is not easy to give a simple and formal definition to cover all of them. However, they share a common idea and usually work as follows.

1. To trace a ciphertext c_i, an adversary computes one or more ciphertexts encrypting messages related to the message encrypted in c_i. The ciphertexts are mixed with the normal and valid input ciphertexts and are shuffled together. They may appear as input ciphertexts to a mix network and then be shuffled by all the mixers or be inserted into the mix network by a dishonest mixer and replace some ciphertexts received by the mixer and then be shuffled by the following mixers.

---

[5]The concrete countermeasures are not described here. Interested readers are referred to the papers describing these attacks and fixing the attacked mix networks [100, 72, 8, 7].

2. The key idea of the attack is that there are some special relations between the message in c_i and the messages in the ciphertexts generated by the adversary. The special relations are chosen by the adversary A and can be recognised by A.

3. After the output messages of the mix network are published, the adversary finds the special relations among them and identifies the message in c_i in polynomial time according to recognised relations.

In summary, a relation attack generates some special relations between some output messages so that an adversary can recognise the relation and trace one of the messages to its corresponding input ciphertext. We have to emphasize that the special relation is not limited to normal algebraic relations and includes a very wide range of relations. Any relation distinguishing the attacked message from other messages can be employed. Actually, a relation useful in a relation attack can be defined as follows.

- A relation is in the form $R(m, m_1, m_2, \ldots, m_\delta)$ where m is the attacked and traced message, $\delta \geq 1$ and $m_1, m_2, \ldots, m_\delta$ are some messages in the output result of the mix network. The domain of $R()$ is a definite set and if necessary such a set with τ elements can be represented in the form $\{0, 1, \ldots, \tau - 1\}$.

- A relation $R(m, m_1, m_2, \ldots, m_\delta)$ is useful in a relation attack if for any m' not equal to m in the output messages $R(m, m_1, m_2, \ldots, m_\delta) \neq R(m', m_1, m_2, \ldots, m_\delta)$.

The following two examples of useful relations will be employed in the two examples of relation attacks later in this section.

- One message is t times of another message:

$$R(m, m_1) = \begin{cases} 1 & \text{if} \quad m_1 = tm \\ 0 & \quad otherwise \end{cases}$$

- One message is the only valid message, or (speaking like a relation) m is more valid than the other messages:

$$R(m, m_1, m_2, \ldots) = \begin{cases} 1 & \text{if} \quad m \text{ is a valid vote and} \\ & \quad m_1, m_2, \ldots \text{ are invalid} \\ 0 & \quad otherwise \end{cases}$$

If this abstract definition is not easy to follow, readers can use a simpler method to identify relation attacks: all the already known and newly discovered relation attacks are presented in Table 3.2.

As stated before, unless an appropriate countermeasure is employed to break malleability, any existing mix network has to deal with relation attacks as they employ malleable encryption algorithms. Some mix networks [48, 56] try to protect privacy from attack without breaking malleability. Golle et al. [48] employ two special mechanisms, double encryption and additional tags, to strengthen privacy. In [56] cut-and-choose, tags and dummy inputs are employed as extra efforts to provide immunity to attacks against privacy. However, as demonstrated in [100, 8, 7], they are still vulnerable to relation attacks.

Some discovered relation attacks and their simple variants are listed in Table 3.2. Among them, Attack 1 and Attack 2 are the most common relation attacks. A simple example of these two attacks is that a corrupted polynomial party (the first mixer or a sender) inserts c^t into the input list where the attacked input is a ciphertext c, t is an integer randomly chosen by the adversary and El Gamal encryption is employed (and such that $c = (a, b)$ is related to $c^t = (a^t, b^t)$). The adversary finds in the output message list two messages m_i and m_j such that $m_i = m_j^t$ and deduces that m_j is the message encrypted in c. Note that the special case $t = 1$ has not been explicitly described in the literature. Attack 1 and Attack 2 can be developed into attacking protocols with different specifications in details. Attacks 3, 4, 5 and 6 are concrete enough in Table 3.2 and more details about them can be found in the given references.

There is a special relation attack, which has not been mentioned in existing literature to our knowledge. It is quite simple and can work when illegal ciphertexts cannot be detected in a mix network. Suppose the first mixer, M_1, under the control of a polynomial adversary, wants to break privacy of a certain encrypted vote. M_1 modifies all the encrypted votes but the chosen vote to illegal ciphertexts. Then the only legal vote discovered in the end is the content of the attacked vote. For example, M_1 keeps encrypted vote c and replaces any other encrypted vote with $E(m')$ where m' is an invalid vote and $E()$ is the vote encryption algorithm. In this way the vote encrypted in c must be the only legally opened vote. This attack is easier to detect than the other relation attacks if the employed mix network employs instant and complete public verification. If the employed mix network only employs a final public verification, this attack can only be detected in the final verification of the mix network when the votes have been decrypted and published and thus the attacked vote has been revealed. This is called Attack 7 and also included in Table 3.2. At present, to our knowledge there is no countermeasure against this attack in mix networks employing final verification.

A simple countermeasure to attacks exploiting malleability of encryption is to introduce redundancy into the messages. However, it has been illustrated in [94] that countermeasures to prevent relation attack through redundancy in the messages are either ineffective or impractical. In [100, 8, 7] ZK proof of every sender's knowledge of his message (or ZK proof of every sender's knowledge of some secret integer used in his encryption, which implies knowledge of the message) is recommended as a general countermeasure against relation attacks. A concrete ZK proof of senders' knowledge of their messages is spec-

Table 3.2: Relation attacks

Attack	Reference	Attacked Scheme	Condition	Specification
1	Active attack in [94]	Any mix when instant and complete verification of shuffling is not provided	At least first mixer is corrupted	Corrupted mixers insert ciphertext related to attacked input
2	Active attack in [94]	Any mix when sender's knowledge of message is not proved	Sender is corrupted and can submit later than attacked sender	Corrupted sender submits input related to attacked input
3	First attack in [100]	[48]	Two corrupted senders	Two related inputs encrypting first ciphertext of attacked input
4	Second attack in [100] and independently in [8, 7]	[48]	First mixer is corrupted; there are two mix sessions	In first session the first mixer exchanges tags of two attacked inputs; in second session one of first two attacks is employed
5	Fourth attack in [100]	[48, 56]	First mixer and last mixer are corrupted	First mixer tampers with two inputs and last mixer detects and corrects them
6	Attack 2 in [8, 7]	[48]	One sender is corrupted	Corrupted sender sends invalid input with same tag as attacked input
7	Unknown	Any mix which cannot detect invalid ciphertext	First mixer is corrupted	First mixer tampers with all votes except vote to attack

ified in [21]. Non-malleable encryption is employed in [57, 33] as a general countermeasure against relation attacks. In [8, 7], CCA secure encryption algorithms are employed as a general countermeasure against relation attacks and vulnerability against relation attacks is formally abstracted into CCA security of multiple encryptions. All these general countermeasures are identical or at least similar in essence. The non-malleable encryption algorithm in [57, 33] is specified through ZK proof of senders' knowledge of their messages. Although no specification of CCA secure encryption algorithm is provided in [8, 7], it faces the same problem of non-malleable encryption. In general, CCA secure encryption is implemented through ZK proof of a sender's knowledge of his message or other similar ZK proof primitives. Even if some CCA secure encryption algorithms do not need zero knowledge proof of knowledge on the encryption performer's (voter's) side, they usually extend the length of ciphertext and greatly increase the cost of shuffling the ciphertexts. Moreover, they usually cannot be used in shuffling, which re-encrypts and randomises some ciphertexts. All the existing general countermeasures against relation attacks implicitly or explicitly employ costly ZK proof techniques or other costly operations.

Moreover, the existing general countermeasures can only prevent relation attacks launched by senders solely like Attack 2, Attack 3 and Attack 6. If malicious mixers take part in a relation attack like Attack 1, Attack 4, Attack 5 and Attack 7, these general countermeasures based on the senders' ZK proof of their knowledge of their messages are not enough. The reason is simple: although no sender can submit any ciphertext related to an input, malicious mixers (e.g., the first mixer) can insert a ciphertext related to the input into the ciphertext list. The mixer's malicious behaviour may be detected in time to stop a relation attack on some mix networks through immediate and complete verification of shuffling. Mix networks which do not employ complete verification [81] or immediate verification [84, 56, 48] of shuffling cannot prevent the relation attack in time. The general countermeasures based on the senders' ZK proof of their knowledge of their messages implicitly need support of other operations (e.g., complete and instant verification of shuffling) and cannot protect the mix networks from many relation attacks without the supporting operations. In addition, when the existing general countermeasures are employed to prevent certain relation attacks like Attack 2, other special operations (e.g., untransferable ZK proof to prevent Attack 2) are needed.

There are some special countermeasures against certain relation attacks. For example, instant and complete proof and verification of shuffling prevent Attack 1, Attack 4 and Attack 5. In another example if the encrypted inputs to a mix network are committed in an additional round of communication and then opened in the submission session as the inputs, Attack 2 and Attack 6 can be prevented. It is mentioned in [100, 8, 7] that double encryption with different keys can prevent Attack 3. However, these existing special countermeasures only handle some special relation attacks in certain mix networks and cannot provide a general solution. Moreover, they are usually inefficient in either computation or communication. For example, although more efficient proof and verification techniques [41, 90] have been proposed to instantly verify validity of shuffling, mix networks with instant and complete proof and verification of shuffling are still inefficient in comparison with mix networks with partial verification of shuffling like [48] or mix networks with only a final verification of shuffling like [84]. In the second example, one more round of communication and additional commitments reduces efficiency of communication. Although double encryption with different keys is not so inefficient, it is so special that it can only prevent Attack 3.

There is a semi-general countermeasure in [96], which can prevent any relation attack in an e-voting application employing any mix network. Although it can only work in e-voting applications and cannot work in general-purpose mix networks, it is more general than the special countermeasures. In [96] a counting center selects different ciphertexts standing for the same possible choices in the election for different voters, shuffles them into a random order and proves their validity using ZK proof primitives. Then the mixers form a reverse-direction mix network, through which the ciphertexts are shuffled and sent to the voters. At the same time, the counting center and the mixers send their permutations on the ciphertexts for each voter to the corresponding voter through an "untapped secure channel". Finally, the voters submit the ciphertexts standing for their choices to the mixers, who then shuffle them as in a normal mix-based e-voting scheme. An obvious drawback of [96] is very low efficiency. Before n votes are mixed, kn ciphertexts must be mixed in a reverse mix network where k is the number of possible choices in the election, not to mention transmission of $n(m + 1)$ k-dimension permutations through the additional "untapped secure channel" between the counter center, mixers and the voters must be specified with costly cryptographic operations where m is the number of mixers. Even if the simplest election rule is used and $k = 2$ as in the example in [96], efficiency is very low. When a more general election is involved and k is larger, the cost of this countermeasure is intolerable.

In summary, except for a special countermeasure handling only a single special attack all the existing countermeasures to relation attacks are inefficient. In addition, it is difficult to design a general countermeasure to protect various mix networks from any relation attack. In general there is no efficient solution to relation attacks in mix networks.

3.3.2   Main Idea of the New Countermeasure

An idea of Sako and Kilian [96] is inspiring: although it is difficult to design a general countermeasure against relation attacks in general-purpose mix networks, it may be easier to design a general countermeasure against relation attacks in e-voting-oriented mix networks as the vote space in e-voting applications is usually small. Of course the extremely inefficient solution in [96] is not inherited. Instead we employ a very efficient approach. We specially design a new encryption algorithm in an e-voting-oriented mix network such that any ciphertext is decrypted into a small vote space, each element in which stands for a legal choice in the election. More precisely,

- If a legal choice is encrypted into a ciphertext and shuffled in the mix network after being shuffled it will be recovered correctly.

- If a ciphertext encrypting an illegal choice is shuffled in the mix network, whether it is generated by a malicious voter or inserted into the mix network by a malicious mixer, it will either be detected before being decrypted or be recovered as a legal choice by a deterministic function.

No matter how the input ciphertexts are generated, modified or how special they are, only legal votes are decrypted and published in the end, while the legal votes are in a small set in normal e-voting applications. Therefore, although a very large number (e.g., larger than 2^{1024}) of possible inputs may be submitted or inserted into the mix network and various relations may exist among them, most relations will vanish after they are processed in the mix network. An adversary in a relation attack can only base his attack on relations able to survive the mix network: relation between legal votes. As usually many voters have the same choice in an election, many votes satisfy those surviving relations and the attacked vote and the vote related to it cannot be distinguished from other votes equal to them. As a result, the relation attacks in e-voting applications are prevented.

As the new countermeasure employs an efficient encryption algorithm and needs no costly operation, it is highly efficient. Especially, it does not assume existence of any costly additional operation, which may cause hiding cost. Moreover, it is a general solution. It can be applied to any mix network on the condition that it only handles messages in small sets like e-voting applications. No matter whether re-encryption or decryption or both are employed in the shuffling, whether single encryption or double encryption is employed, whether verifiability is achieved to guarantee correctness or not, how verifiability is achieved and correctness is guaranteed, the new countermeasure can work. Although different mix networks may have different levels of robustness and some may be vulnerable to various other attacks, once our new countermeasure is applied, all of them will be invulnerable to relation attacks in e-voting applications. Moreover, the new countermeasure is consistent with other countermeasures against other attacks in mix networks.

A new security model defining robustness against relation attacks in shuffling-based e-voting is proposed in Definition 4 and Definition 5. The first condition, Definition 2, guarantees that in any relation attack any ciphertext is not helpful and the only information to exploit is the decrypted votes. The second condition guarantees that each decryption output a legal vote and the illegal state cannot be exploited in any relation attack. The third condition further specifies the second one and guarantees that the decrypted votes only reveal the voters' election choices, so that no other information can be used by any relation attack. The fourth condition guarantees that with a very large probability there are multiple instances of each election choice in the recovered votes, such that the votes involved in a relation attack are untraceable. Theorem 11 illustrates that the four conditions are sufficient to prevent relation attack and they guarantee that the probability that a vote is traceable is vanishingly small.

Definition 4 *A vote is traceable if a link between its content and its origin can be found. Suppose a vote appears as an encryption or commitment η_1 when it is cast and its content is published as η_2 in the tallying phase. The vote is traceable if η_2 can be linked to η_1 and thus linked to the corresponding voter.*

Definition 5 *A mix network-based e-voting scheme is robust against relation attacks if the following four conditions are satisfied.*

- *The encryption algorithm employed to encrypt the votes is semantically secure.*

- *An encrypted vote is decrypted only if it contains a legal election choice.*

- *No other information than the submitted election choices is extracted from the votes. More formally and precisely, the following two vote transcripts are indistinguishable. The first vote transcript contains the decryption results of an instance of the optimised e-voting scheme, where every participant is honest and strictly follows the e-voting protocol and no relation attack is launched. The second vote transcript contains the decryption results of an instance of the optimised e-voting scheme, where the participants are dishonest and may launch any relation attack.*

- *The vote space is much smaller than the number of voters such that many voters have the same vote.*

Theorem 11 *Satisfaction of the the four conditions in Definition 5 is sufficient to prevent any relation attack.*

Before Theorem 11 is proved, a lemma is proved first.

Lemma 11 *The probability that a vote is traceable is negligible when the number of voters n is much larger than ρ, the number of valid voting choices.*

Proof: A vote can be traced only if no other vote contains the same voting choice with it. We assume that every vote is chosen randomly with some fixed positive probability. So a vote can be traced with a probability

$$(1 - \upsilon)^{n-1}$$

where υ is the probability that the choice in the vote is chosen by a common voter. When n is large and much larger than ρ, it is a very small probability. For example, if $\upsilon = 1/\rho$, the probability is

$$(1 - 1/\rho)^{n-1} = ((1 - 1/\rho)^\rho)^{n-1/\rho}$$

As $(1 - 1/\rho)^\rho$ is a small value asymptotically approaching $1/e$ and n is much larger than ρ, $(1 - 1/\rho)^{n-1}$ is overwhelmingly small in terms of n/ρ and negligible. □

Even if the choice in the vote is unpopular and v is much smaller than $1/\rho$ (e.g., $v = 0.01$ in a five-candidate election), in a large scale election (e.g., millions of voters) the probability is still small and negligible. In practice, only one different vote with the same choice may not be enough to satisfactorily hide an attacked vote and thus a vote is regarded as untraceable if and only if there are other votes containing the same choice. Suppose γ is a security parameter and it is required that at least γ other votes contain the same choice. Usually, γ only needs to be large enough to hide the attacked vote among $\gamma + 1$ votes with the same choice, so γ can be much smaller than n. The probability that there are less than γ other votes containing the same voting choice is

$$((\rho - 1)^{n-1} + \binom{n-1}{1}(\rho - 1)^{n-2} + \binom{n-1}{2}(\rho - 1)^{n-3} + \dots$$
$$+ \binom{n-1}{\gamma-1}(\rho - 1)^{n-\gamma})/\rho^{n-1}$$

where $\binom{a}{b}$ denotes the number of possible choices of b elements from a candidate elements.

As $\rho^{n-1} = (\rho - 1 + 1)^{n-1} = \sum_{i=0}^{n-1} \binom{n-1}{i}(\rho - 1)^{n-1-i}$ and n is much larger than ρ and γ, the probability that there are less than γ other votes containing the same voting choice is negligible.

Proof of Theorem 11: As the first condition is satisfied, any ciphertext published in the e-voting scheme is not helpful in any relation attack against it as it reveals no information and is indistinguishable from a random ciphertext. Any relation attack can only exploit the published plaintexts, namely the finally published votes in the e-voting scheme. Satisfaction of Condition 2 and Condition 3 guarantees that all the published votes are legal election choices and their distribution has no difference from that of the votes in an unattacked e-voting scheme. Any relation attack can only exploit the relations between legal and normal votes. Lemma 11 illustrates that satisfaction of the fourth condition guarantees that the relations between legal and normal votes cannot identify any vote as it is indistinguishable from the other votes with the same election choice. □

3.3.3 A Prototype and Its Drawbacks

In this section, an example is given to specify the new idea in a prototype. This prototype is not secure enough and used only to demonstrate the new idea. In the prototype, the modified El Gamal encryption in [67] is employed. However, there is a drawback to overcome in the modified El Gamal encryption: its decryption is inefficient as a costly search for discrete logarithm is employed in its decryption function. The modified El Gamal encryption in [67] is further modified in our design such that efficient decryption and limited output space of decryption function are achieved simultaneously. The new modified El Gamal encryption is as follows.

- p is a large prime. q is a small prime divisor of $p-1$ such that $q \geq 2\xi$ where ξ is the number of choices in the election. g is a generator of the cyclic subgroup with order $(p-1)/q$ and g' is the generator of the cyclic subgroup with order q.

- The private key is an integer x and the public key is y where $y = g^x$ mod p. The private key is generated in a distributed manner [36, 85, 43] such that it is shared among some decryption authorities: $A_1, A_2, \ldots$ without being revealed to any one.

- Encryption: a message m in Z_q is encrypted into $c = (a, b) = (g^r$ mod $p,\ g'^m y^r$ mod $p)$ where r is randomly chosen from Z_{p-1}.

- Decryption of a ciphertext $c = (a, b)$ is denoted as $D(c)$.

Note that order of g' is a small integer q. So the decryption function in this new modified El Gamal encryption is much more efficient than in [67]. Moreover, the message space is limited in Z_q and any ciphertext is decrypted into Z_q.

Any mix-based e-voting scheme employing El Gamal encryption can be optimised by employing the modified El Gamal encryption above and modifying vote format as follows to prevent relation attacks exploiting relations between the decrypted votes.

1. Suppose there are ξ possible choices in the election application. The integers in Z_q are evenly divided into ξ subsets, each standing for an election choice. When Z_q is divided, both odd integers and even integers in it are respectively divided into the ξ subsets as evenly as possible. To elect a choice, a voter randomly chooses an integer from the subset corresponding to his choice and seals it in his vote using the modified El Gamal encryption algorithm presented in this section.

2. Any mix network supporting El Gamal encryption (e.g., [52, 93, 90, 42, 41, 102]) can be employed to shuffle the encrypted votes.

3. The mixed votes are decrypted and recovered.

4. Among the decrypted results, the legal votes are counted, while the illegal results recovered from illegal encrypted votes are ignored.

In the modified e-voting scheme,

- If a vote is generated as described in the voting protocol, it will be recovered without any change.

- If a vote is invalid (e.g., submitted by a voter or inserted by a malicious mixer launching a relation attack), it will be recovered as illegal.

Although the prototype prevents all the other relation attacks in Table 3.2, it is vulnerable to Attack 7 when instant verification of validity of shuffling is not employed in the mix network. If the employed mix network is instantly verified, any illegal result must be from a dishonest or careless voter and cannot be the result of a relation attack by a dishonest mixer. The voter only invalidates his own vote and cannot launch a harmful relation attack. However, if the employed mix network is not instantly verified, Attack 7 can be successfully carried out by the first mixer. Moreover, besides relation attack, there is another attack to extract the votes in the prototype as follows where it is supposed that $p - 1 = q\mu$ and there is an encrypted vote c in the form of (a, b).

1. An adversary calculates $a' = a^\mu \bmod p$.

2. The adversary searches for discrete logarithm $r' = \log_{g'} a'$, which is feasible for a polynomial adversary as q is small.

3. The adversary calculates $b' = b^\mu / y^{\mu r'} \bmod p$.

4. The adversary searches for discrete logarithm $m = \log_{g'^\mu} b'$, which is the vote encrypted in c. As q is small, the search is feasible for a polynomial adversary.

3.3.4   Optimization and Security Analysis

The prototype is optimised such that the drawbacks in it can be overcome. Firstly, a novel encryption algorithm is designed as follows.

- Parameter setting
  N is a large public composite with unknown factorization and the largest cyclic group in Z_N^* has an order $2q\alpha\beta$ where q is not a divisor of N. α and β are secret large primes with similar size. q is a public prime no smaller than ρ where ρ is the number of possible choices in the election. Note that such parameter setting is easy and practical as

  - In most practical e-voting applications, ρ is not large and q can be much smaller than α and β

  - Generation of N is straightforward by satisfying that $N = PQ$, $2q\alpha$ divides $P - 1$ and 2β divides $Q - 1$.

g is a generator of G_1, the cyclic subgroup with order $q\alpha$. h is a generator of G_2, the cyclic subgroup with order α. $g' = g^\alpha$ and thus g' is a generator of G, the cyclic subgroup with order q. The three integers, g, h, g', are publicly known.

- Setting of keys
  The private key is α and the public key is g'.

- Key sharing
  The verifiable t-out-of-m secret sharing function [85] is employed to share α among the talliers $A_1, A_2, \ldots, A_m$ where α_j is the share held by A_j. $\theta_j = g^{\alpha_j}$ for $j = 1, 2, \ldots, m$ are published.

- Encryption: a message m in Z_q is encrypted into $c = E(m) = g^m h^r \bmod N$ where r is a random integer in Z_l and l is a large security parameter.

- Re-encryption: a ciphertext c in Z_q is re-encrypted into $c' = c h^{r'} \bmod N$ where r' is a random integer in Z_l.

- Decryption function

  1. The talliers receive a ciphertext c and cooperate to calculate $d = \prod_{j \in S} c_j^{w_j} \bmod N$ where A_j publishes $c_j = c^{\alpha_j} \bmod N$, $w_j = \prod_{k \in S, k \neq j} \frac{k}{k-j}$ and set S contains the indices of $t + 1$ cooperating talliers. Each A_j proves correctness of his partial decryption by proving $\log_c c_j = \log_g \theta_j$ using zero knowledge proof of equality of logarithms.

  2. Search for $\log_{g'} d$ in Z_q. If $\log_{g'} d$ is found in Z_q, it is output as the decryption result. If $\log_{g'} d$ does not exist, c is declared as an illegal ciphertext and an illegal result is output. When c is declared illegal, anyone can test whether $d^q \neq 1 \bmod N$ to verify.

This new encryption algorithm has similarity with [16] in the main idea, but has its own special design and a certain advantage in preventing relation attacks. Its security is specified in Definition 6 and Definition 7 and proved in Theorem 13. Note that for convenience of formal analysis the definition of semantic security slightly differs from the universally accepted definition of semantic security recalled in Definition 8. However, all the definitions are the same in essence as illustrated in Theorem 12 although they differ in presentation.

Definition 6 *(New definition of semantic security) A challenger chooses a message m and a ciphertext c in any way he likes and asks a polynomial party to tell whether $E(m) = c$ where $E()$ is an encryption algorithm. Suppose the message encrypted in c is m' and c is uniformly distributed in $\{C \mid D(C) = m'\}$ and the probability that the polynomial party correctly answers that question is ω. The encryption algorithm is semantically secure if $\omega - 0.5$ is negligible no matter how m is chosen in the message space and c is chosen in the ciphertext space.*

Definition 7 *Hardness of decision subgroup problem: given N, g, g', h and an integer in G_1, it is hard to tell whether it is in G_2.*

Definition 8 *(Universally accepted definition of semantic security) A party chooses two messages m_1 and m_2 in any way he likes in the message space and sends them to an encryption oracle. The encryption oracle randomly chooses i from $\{1,2\}$ and returns $c = E(m_i)$ to the party where the probabilistic operation in the encryption is randomly performed. Suppose the probability that the party finds out i in polynomial time is ω. The encryption algorithm is semantically secure if $\omega - 0.5$ is negligible.*

Theorem 12 *The definition of semantic security in Definition 6 is the same in essence as the universally accepted definition in Definition 8.*

Proof: Suppose semantic security in Definition 6 is broken by a polynomial algorithm B. Then a polynomial algorithm can be designed as follows to break semantic security in the universally accepted definition by querying B.

1. With two messages m_1 and m_2 chosen by itself and a ciphertext $c = E(m_i)$, a polynomial party is asked to find i.

2. The polynomial party sends query (m_1, c) to B.

3. The polynomial party return 1 if B returns YES. Otherwise he returns 2.

Suppose semantic security in the universally accepted definition is broken by a polynomial algorithm A. Then a polynomial algorithm can be designed as follows to break semantic security in Definition 6 by querying A.

1. Given a message m and a ciphertext c, a polynomial party is asked to tell whether $E(m) = c$.

2. The polynomial party randomly chooses another message m' and sends query (m_1, m_2, c) to A where $m_1 = m$ and $m_2 = m'$.

3. The polynomial party answers YES if A returns 1. Otherwise (no matter A returns 2 or "Invalid Input") he answers NO.

Semantic security satisfied in either definition deduces semantic security satisfied in the other definition. Therefore, the two definitions are the same in essence. $\qquad\square$

Theorem 13 *The new encryption algorithm is semantically secure as defined in Definition 6 if the decision subgroup problem in Definition 7 is hard.*

Proof: If the new encryption algorithm is not semantically secure, there must exist a polynomial algorithm A and a message m' such that A can correctly tell whether m' is encrypted in a given ciphertext with a probability non-negligibly larger than a random guess can do. A can be employed in the following algorithm to break the decision subgroup problem.

1. Given an integer z in G_1, a polynomial party wants to tell whether it is in G_2 or not.

2. It inputs message m' and ciphertext $c' = g^{m'} z$ to A.

3. If A concludes that $E(m') = c'$, the party concludes that z is in G_2; if A concludes that $E(m') \neq c'$, the party concludes that z is not in G_2.

Note that $g^{m'} z$ is independent of m' when z is not in G_2. As $E(m') = c'$ if and only if z is in G_2, the probability that the party correctly tells whether z is in G_2 equals the probability that A correctly tells whether $E(m') = c'$. The probability that the party's guess correctly tells whether z is in G_2 is non-negligibly larger than a random guess can indicate. Therefore, the decision subgroup problem is broken. This contradiction implies that the new encryption algorithm is semantically secure.   □

Decision subgroup problems are generalizations of a widely accepted hard quadratic residuosity problem. In a quadratic residuosity problem, it is required to decide whether an integer is a quadratic residue. It is widely recognised and accepted that when the factorization of the multiplicative modulus is secret, a quadratic residuosity problem is hard. Many cryptographic techniques (e.g., Goldwasser-Micali encryption [46]) depend on hardness of quadratic residuosity problems. Decision subgroup problems in this section are actually q-ic residuosity problems as an integer is in G_2 if and only if it is a q-ic residue. When $q = 2$, a decision subgroup problem actually becomes a quadratic residuosity problem. Note that the hardness of decision subgroup problem is widely recognised [76, 105].

This new encryption algorithm is semantically secure as illustrated in Theorem 13. Note that in the new encryption algorithm the final search for discrete logarithm is in a small set Z_q and thus is quite efficient. The new encryption algorithm is homomorphic and thus suitable for nearly all the existing mix networks, most of which require that the employed encryption algorithm must be either additive homomorphic or multiplicative homomorphic. More precisely,

- With encryption algorithm $c = g^m h^r$ and the corresponding decryption function $D()$ to recover m from c, the new encryption algorithm is additive homomorphic as $D(c_1 c_2) = D(c_1) + D(c_2)$ for any ciphertexts c_1 and c_2.

- If g^m is regarded as the message and $D'()$ stands for the decryption function to recover it from c, the new encryption algorithm is multiplicative homomorphic as $D'(c_1 c_2) = D'(c_1) D'(c_2)$ for any ciphertexts c_1 and c_2.

Moreover, the new encryption algorithm is simpler and more efficient than the existing encryption algorithms used in mix networks like Paillier encryption [83] and El Gamal encryption. The optimised e-voting scheme employs the new encryption algorithm and is as follows where batch verification is employed to verify validity of the votes before they are decrypted.

1. The new encryption described above is set up with encryption function $E()$. The private key is shared by the talliers.

2. The election rule is declared and Z_q is the vote space, which is evenly divided[6] by the talliers into ρ sets $S_1, S_2, \ldots, S_\rho$, each representing a choice in the election.

3. For $i = 1, 2, \ldots, n$ each voter V_i randomly chooses an integer v_i from the set representing his choice and submits $c_i = E(v_i)$ to the talliers.

4. A mix network is employed to shuffle the encrypted votes into $c'_1, c'_2, \ldots, c'_n$ by re-encrypting and re-ordering them, while the talliers can act as the mixers.

5. The mixed encrypted votes $c'_1, c'_2, \ldots, c'_n$ are sent to the talliers for the final decryption. The talliers cooperate to decrypt them and publicly prove validity of the decryption. Before any decryption is performed the talliers must cooperate to verify that none of the output ciphertexts from the mix network is illegal by checking

$$\prod_{i=1}^{n} c'^{t_i}_i \text{ is decrypted into}$$
$$\text{a legal message in } Z_q \tag{3.15}$$

   where integers $t_1, t_2, \ldots, t_n$ are L-bit random integers (e.g., generated by a pseudorandom hash function) and 2^L is no larger than β. Soundness of the verification is guaranteed by Theorem 14. The output ciphertexts are decrypted and published as the recovered votes only if the two conditions are satisfied. Note the following two explanations.

   - Although β is secret, L is easy to choose. β must be large enough such that that factorization of $2q\alpha\beta$ is hard. So we only need to set L as an integer smaller than the lower bound of β.

   - Although when either of the two conditions is not satisfied rewinding is necessary, probability of this incident can be minimized. When this incident happens each participant is required to prove validity of his operation. Any participant whose validation fails will be removed from the voting scheme which will have to be rerun.

6. The decrypted votes are counted.

Analysis of resistance against relation attacks in the optimised e-voting scheme is based on the formal standard in Definition 5. The first condition

---

[6]Z_q is divided into the ρ sets such that the number of elements in each set is equal or at least as equal as possible.

has been demonstrated to be satisfied in Theorem 13. The second condition is satisfied as illustrated in Theorem 14. The third condition is demonstrated to be satisfied in Theorem 15. The fourth condition is satisfied in most e-voting applications. The first condition guarantees that no information about any vote is revealed from any ciphertext to any polynomial party. On one hand, it guarantees that the vote privacy is protected before the tallying phase. On the other hand, it implies that any polynomial adversary can only base his relation attack on the decrypted votes while the encrypted votes are useless to him. The second condition guarantees that the illegal state cannot be exploited in any relation attack. The third condition and the fourth condition guarantee that when the encrypted and shuffled votes are decrypted the decryption result reveals no information but the submitted election choices, which are in a small set and thus useless in relation attacks. Therefore, satisfaction of the four conditions simultaneously prevents any relation attack.

Theorem 14 *If decryption of $\prod_{i=1}^{n} c'^{t_i}_i$ mod N is in Z_q with a probability larger than 2^{-L}, then any c'_i is in G_1 for $i = 1, 2, \ldots, n$.*

Proof: Suppose f is a generator of the largest cyclic group. c'_i can be denoted as f^{d_i} mod N for $i = 1, 2, \ldots, n$ where d_i is an even integer. As decryption of $\prod_{i=1}^{n} c'^{t_i}_i$ mod N is in Z_q with a probability larger than 2^{-L} and

$$\prod_{i=1}^{n} c'^{t_i}_i = f^{\sum_{i=1}^{n} d_i t_i} \bmod p$$

$\alpha \sum_{i=1}^{n} d_i t_i$ is a multiple of $2\alpha\beta$ with a probability larger than 2^{-L}. Namely, $\sum_{i=1}^{n} d_i t_i$ is a multiple of 2β with a probability larger than 2^{-L}. So for any integer k in $\{1, 2, \ldots, n\}$ there must exist a combination of $t_1, t_2, \ldots, t_{k-1}, t_{k+1}, \ldots, t_n$ such that there are two choices for t_k in Z_{2^L}, $t_{k,1}$ and $t_{k,2}$, to satisfy that $\sum_{i=1}^{n} d_i t_i$ is a multiple of 2β. More precisely, there must exist $t_1, t_2, \ldots, t_{k-1}, t_{k+1}, \ldots, t_n, t_{k,1}$ and $t_{k,2}$, each in Z_{2^L} to satisfy the following two statements.

$$\sum_{i=1}^{k-1} d_i t_i + d_k t_{k,1} + \sum_{i=k+1}^{n} d_i t_i$$
$$\text{is a multiple of } 2\beta \tag{3.16}$$

$$\sum_{i=1}^{k-1} d_i t_i + d_k t_{k,2} + \sum_{i=k+1}^{n} d_i t_i$$
$$\text{is a multiple of } 2\beta \tag{3.17}$$

Otherwise, for any combination of $t_1, t_2, \ldots, t_{k-1}, t_{k+1}, \ldots, t_n$, there is at most one choice for t_k in Z_{2^L} to satisfy that $\sum_{i=1}^{n} d_i t_i$ is a multiple of 2β, which leads to a contradiction: the probability that $\sum_{i=1}^{n} d_i t_i$ is a multiple of 2β is no more than 2^{-L}. (3.16) and (3.17) imply that

$$d_k(t_{k,1} - t_{k,2}) \text{ is a multiple of } 2\beta$$

As $t_{k,1} < 2^L$, $t_{k,2} < 2^L$, $2^L \leq \beta$ and β is prime, d_k is a multiple of β. Therefore, as d_k is even, c'_k is in G_1. As k can be any integer in $\{1, 2, \ldots, n\}$, c'_i is in G_1 for $i = 1, 2, \ldots, n$. □

Theorem 15 *The two vote transcripts defined in the third condition in Definition 5 are indistinguishable.*

Proof: The first vote transcript defined in the third condition in Definition 5 is in the form $(a_1, b_1, a_2, b_2, \ldots, a_n, b_n)$ where a_i stands for a recovered election choice and is uniformly distributed in Z_q and $b_i = g'^{a_i} \bmod N$ for $i = 1, 2, \ldots, n$. Theorem 14 guarantees that only legal votes are decrypted. So although dishonest voters and mixers can submit or insert special votes into the e-voting system, the final decryption result only contains legal votes. In the second transcript defined in the third condition in Definition 5, each decryption in the tallying phase reveals (a, b) in its two-step procedure where a is uniformly distributed in Z_q and $b = g'^{a} \bmod N$. The second vote transcripts are in the form $(a_1, b_1, a_2, b_2, \ldots, a_n, b_n)$ where a_i stands for a recovered election choice and is uniformly distributed in Z_q and $b_i = g'^{a_i} \bmod N$ for $i = 1, 2, \ldots, n$. As the two vote transcripts have the same distribution, they are indistinguishable. □

The optimised e-voting scheme not only prevents relation attacks but also achieves high efficiency. Theorem 14 illustrates that t_i is not necessary to be a full length (e.g., 1024 bits long) integer in practical applications. For example, when $L = 30$, 2^{-L} is smaller than one out of one billion and thus the probability that any c' is an invalid ciphertext can be ignored even in e-voting applications with very high security requirements. Test of (3.15) is much more efficient than the existing countermeasures against relation attacks. As the new encryption algorithm does not compromise efficiency, the optimised e-voting scheme is more efficient than the existing countermeasures against relation attacks. Its advantages over the existing countermeasures against relation attacks is demonstrated in Table 3.3, which summarizes the analysis in Section 3.3.1 and this section.

3.4 Off-Line Pre-Computation in Mix Networks

There are two costly operations in a shuffle: re-encryption of the n ciphertexts and public proof and verification of validity of shuffle. The existing shuffling schemes (including [5, 6, 74, 42, 52, 93, 77, 78, 90, 102, 51, 50, 89] and some other less famous schemes where the scheme in [41] is an extended journal version of [42] and the scheme in [75] is a formal publication of [74]) usually try their best to make the public proof and verification as efficient as possible. An important method used by the recent shuffling schemes

Table 3.3: Comparison of countermeasures against relation attacks

Scheme	Effectiveness	Efficiency
Redundancy in messages	Ineffective as illustrated in [94]	High
ZK proof of every sender's knowledge	Preventing Attack 2, Attack 3, Attack 6 and Attack 2	Costly operations like ZK proof costing $O(n)$ full length exponentiations
Non-malleable encryption	Preventing Attack 2, Attack 3, Attack 6 and Attack 2	Costly operations like ZK proof costing $O(n)$ full length exponentiations
CCA secure encryption	Preventing Attack 2, Attack 3, Attack 6 and Attack 2	Costly operations like ZK proof costing $O(n)$ full length exponentiations
Special countermeasures	Each preventing certain attacks	Costly operations like instant and complete proof and additional communication
Semi-general countermeasure in [96]	Preventing any relation attack in e-voting	Additional shuffling costing $O(kn)$ full length exponentiations and $n(m+1)k$ full-length integers in communication
New countermeasure	Preventing any relation attack in e-voting	Very efficient and only costing $O(1)$ full length exponentiations

[93, 90, 102, 77, 78, 51, 89] to improve computational efficiency is employ-ment of small exponents. They notice that the exponentiation computations in cryptographic operations usually employ very large exponents (hundreds of bits long) and sometimes the exponents are not necessary to be so large. Ac-tually in many practical applications the exponents can be much smaller (e.g., scores of bits long) but still large enough to guarantee very strong security (e.g., to control the probability of failure under one out of billions). The recent shuffling schemes employ many small exponents in proof and verification of validity of shuffle and estimate their computational cost in the proof and ver-ification in terms of the number of separate exponentiations with full-length exponents. More precisely, they set the computational cost of an exponenti-ation with a full-length exponent as the basic unit in efficiency analysis and estimate how many basic units cost the same as their operations.[7] In this way, their efficiency advantage over the previous shuffling schemes is obviously and vividly demonstrated.

The existing shuffling schemes do not worry for the cost of re-encryption as most of the computations in the n instances of re-encryption can be carried out offline in advance (as demonstrated in Section 3.4.3 and Section 3.4.4) and so will not affect real-time efficiency. For example, in recent shuffles like [51], the cost of proof and verification of validity of shuffle has been reduced to a quite low level while no attempt is made to reduce the cost of re-encryption. Although the existing shuffling schemes give different priorities to inevitable online operations and operations possible to be carried out offline in advance and only pursue high efficiency in the online operations, they ignore two more subtle strategies. Firstly, they do not consider a better trade-off between online cost and offline cost by reducing the former and increasing the latter. Secondly, they do not give difference priorities to the cost for a prover (shuffling node) and the cost of a verifier. Note that the shuffling nodes in an anonymous com-munication network usually have much more powerful computation capability than the verifiers. For example, in the most important application of shuffles, e-voting, the talliers (who shuffle the encrypted votes) are professional elec-tion officials and have powerful computational capability. In comparison, the verifiers (voters and observers) include many common citizens and many of them may have limited computational capability. Moreover, in applications like e-voting, many verifiers are expected to take part to guarantee credibility. Efficiency of verifiers should have a higher priority in shuffles.

A new shuffling protocol is designed in this section. On one hand, it inher-its the two useful strategies in the existing shuffling schemes: higher priority in efficiency improvement for online operations and employment of small expo-nents to improve efficiency. On the other hand, the two more subtle strategies ignored in the existing shuffling schemes are adopted as well. In our new shuf-fling protocol, all the costly operations of the shuffling node are carried out

---

[7]Namely, multiple exponentiations with small exponents are counted as one exponenti-ation with a full-length exponent that has the same cost.

offline in advance, while a verifier's computation can be batched and is very efficient when small exponents are employed. Its online computational cost is much lower than those of the existing shuffling schemes and so it has an advantage in practical efficiency. As the proof and verification techniques in the new shuffling scheme are very simple, its formal security can be illustrated in a simple way without any other computational assumption than the basic assumption, which is inevitable in any shuffle.

3.4.1   Security Model of Shuffles

The proof of validity of a shuffle is modeled as a ZK proof in [50] as follows. A proof protocol like a proof of validity of a shuffle is denoted in the form of a triple (K, P, V) where the following parameters are used.

- G is a set-up algorithm and gk is the set-up information it generates.

- (P, V) are a pair of probabilistic polynomial time interactive algorithms presenting the prover and the verifier, while they may have access to a common random string σ generated by a probabilistic polynomial time key generation algorithm K.

- R is a polynomial time decidable ternary relation and for an element x we call w a witness if $(gk, x, w) \in R$.

- L_{gk} is the language consisting of elements x that have a witness w such that $(gk, x, w) \in R$.

- $tr \leftarrow \langle P(x), V(y) \rangle$ stands for the public transcript produced by P and V when interacting on inputs x and y together with the randomness used by V.

- $Ptr \leftarrow \langle P(x) \rangle$ stands for the public transcript produced by P in the proof.

- $Vtr \leftarrow \langle V(y) \rangle$ stands for the public transcript produced by V in the proof.

- $Pr[E]$ stands for the probability that an event E happens.

(K, P, V) is called a proof for relation R with setup G if for all non-uniform polynomial time interactive adversaries A it is complete and sound as defined in Definition 9 and Definition 10. Its ZK is defined in Definition 11 and Definition 12.

Definition 9 *(Completeness) (K, P, V) is complete regarding A if*

$$Pr[gk \leftarrow G(1^k); \sigma \leftarrow K(gk); (x, w) \leftarrow A(gk, \sigma) :$$
$$(gk, s, w) \notin R \text{ or } \langle P(gk, \sigma, x, w), V(gk, \sigma, x) \rangle = 1] \approx 1$$

Definition 10 *(Soundness) (K, P, V) is sound regarding A if*

$$Pr[gk \leftarrow G(1^k); \sigma \leftarrow K(gk); x \leftarrow A(gk, \sigma) : x \notin L_{gk} \text{ and}$$
$$\langle A, V(gk, \sigma, x) \rangle = 1] \approx 0$$

Definition 11 *(Public coin) A proof is public coin if the verifier's messages are chosen uniformly at random independently of the messages sent by the prover and the setup parameters.*

Definition 12 *(HVZK) The public coin proof (K, P, V) is called a special honest verifier zero-knowledge proof for R with setup G if there exists a probabilistic polynomial time simulator S such that for all non-uniform polynomial time adversaries A we have*

$$Pr[gk \leftarrow G(1^k); \sigma \leftarrow K(gk); (x, w, \rho) \leftarrow A(gk, \sigma);$$
$$tr \leftarrow < P(gk, \sigma, x, w), V(gk, \sigma, x, \rho) >: (gk, x, w) \in R \text{ and } A(tr) = 1]$$
$$= Pr[gk \leftarrow G(1^k); \sigma \leftarrow K(gk); (x, w, \rho) \leftarrow A(gk, \sigma);$$
$$tr \leftarrow S(gk, \sigma, x, w) : (gk, x, w) \in R \text{ and } A(tr) = 1]. \quad (3.18)$$

In proof of validity of a shuffle, the relation R is actually $c'_i = RE(c_{\pi(i)})$ for $i = 1, 2, \ldots, n$ and the secret witnesses of this relation include $\pi()$ and the secret random integers used in the n instances of re-encryption .

3.4.2 The Basic Design

In our new shuffling protocol, the shuffled messages are encrypted with Paillier encryption where the private key is shared among decryption authorities (e.g., all the shuffling nodes) in an anonymous communication network. Usually a threshold secret sharing mechanism is employed to share the private key (see [37] for more details) such that decryption is feasible if and only if the number of cooperating decryption authorities is over the threshold. The message space of Paillier encryption is Z_N where N is a composite with two large secret factors p' and q'. The multiplicative modulus is N^2 and the public key is g, a large number with secret order modulo N^2. Encryption of a message m is $g^m r^N \mod N^2$ where r is randomly chosen from Z_N^*. More details about the parameter setting can be found in [37]. The basic idea in the new shuffling protocol is cut-and-choose. Some more instances of re-ordered re-encryptions of $c_1, c_2, \ldots, c_n$ are published by the shuffling node that must show that a randomly chosen subset of them are shuffles of $c_1, c_2, \ldots, c_n$ and the remaining subset of them are shuffles of $c'_1, c'_2, \ldots, c'_n$. The new shuffling protocol is described as follows.

1. Receiving Paillier ciphertexts $c_1, c_2, \ldots, c_n$, the shuffling node calculates and publishes $c'_i = c_{\pi(i)} r_i^N \mod N^2$ for $i = 1, 2, \ldots, n$ where $\pi()$ is a random permutation of $\{1, 2, \ldots, n\}$ and every r_i is randomly chosen from Z_N^*.

2. To prove validity of $c_1', c_2', \ldots, c_n'$, the shuffling node publishes another T instances of re-ordered re-encryption of $c_1, c_2, \ldots, c_n$:

$$C_{j,i} = c_{\pi_j(i)} r_{j,i}^N \bmod N^2 \text{ for } j = 1, 2, \ldots, T \text{ and } i = 1, 2, \ldots, n$$

where T is a security parameter to guarantee that $1/2^T$ is a negligible probability, $\pi_j()$ is a random permutation of $\{1, 2, \ldots, n\}$ for $j = 1, 2, \ldots, T$ and every $r_{j,i}$ is randomly chosen from Z_N^*.

3. A random subset P_1 is chosen from $\{1, 2, \ldots, T\}$ by some verifier(s) or as a (pseudo)random function (e.g., hash function of $c_1, c_2, \ldots, c_n, c_1', c_2', \ldots, c_n', C_{1,1}, C_{1,2}, \ldots, C_{T,n}$). The left integers in $\{1, 2, \ldots, T\}$ are included a set $P_2 = \{1, 2, \ldots, T\} - P_1$.

4. For $j \in P_1$, the shuffling node publishes $\pi_j()$ and $r_{j,1}, r_{j,2}, \ldots, r_{j,n}$ and anyone can publicly verify

$$C_{j,i} = c_{\pi_j(i)} r_{j,i}^N \bmod N^2 \text{ for } j \in P_1 \text{ and } i = 1, 2, \ldots, n. \quad (3.19)$$

5. For $j \in P_2$, the shuffling node publishes $\pi_j'() = \pi\pi_j^{-1}()$ and $r_{j,i}' = r_i/r_{j,\pi_j'(i)} \bmod N$ for $i = 1, 2, \ldots, n$ where $\pi\pi_j^{-1}(k) = \pi(\pi_j^{-1}(k))$ for any k in $\{1, 2, \ldots, n\}$. Anyone can publicly verify

$$c_i' = C_{j,\pi_j'(i)} r_{j,i}'^N \bmod N^2 \text{ for } j \in P_2 \text{ and } i = 1, 2, \ldots, n. \quad (3.20)$$

Completeness of the new shuffling protocol is straightforward and any interested reader can follow it step by step to verify that it ends successfully when the shuffling node is honest and strictly follows it. Its soundness and privacy are formally guaranteed by Theorem 16 and Theorem 17 respectively.

Theorem 16 *The new shuffling protocol achieves soundness. More precisely, if it satisfies Equations (3.19) and (3.20) with a probability larger than 2^{-T}, then $D(c_1'), D(c_2'), \ldots, D(c_n')$ is a permutation of $D(c_1), D(c_2), \ldots, D(c_n)$.*

Proof: Since Equations (3.19) and (3.20) are satisfied with a probability larger than 2^{-T}, there must exist integer J in $\{1, 2, \ldots, T\}$, such that

$$C_{J,i} = c_{\pi_J(i)} r_{J,i}^N \bmod N^2 \text{ for } i = 1, 2, \ldots, n \quad (3.21)$$

$$c_i' = C_{J,\pi_J'(i)} r_{J,i}'^N \bmod N^2 \text{ for } i = 1, 2, \ldots, n \quad (3.22)$$

Otherwise, for any integer J in $\{1, 2, \ldots, T\}$ at most one of the two equations (3.21) and (3.22) is satisfied and thus Equations (3.19) and (3.20) are satisfied only when every j in P_1 happens to be a J satisfying (3.21) and every j in P_2 happens to be a J satisfying (3.22), which leads to a contradiction by implying that the probability that Equations (3.19) and (3.20) are satisfied is no larger than 2^{-T} as P_1 is a random subset of $\{1, 2, \ldots, T\}$.

Equations (3.21) and (3.22) imply

$$c'_i = c_{\pi_J \pi'_J(i)}(r_{J,\pi'_J(i)} r'_{J,i})^N \bmod N^2 \text{ for } i = 1, 2, \ldots, n$$

and thus

$$D(c'_i) = D(c_{\pi_J \pi'_J(i)}) \text{ for } i = 1, 2, \ldots, n$$

$\square$

Theorem 17 *The new shuffling protocol achieves HVZK.*

Proof: The shuffling node's proof of validity of its shuffle has a proof transcript $C_{j,i}$ for $j = 1, 2, \ldots, T$ and $i = 1, 2, \ldots, n$; P_1; $\pi_j()$, $r_{j,1}, r_{j,2}, \ldots, r_{j,n}$ for $j \in P_1$; $\pi'_j()$, $r'_{j,1}, r'_{j,2}, \ldots, r'_{j,n}$ for $j \in P_2$. A party without any knowledge of the shuffling node's secret can simulate this proof transcript as follows.

1. He randomly chooses P_1 as a subset of $\{1, 2, \ldots, T\}$.

2. He randomly chooses $r_{j,1}, r_{j,2}, \ldots, r_{j,n}$ from Z_N^* for $j \in P_1$.

3. He randomly chooses $r'_{j,1}, r'_{j,2}, \ldots, r'_{j,n}$ from Z_N^* for $j \in P_2$ where $P_2 = \{1, 2, \ldots, T\} - P_1$.

4. He calculates

$$C_{j,i} = c_{\pi_j(i)} r_{j,i}^N \bmod N^2 \text{ for } j \in P_1 \text{ and } i = 1, 2, \ldots, n$$
$$C_{j,\pi'_j(i)} = c'_i r'^{-N}_{j,i} \bmod N^2 \text{ for } j \in P_2 \text{ and } i = 1, 2, \ldots, n$$

This simulating transcript has the following distribution.

- P_1 is uniformly distributed in all the subsets of $\{1, 2, \ldots, T\}$.

- $r_{j,1}, r_{j,2}, \ldots, r_{j,n}$ is uniformly distributed in Z_N^* for $j \in P_1$.

- $r'_{j,1}, r'_{j,2}, \ldots, r'_{j,n}$ is uniformly distributed in Z_N^* for $j \in P_2$ where $P_2 = \{1, 2, \ldots, T\} - P_1$.

- $C_{j,1}, C_{j,2}, \ldots, C_{j,n}$ is uniformly distributed in $\{C_{j,1}, C_{j,2}, \ldots, C_{j,n} \mid C_{j,i} = c_{\pi_j(i)} \hat{r}_{j,i}^N \bmod N^2$ for $i = 1, 2, \ldots, n, \pi_j()$ is uniformly distributed in all the possible permutations of $\{1, 2, \ldots, n\}$ and $\hat{r}_{j,i}$ is uniformly distributed in $Z_N^*\}$ for $j = 1, 2, \ldots, T$.

- Equations (3.19) and (3.20) are satisfied.

In the shuffling node's proof of validity of its shuffle, when the public coin model defined in Definition 11 is employed, the real proof transcript has the same distribution as the simulating transcript above. As the two transcripts have just the same distribution, the condition in (3.18) is satisfied and HVZK is achieved according to Definition 12. $\square$

3.4.3 Off-Line Pre-Computation and Batch Verification

The basic design in Section 3.4.2 is simple and secure, but not efficient. To improve its efficiency, offline pre-computation can be arranged for the shuffling node and batch verification can be adopted for the verifiers. With these two efficiency improvement mechanisms, the basic design can be optimised as follows.

1. Before doing any shuffle, the shuffling node carries out some off-line pre-computation when free. It chooses random integers $R_1, R_2, R_3, \ldots \ldots$ from Z_N^* and calculates $A_1 = R_1^N \bmod N^2$, $A_2 = R_2^N \bmod N^2$, $A_3 = R_3^N \bmod N^2$, $\ldots \ldots$ In this way, it builds up two pre-encryption databases $\Phi = \{R_1, R_2, R_3 \ldots \ldots\}$, $S = \{A_1, A_2, A_3 \ldots \ldots\}$ and an empty database $\Psi = \{\}$.

2. Receiving Paillier ciphertexts $c_1, c_2, \ldots, c_n$, the shuffling node calculates and publishes $c_i' = c_{\pi(i)} b_i \bmod N^2$ for $i = 1, 2, \ldots, n$ where $\pi()$ is a random permutation of $\{1, 2, \ldots, n\}$ and every b_i is randomly chosen from S. Every used b_i is immediately deleted from S after it is picked out and new data $(b_i^{1/N}, b_i)$ is then inserted into Ψ where $b_i^{1/N}$ is taken as the data in Φ corresponding to b_i in A.

3. To prove validity of $c_1', c_2', \ldots, c_n'$, the shuffling node publishes more T instances of re-ordered re-encryption of $c_1, c_2, \ldots, c_n$:

$$C_{j,i} = c_{\pi_j(i)} b_{j,i} \bmod N^2 \text{ for } j = 1, 2, \ldots, T \text{ and } i = 1, 2, \ldots, n$$

where $\pi_j()$ is a random permutation of $\{1, 2, \ldots, n\}$ for $j = 1, 2, \ldots, T$ and every $b_{j,i}$ is randomly chosen from S. Every used $b_{j,i}$ is immediately deleted from S after it is picked out and new data $(d_{j,i}, b_{j,i})$ is then inserted into Ψ where $d_{j,i}$ is the data in Φ corresponding to $b_{j,i}$ in A and thus equal to $b_{j,i}^{1/N}$.

4. A random subset P_1 is chosen from $\{1, 2, \ldots, T\}$ in the same way as in the basic design.

5. For $j \in P_1$, the shuffling nodes finds $(d_{j,i}, b_{j,i})$ for $i = 1, 2, \ldots, n$ in Ψ and publishes $\pi_j()$ and $r_{j,i} = d_{j,i}$ for $i = 1, 2, \ldots, n$.

6. For $j \in P_2$, the shuffling nodes finds $(d_{j,i}, b_{j,i})$ for $i = 1, 2, \ldots, n$ in Ψ and then publishes $\pi_j'() = \pi \pi_j^{-1}()$ and $r_{j,i}' = r_i / d_{j,\pi_j'(i)} \bmod N$ for $i = 1, 2, \ldots, n$ where $r_i = b_i^{1/N}$, which is found in Ψ corresponding to b_i.

7. Verification of (3.19) and (3.20) is batched into verification of

$$\prod_{j \in P_1, 1 \leq i \leq n} (C_{j,i}/c_{\pi_j(i)})^{t_{j,i}} \prod_{j \in P_2, 1 \leq i \leq n} (c_i'/C_{j,\pi_j'(i)})^{t_{j,i}}$$
$$= (\prod_{j \in P_1, 1 \leq i \leq n} r_{j,i}^{t_{j,i}} \prod_{j \in P_2, 1 \leq i \leq n} r_{j,i}'^{t_{j,i}})^N \bmod N^2 \qquad (3.23)$$

where every $t_{j,i}$ is a random L-bit integer chosen by the verifier or generated as as a (pseudo)random function and L is a security parameter smaller than p' and q' to be instantiated later.

Completeness of this optimised shuffling protocol is straightforward and anyone can check it. According to Theorem 18, with an overwhelmingly large probability, satisfaction of (3.23) guarantees that $C_{j,i}/c_{\pi_j(i)}$ for $j \in P_1$ and $c'_i/C_{j,\pi'_j(i)}$ for $j \in P_2$ are N^{th} residues and thus

$$D(C_{j,i}) = D(c_{\pi_j(i)}) \text{ for } j \in P_1 \text{ and } i = 1, 2, \ldots, n$$
$$D(c'_i) = D(C_{j,\pi'_j(i)}) \text{ for } j \in P_2 \text{ and } i = 1, 2, \ldots, n$$

Theorem 16 still works after the optimisation and soundness of the optimised shuffling protocol are guaranteed. Pre-computation and batch verification do not change the proof transcript, which still consists of $C_{j,i}$ for $j = 1, 2, \ldots, T$ and $i = 1, 2, \ldots, n$; P_1; $\pi_j()$, $r_{j,1}, r_{j,2}, \ldots, r_{j,n}$ for $j \in P_1$; $\pi'_j()$, $r'_{j,1}, r'_{j,2}, \ldots, r'_{j,n}$ for $j \in P_2$. Their distribution is unchanged as well. Theorem 17 still works after the optimisation and privacy of the optimised shuffling protocol are guaranteed.

Theorem 18 *Suppose $y_1, y_2, \ldots, y_n$ are in Z_{N^2}, $x_1, x_2, \ldots, x_n$ are in Z_N^*, $t_1, t_2, \ldots, t_n$ are randomly chosen from $\{0, 1, \ldots, 2^L - 1\}$ and $2^L < min(p', q')$. If $\prod_{i=1}^n y_i^{t_i} = (\prod_{i=1}^n x_i^{t_i})^N \bmod N^2$ with a probability larger than 2^{-L}, then $y_1, y_2, \ldots, y_n$ are N^{th} residues.*

Proof: $\prod_{i=1}^n y_i^{t_i} = (\prod_{i=1}^n x_i^{t_i})^N \bmod N^2$ with a probability larger than 2^{-L} implies that for any given integer v in $\{1, 2, \ldots, n\}$ there must exist integers $t_1, t_2, \ldots, t_n \in \{0, 1, \ldots, 2^L - 1\}$ and $t'_v \in \{0, 1, \ldots, 2^L - 1\}$ such that

$$\prod_{i=1}^n y_i^{t_i} = \prod_{i=1}^n x_i^{N t_i} \bmod N^2 \tag{3.24}$$

$$(\prod_{i=1}^{v-1} y_i^{t_i}) y_v^{t'_v} \prod_{i=v+1}^n y_i^{t_i} = (\prod_{i=1}^{v-1} x_i^{N t_i}) x_v^{N t'_v} \prod_{i=v+1}^n x_i^{N t_i} \bmod N^2 \tag{3.25}$$

Otherwise, for any $(t_1, t_2, \ldots, t_{v-1}, t_{v+1}, \ldots, t_n)$ in $\{0, 1, \ldots, 2^L - 1\}^{n-1}$, there is at most one t_v in $\{0, 1, \ldots, 2^L - 1\}$ to satisfy $\prod_{i=1}^n y_i^{t_i} = \prod_{i=1}^n x_i^{N t_i} \bmod N^2$, which implies that among the 2^{nL} possible choices for $\{t_1, t_2, \ldots, t_n\}$ there are at most $2^{(n-1)L}$ choices to satisfy $\prod_{i=1}^n y_i^{t_i} = \prod_{i=1}^n x_i^{N t_i} \bmod N^2$ and leads to a contradiction to the assumption that $\prod_{i=1}^n y_i^{t_i} = (\prod_{i=1}^n x_i^{t_i})^N \bmod N^2$ with a probability larger than 2^{-L}.

Equations (3.24)/(3.25) yield

$$y_v^{t_v - t'_v} = x_v^{N(t_v - t'_v)} \bmod N^2$$

According to the Euclidean algorithm there exist integers α and β to satisfy $\beta(t_v - \hat{t}_v) = \alpha N + GCD(N, t_v - \hat{t}_v)$. Note that $GCD(N, t_v - \hat{t}_v) = 1$ as $t_v, \hat{t}_v < 2^L < min(p', q')$, and so $y_v^{\beta(t_v - \hat{t}_v)} = y_v^{\alpha N} y_v$. Thus,

$$y_v = y_v^{\beta(t_v - \hat{t}_v)} / y_v^{\alpha N} = (y_v^{(t_v - \hat{t}_v)})^\beta / y_v^{\alpha N}$$
$$= x_v^{N(t_v - \hat{t}_v)\beta} / (y_v^\alpha)^N = (x_v^{(t_v - \hat{t}_v)\beta} / y_v^\alpha)^N \bmod N^2$$

So y_v is an Nth residue. Therefore, $y_1, y_2, \ldots, y_n$ are N^{th} residues as v can be any integer in $\{1, 2, \ldots, n\}$.   □

With this optimisation, online efficiency of the shuffling node is greatly improved. It does not need to compute any exponentiation online. For a verifier, the total computational cost includes a full-length exponentiation (with exponent N) and two instances of computation of product of nT exponentiations with L-bit exponents. Note that as in the efficiency analysis in most existing shuffling schemes, we only count the number of exponentiations in terms of multiples of n and their remainder modulo n is ignored. According to [11], computing each of the two instances of product of exponentiations costs about $2^{W-1}(nT + 1) + L + nTL/(W + 1)$ multiplications where $|N|$ is the bit length of N and W is a parameter in the W-bit sliding window exponentiation method and is normally set as 3. When the standard W-bit sliding window exponentiation method is employed, a full-length exponentiation costs $2^{W-1} + |N| + |N|/(W + 1)$ multiplications. So the computational cost of a verifier is approximately equal to

$$2(2^{W-1}(nT + 1) + L + nTL/(W + 1))/(2^{W-1} + |N| + |N|/(W + 1)) + 1$$

full-length exponentiations. When $T = L = 40$, 2^{-T} and 2^{-L} are smaller than one out of one trillion and thus negligible in any practical application. In this case, when $|N|=1024$, the computational cost of a verifier is approximately equal to $0.31n$ full-length exponentiations.

3.4.4   The Final Shuffling Protocol: Modifying Encryption and Further Improving Efficiency

To further improve efficiency of a verifier, the employed Paillier encryption can be slightly modified such that the batch verification can be optimised. The modified Paillier encryption has a slightly different public key (g, h, N) where h is an integer in Z_N^* with a large multiplicative order modulo N^2 and its order has no small factor. The encryption function is slightly modified: a message m is encrypted into $g^m h^{rN} \bmod N^2$ where r is randomly chosen from Z_N. The decryption function is unchanged. With this modified encryption algorithm, the shuffling protocol is finally optimised as follows.

1. Before doing any shuffle, the shuffling node carries out some offline pre-computation when free. It chooses random integers $R_1, R_2, R_3, \ldots \ldots$ from Z_N and calculates $A_1 = h^{R_1 N} \bmod N^2$, $A_2 = h^{R_2 N} \bmod N^2$, $A_3 = h^{R_3 N} \bmod N^2, \ldots \ldots$. In this way, it builds up two pre-encryption databases $\Phi = \{R_1, R_2, R_3 \ldots \ldots\}$, $S = \{A_1, A_2, A_3 \ldots \ldots\}$ and an empty database $\Psi = \{\}$.

2. Receiving ciphertexts $c_1, c_2, \ldots, c_n$, the shuffling node calculates and publishes $c_i' = c_{\pi(i)} b_i \bmod N^2$ for $i = 1, 2, \ldots, n$ where $\pi()$ is a random

permutation of $\{1, 2, \ldots, n\}$ and every b_i is randomly chosen from S. Every used b_i is immediately deleted from S after it is picked out and new data $(\log_{h^N} b_i, b_i)$ is then inserted into Ψ where $\log_{h^N} b_i$ is taken as the data in Φ corresponding to b_i in A.

3. To prove validity of $c'_1, c'_2, \ldots, c'_n$, the shuffling node publishes another T instances of re-ordered re-encryption of $c_1, c_2, \ldots, c_n$:

$$C_{j,i} = c_{\pi_j(i)} b_{j,i} \bmod N^2 \text{ for } j = 1, 2, \ldots, T \text{ and } i = 1, 2, \ldots, n$$

where $\pi_j()$ is a random permutation of $\{1, 2, \ldots, n\}$ for $j = 1, 2, \ldots, T$ and every $b_{j,i}$ is randomly chosen from S. Every used $b_{j,i}$ is immediately deleted from S after it is picked out and new data $(d_{j,i}, b_{j,i})$ is then inserted into Ψ where $d_{j,i}$ is the data in Φ corresponding to $b_{j,i}$ in A and thus equal to $\log_{h^N} b_{j,i}$.

4. A random subset P_1 is chosen from $\{1, 2, \ldots, T\}$ in the same way as in the basic design.

5. For $j \in P_1$, the shuffling nodes finds $(d_{j,i}, b_{j,i})$ for $i = 1, 2, \ldots, n$ in Ψ and publishes $\pi_j()$ and $r_{j,i} = d_{j,i}$ for $i = 1, 2, \ldots, n$.

6. For $j \in P_2$, the shuffling nodes finds $(d_{j,i}, b_{j,i})$ for $i = 1, 2, \ldots, n$ in Ψ and then publishes $\pi'_j() = \pi \pi_j^{-1}()$ and $r'_{j,i} = r_i - d_{j,\pi'_j(i)} \bmod N$ for $i = 1, 2, \ldots, n$ where $r_i = \log_{h^N} b_i$, which is found in Ψ corresponding to b_i.

7. Anyone can publicly verify

$$C_{j,i} = c_{\pi_j(i)} h^{r_{j,i}N} \bmod N^2 \text{ for } j \in P_1 \text{ and } i = 1, 2, \ldots, n \quad (3.26)$$
$$c'_i = C_{j,\pi'_j(i)} h^{r'_{j,i}N} \bmod N^2 \text{ for } j \in P_2 \text{ and } i = 1, 2, \ldots, n \quad (3.27)$$

which is batched into verification of

$$\prod_{j \in P_1, 1 \le i \le n} (C_{j,i}/c_{\pi_j(i)})^{t_{j,i}} \prod_{j \in P_2, 1 \le i \le n} (c'_i/C_{j,\pi'_j(i)})^{t_{j,i}}$$
$$= h^{N(\sum_{j \in P_1, 1 \le i \le n} r_{j,i}t_{j,i} + \sum_{j \in P_2, 1 \le i \le n} r'_{j,i}t_{j,i})} \bmod N^2 \quad (3.28)$$

where every $t_{j,i}$ is a random L-bit integer generated in the same way as in the first optimisation and 2^L is smaller than any factor of the order of h.

Completeness of this final shuffling protocol is straightforward and anyone can check it. According to Theorem 19, satisfaction of (3.28), with an overwhelmingly large probability, guarantees satisfaction of (3.26) and (3.27) and thus satisfaction of

$$D(C_{j,i}) = D(c_{\pi_j(i)}) \text{ for } j \in P_1 \text{ and } i = 1, 2, \ldots, n$$
$$D(c'_i) = D(C_{j,\pi'_j(i)}) \text{ for } j \in P_2 \text{ and } i = 1, 2, \ldots, n$$

Theorem 16 still works after the final optimisation and soundness of the final shuffling protocol is guaranteed. As the proof transcript is changed in this final optimisation, its privacy is illustrated in a new theorem, Theorem 20.

Theorem 19 *Suppose $H, y_1, y_2, \ldots, y_n$ are in $Z_{N^2}, t_1, t_2, \ldots, t_n$ are randomly chosen from $\{0, 1, \ldots, 2^L - 1\}$ and 2^L is smaller than any factor of the order of H. If $\prod_{i=1}^{n} y_i^{t_i} = H^{\sum_{i=1}^{n} x_i t_i} \bmod N^2$ with a probability larger than 2^{-L}, then $y_i = H^{x_i}$ for $i = 1, 2, \ldots, n$.*

Proof: $\prod_{i=1}^{n} y_i^{t_i} = H^{\sum_{i=1}^{n} x_i t_i} \bmod N^2$ with a probability larger than 2^{-L} implies that for any given integer v in $\{1, 2, \ldots, n\}$ there must exist integers $t_1, t_2, \ldots, t_n \in \{0, 1, \ldots, 2^L - 1\}$ and $t_v' \in \{0, 1, \ldots, 2^L - 1\}$ such that

$$\prod_{i=1}^{n} y_i^{t_i} = H^{\sum_{i=1}^{n} x_i t_i} \bmod N^2 \tag{3.29}$$

$$(\prod_{i=1}^{v-1} y_i^{t_i}) y_v^{t_v'} \prod_{i=v+1}^{n} y_i^{t_i} = H^{(\sum_{i=1}^{v-1} x_i t_i) + x_v t_v' + \sum_{i=v+1}^{n} x_i t_i} \bmod N^2 \tag{3.30}$$

Otherwise, for any $(t_1, t_2, \ldots, t_{v-1}, t_{v+1}, \ldots, t_n)$ in $\{0, 1, \ldots, 2^L - 1\}^{n-1}$, there is at most one t_v in $\{0, 1, \ldots, 2^L - 1\}$ to satisfy $\prod_{i=1}^{n} y_i^{t_i} = H^{\sum_{i=1}^{n} x_i t_i} \bmod N^2$, which implies that among the 2^{nL} possible choices for $\{t_1, t_2, \ldots, t_n\}$ there are at most $2^{(n-1)L}$ choices to satisfy $\prod_{i=1}^{n} y_i^{t_i} = H^{\sum_{i=1}^{n} x_i t_i} \bmod N^2$ and leads to a contradiction to the assumption that $\prod_{i=1}^{n} y_i^{t_i} = H^{\sum_{i=1}^{n} x_i t_i} \bmod N^2$ with a probability larger than 2^{-L}.

Equations (3.29)/(3.30) yield

$$y_v^{t_v - \hat{t}_v} = H^{(t_v - \hat{t}_v) x_v} \bmod N^2$$

Note that t_v and $\hat{t}_v$ are L-bit integers and 2^L is smaller than any factor of the order of H. So $(t_v - \hat{t}_v)^{-1}$ modulo the order of H exists and thus

$$y_v = H^{x_v} \bmod N^2$$

Therefore, $y_i = H^{x_i}$ for $i = 1, 2, \ldots, n$ as v can be any integer in $\{1, 2, \ldots, n\}$.
$\square$

Theorem 20 *The final shuffling protocol achieves HVZK.*

Proof: The shuffling node's proof of validity of his shuffle has a proof transcript $C_{j,i}$ for $j = 1, 2, \ldots, T$ and $i = 1, 2, \ldots, n$; P_1; $\pi_j()$, $r_{j,1}, r_{j,2}, \ldots, r_{j,n}$ for $j \in P_1$; $\pi_j'()$, $r_{j,1}', r_{j,2}', \ldots, r_{j,n}'$ for $j \in P_2$. A party without any knowledge of the shuffling node's secret can simulate this proof transcript as follows.

1. He randomly chooses P_1 as a subset of $\{1, 2, \ldots, T\}$.

2. He randomly chooses $r_{j,1}, r_{j,2}, \ldots, r_{j,n}$ from Z_N for $j \in P_1$.

3. He randomly chooses $r_{j,1}', r_{j,2}', \ldots, r_{j,n}'$ from Z_N for $j \in P_2$ where $P_2 = \{1, 2, \ldots, T\} - P_1$.

4. He calculates

$$C_{j,i} = c_{\pi_j(i)} h^{r_{j,i}N} \bmod N^2 \text{ for } j \in P_1 \text{ and } i = 1, 2, \ldots, n$$
$$C_{j,\pi'_j(i)} = c'_i h^{-r'_{j,i}N} \bmod N^2 \text{ for } j \in P_2 \text{ and } i = 1, 2, \ldots, n$$

This simulating transcript has the following distribution.

- P_1 is uniformly distributed in all the subsets of $\{1, 2, \ldots, T\}$.

- $r_{j,1}, r_{j,2}, \ldots, r_{j,n}$ is uniformly distributed in Z_N for $j \in P_1$.

- $r'_{j,1}, r'_{j,2}, \ldots, r'_{j,n}$ is uniformly distributed in Z_N for $j \in P_2$ where $P_2 = \{1, 2, \ldots, T\} - P_1$.

- $C_{j,1}, C_{j,2}, \ldots, C_{j,n}$ is uniformly distributed in $\{C_{j,1}, C_{j,2}, \ldots, C_{j,n} \mid C_{j,i} = c_{\pi_j(i)} h^{\hat{r}_{j,i}N} \bmod N^2$ for $i = 1, 2, \ldots, n, \pi_j()$ is uniformly distributed in all the possible permutations of $\{1, 2, \ldots, n\}, \hat{r}_{j,i}$ is uniformly distributed in $Z_N\}$ for $j = 1, 2, \ldots, T$.

- Equations (3.26) and (3.27) are satisfied.

In the shuffling node's proof of validity of his shuffle, when the public coin model set in Definition 11 is employed, the real proof transcript has the same distribution as the simulating transcript above. As the two transcripts have just the same distribution, the condition in (3.18) is satisfied and HVZK is achieved according to Definition 12. □

With this final optimisation, online computation of the shuffling node still needs no exponentiation and the total computational cost of a verifier is further improved. In terms of multiples of n, the computational cost of a verifier includes a full-length exponentiation and computation of a product of nT exponentiations with L-bit exponents. So the computational cost of a verifier is approximately equal to

$$2^{W-1}(nT + 1) + L + nTL/(W + 1))/(2^{W-1} + |N| + |N|/(W + 1) + 1$$

full-length exponentiations. When $T = L = 40$, and $|N|=1024$, the result is approximately equal to $0.16n$ full-length exponentiations.

3.4.5 Comparison and Conclusion

A comparison between the new shuffling scheme and the recent shuffling schemes is given in Table 3.4, where "no additional assumption" means that only the basic assumption inevitable in any shuffle is needed. Among the two similar mix network designs in [77, 78], the optimised final version in [78] is included in the comparison. The not so recent shuffling schemes like [5, 6, 74, 42] are not included as they are not so advanced in security and efficiency. As the

Table 3.4: Comparison of shuffling schemes

Shuffle	Additional computa-tional assumption	Shuffler's online computation	Verifier's computation
[52][1]	Additional assumption for $com()$ and $mcom()$	$6n + 3n/\kappa$	$6n + 3n/\kappa$
[90]	No	$5.5n$	$4.3n$
[102][2]	Strong RSA assumption besides DDH assumptions needed in El Gamal encryption	$2.3n$	$1.5n$
[78]	Additional assumption for its DL-based commitment function	$3.4n$	$5.4n$
[51][3]	Additional assumptions for security of $com()$ besides basic assumption, including DL and factorization assumptions	$0.6n$	$0.3n$
[50][4]	No	$3\hat{m}n + 5n$	$4n + 3\hat{n}$
[89][5]	Factorization assumption besides DDH assumptions needed in El Gamal encryption	$3n$	$3n$
New	No	No online exponentiation	$0.16n$

[1] κ is a parameter integer. Detailed definition of the two functions $com()$ and $mcom()$ can be found in [52].

[2] The figures in [102] are amended in [51] and we adopt the amended figures.

[3] Detailed definition of the function $com()$ can be found in [51].

[4] $\hat{m}$ and $\hat{n}$ are two factors of n such that $n = \hat{m}\hat{n}$.

[5] The final proposal in Section 5 of [89].

shuffling scheme in [75] is a slight modification of the work in [74] and [52] and the shuffling scheme in [41] is a slight modification of the work in [42], [75] and [41] are not included either. The shuffling scheme in [93] does not support a complete permutation and only achieves weak privacy and so is not included. As in the efficiency analysis in most shuffling schemes, only exponentiations are counted in the efficiency analysis in Table 3.4, while much less costly multiplications and additions are omitted. For the sake of simplicity, the figures are given in terms of multiples of n and their remainders modulo n are ignored. Our efficiency analysis only covers the online computations, so for fairness, computations which can be carried out offline in advance in the existing shuffling schemes are not included in our analysis. More precisely, although most existing shuffling schemes do not explicitly mention offline pre-computation of the exponentiations in their re-encryption operations, we assume that those exponentiations are carried out offline as in our new shuffling scheme and do not include them in online computation of any shuffling scheme.

Table 3.4 shows that our new shuffling scheme has an obvious advantage in online computational efficiency over the existing shuffling schemes and is suitable for applications requiring high efficiency. Moreover, it only needs the basic assumption and thus achieves the strongest security possible in shuffling.

Chapter 4

Onion Routing

Onion routing [20, 44, 45] employs the idea of multiple-node routing and multiple-layer encryption. It employs multiple nodes to route a message, where each message is contained in a packet called an onion. In the packet, a message is encrypted layer by layer using the encryption keys of all the routers on its route and the receiver. Each layer of encryption is just like a layer of onion bulb. In onion routing, given a message packet, each router unwraps a layer of encryption by decrypting the message packet using its decryption key, finds out the identity of the next router and forwards the unwrapped message packet to the next router. Unless gaining collusion of all the routers on the routing path of his received message, the receiver cannot trace the message back to the sender, who then obtains anonymity. When a packet is routed together with a large number of other packets in busy traffic, onion routing prevents it from being traced, even if the traffic in the onion network is monitored. However, when the traffic is not busy enough, an onion packet may be traced by a party who can monitor the traffic in the whole onion network. Onion routing is widely employed in anonymous cyber surf activities and a typical example in practice is its simplified and optimised version in Tor [34].

4.1 The Basic Idea

The basic principle of onion routing is systematically introduced in [95] as follows. The onion routing network is accessed via a series of routers. An initiating application makes a connection to an application router. This router messages connection message format (and later data) to a generic form that can be passed through the onion routing network. It then connects to an onion router, which defines a route through the network by constructing a layered data structure called an onion. The onion is passed to the entry funnel, which occupies one of the long-standing connections to an onion router and multiplexes connections to the network at that onion router. That onion router will be the one for whom the outer most layer of the onion is intended. Each layer of the onion defines the next hop in a route. An onion router that receives an onion peels off its layer, identifies the next hop, and sends the embedded onion to that router. The last onion router forwards data to an exit funnel, whose job is to pass data between the onion routing network and the responder.

In addition to carrying next hop information, each onion layer contains key seed material from which keys are generated for crypting data sent forward or backward along the anonymous connection. Once the anonymous connection is established, it can carry data. Before sending data over an anonymous connection, the onion router adds a layer of encryption for each router in the route. As data moves through the anonymous connection, each onion router removes one layer of encryption, so it arrives at the responder as plaintext. This layering occurs in the reverse order for data moving back to the initiator. Data that has passed backward through the anonymous connection must be repeatedly post-crypted to obtain the plaintext.

By layering cryptographic operations in this way, we gain an advantage over link encryption. As data moves through the network it appears different to each onion router. Therefore, an anonymous connection is as strong as its strongest link, and even one honest node is enough to maintain the privacy of the route. In link-encrypted systems, compromised nodes can cooperate to uncover route information. Onion routers keep track of received onions until they expire. Replayed or expired onions are not forwarded, so they cannot be used to uncover route information, either by outsiders or compromised onion routers. Note that clock skew between onion routers can only cause an onion router to reject a fresh onion or to keep track of processed onions longer than necessary. Also, since data is encrypted using stream ciphers, replayed data will look different each time it passes through a properly operating onion router.

As shown in Figure 4.1, onion routing works as follows where a message m is sent by a sender S through n routers $P_1, P_2, \ldots, P_n$ to a receiver P_{n+1}.

1. Each P_i has an encryption algorithm $E_i()$ and a decryption algorithm $D_i()$.

2. The sender encrypts the message m, the route list $P_1, P_2, \ldots, P_{n+1}, S$ into

$$e = E_1(E_2(E_3(\ldots E_{n+1}(m)))\ldots)$$

and

$$c_i = E_1(E_2(E_3(\ldots E_{i-1}(P_{i+1})))\ldots)$$

for $i = 1, 2, \ldots, n$.

3. The sender sends out

$$O_1 = (e_1, c_{1,1}, c_{1,2}, \ldots, c_{1,n}) = (e, c_1, c_2, \ldots, c_n)$$

to P_1.

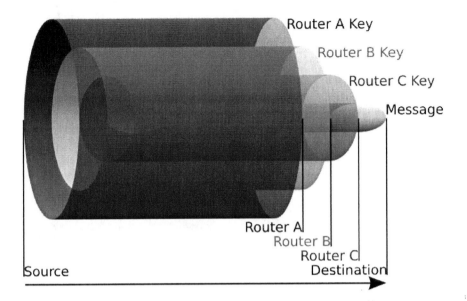

Figure 4.1: Onion Routing

4. For $i = 1, 2, \ldots, n$ each router P_i routes the onion packet as follows where the onion he receives is in the form $O_i = (e_i, c_{i,1}, c_{i,2}, \ldots, c_{i,n})$.

   (a) He calculates $D_i(c_{i,1})$ and finds the identity of P_{i+1}.

   (b) He calculates $e_{i+1} = D_i(e_i)$ and $c_{i+1,j} = D_i(c_{i,j+1})$ for $j = 1, 2, \ldots, n-1$.

   (c) He sends out

$$O_{i+1} = (e_{i+1}, c_{i+1,1}, c_{i+1,2}, \ldots, c_{i+1,n-1}, c_{i+1,n})$$

   to P_{i+1} where $c_{i+1,n}$ is a random ciphertext.

5. Finally, P_n sends

$$O_{n+1} = (e_{n+1}, c_{n+1,1}, c_{n+1,2}, \ldots, c_{n+1,n-1}, c_{n+1,n})$$

   to P_{n+1}.

6. P_{n+1} decrypts $c_{n+1,1}$ and finds nobody's identity, and knows that he is the receiver. He calculates $D_{n+1}(e_{n+1})$ to obtain m.

4.2 Formal Definition of Security

In [20], onion routing is formally defined and modelled into a strict security concept. Especially, a definition of security of an onion routing scheme in the universally composable framework is given in [20]. It is shown that in order to satisfy the universal composability-based definition, it is sufficient to give an onion routing scheme a special cryptographic definition similar to CCA2-security for encryption. As a result, onion routing can be formally illustrated to reveal to an adversarial router any information about onions apart from the prior and the next routers. In particular, the router does not learn how far a given message is from its destination. This property makes traffic analysis a lot harder to carry out, because now any message sent between two onion routers looks the same, even if one of the routers is controlled by the adversary, no matter how close it is to destination.

It is assumed in [20] that there is a network with J players $P_1, \ldots, P_J$. For simplicity, we do not distinguish players as senders, routers, and receivers; each player can assume any of these roles. In fact, making such a distinction would not affect our protocol at all and needs to be considered in its application only. Onion routing is defined in the public key model (i.e., in the hybrid model where a public key infrastructure is already in place) where each player has an appropriately chosen identity P_i, a registered public key PK_i corresponding to this identity, and these values are known to each player.

In each instance of a message that should be sent, for some (s, r), there is a sender P_s (s stands for "sender") sending a message m of length l_m (the length l_m is a fixed parameter, all messages sent must be the same length) to recipient P_r (r stands for "recipient") through $n < N$ additional routers $(P_{o_1}, \ldots, P_{o_n}$ stands for "onion router"), where the system parameter $N - 1$ is an upper bound on the number of route that the sender can choose. How each sender selects his onion routers $P_{o_1}, \ldots, P_{o_n}$ is a non-cryptographic problem independent of the current exposition. The input to the onion sending procedure consists of the message m that P_s wishes to send to P_r, a list of onion routers $P_{o_1}, \ldots, P_{o_n}$, and the necessary public keys and parameters. The input to the onion routing procedure consists of an onion O, the routing party's secret key SK, and the necessary public keys and parameters. In case the routing party is in fact the recipient, the routing procedure will output the message m.

The honest players are modelled by imagining that they obtain inputs (i.e., the data m they want to send, the identity of the recipient P_r, and the identities of the onion routers $P_{o_1}, \ldots, P_{o_n}$) from the environment Z, and then follow the protocol (either the ideal or the cryptographic one). Similarly, the honest players' outputs are passed to the environment.

Following the standard universal composability approach (but dropping most of the formalism and subtleties to keep presentation compact), it is defined that an onion routing protocol is secure if there exists a simulator (ideal-world adversary) S such that no polynomial-time in λ (the security parameter) environment Z controlling the inputs and outputs of the honest players, and the behavior of malicious players, can distinguish between interacting with the honest parties in the ideal model through S or interacting with the honest parties using the protocol.

It is easy to note that the solution presented in [20] is secure in the public key model, i.e., in the model where players publish the keys associated with their identities in some reliable manner. In the proof of security, the simulator S is allowed to generate the keys of all the honest players.

The ideal onion routing process can be defined by assuming that the adversary is static, i.e., each player is either honest or corrupt from the beginning, and the trusted party implementing the ideal process knows which parties are honest and which ones are corrupt. Ideal onion routing needs the following data structures and denotations to support its functionality.

- The Bad set of parties controlled by the adversary.

- An onion O is stored in the form of $(sid, P_s, P_r, m, n, P, i)$ where sid is the identifier, P_s is the sender, P_r is the recipient, m is the message sent through the onion routers, $n < N$ is the length of the onion path, $P = (P_{o_1}, \ldots, P_{o_n})$ is the path over which the message is sent (by convention, $P_{o_0} = P_s$, and $P_{o_{n+1}} = P_r$), and i indicates how much of the path the message has already traversed (initially, $i = 0$). An onion has reached its destination when $i = n + 1$.

- A list L of onions that are being processed by the adversarial routers. Each entry of the list consists of $(temp, O, j)$, where $temp$ is the temporary identifier that the adversary needs to know to process the onion, while $O = (sid, P_s, P_r, m, n, P, i)$ is the onion itself, and j is the entry in P where the onion should be sent next (the adversary does not get to see O and j). This models the replay attack: the ideal adversary is allowed to resend an onion.

- For each honest party P_i, a buffer B_i of onions that are currently being held by P_i. Each entry consists of $(temp', O)$, where $temp'$ is the temporary identifier that an honest party needs to know to process the onion and $O = (sid, P_s, P_r, m, n, P, i)$ is the onion itself (the honest party does not get to see O). Entries from this buffer are removed if an honest party tells the functionality that he or she wants to send an onion to the next party.

The ideal process is activated by a message from router P, from the adversary S, or from itself. There are four types of messages, as follows:

- $(Process\_New\_Onion, P_r, m, n, P)$. Upon receiving such a message from P_s, where $m \in 0, 1^{l_m} \bigcup \{\bot\}$,

    1. If $|P| \geq N$, reject.

    2. Otherwise, create a new session sid identifier and let $O = (sid, \mathbf{P}, P_r, m, n, P, 0)$. Send itself message $(Process\_Next\_Step, O)$.

- $(Process\_Next\_Step, O)$. This is the core of the ideal protocol. Suppose $O = (sid, P_s, P_r, m, n, P, i)$. The ideal functionality looks at the next part of the path. The router P_{o_i} just processed the onion and now it is being passed to $P_{o_{i+1}}$. Corresponding to which routers are honest, and which ones are adversarial, there are two possibilities for the next part of the path:

- Suppose that the next node, $P_{o_{i+1}}$, is honest. Here, the ideal functionality makes up a random temporary identifier *temp* for this onion and sends to S (recall that S controls the network so it decides which messages get delivered): "Onion temp from P_{o_i} to $P_{o_{i+1}}$." It adds the entry $(temp, O, i+1)$ to list.

- Suppose that $P_{o_{i+1}}$ is adversarial. Then there are two cases:

  * There is an honest router remaining on the path to the recipient. Let P_{o_j} be the next honest router. (I.e., $j > i$ is the smallest integer such that P_{o_j} is honest.) In this case, the ideal functionality creates a random temporary identifier *temp* for this onion, and sends the message "Onion temp from P_{o_i}, routed through $(P_{o_{i+1}}, \ldots, P_{o_{j-1}})$ to P_{o_j}" to the ideal adversary S, and stores $(temp, O, j)$ on the list L.

  * P_{o_i} is the last honest router on the path; in particular, this means that Pr is adversarial as well. In that case, the ideal functionality sends the message "Onion from P_{o_i} with message m for P_r routed through $(P_{o_{i+1}}, \ldots, P_{o_n})$" to the adversary S. (Note that if $P_{o_{i+1}} = P_r$, the list $(P_{o_{i+1}}, \ldots, P_{o_n})$ will be empty.

- (*Deliver_Message, temp*) is a message that S sends to the ideal process to notify it that it agrees that the onion with temporary id *temp* should be delivered to its current destination. To process this message, the functionality checks if the temporary identifier *temp* corresponds to any onion O on the list L. If it does, it retrieves the corresponding record $(temp, O, j)$ and update the onion: if $O = (sid, P_s, P_r, m, n, P, i)$, it replaces i with j to indicate that we have reached the j'th router on the path of this onion. If $j < n + 1$, it generates a temporary identifier *temp'*, sends "Onion temp' received" to party P_{o_j} , and stores the resulting pair $(temp', O = (sid, P_s, P_r, m, n, P, j))$ in the buffer B_{o_j} of party P_{o_j}. Otherwise, $j = n+1$, so the onion has reached its destination: if $m \neq \bot$ it sends "Message m received" to router P_r; otherwise it does not deliver anything.

- (*Forward_Onion, temp'*). This is a message from an honest ideal router P_i notifying the ideal process that it is ready to send the onion with id *temp'* to the next hop. In response, the ideal functionality

  1. Checks if the temporary identifier *temp'* corresponds to any entry in B_i. If it does, it retrieves the corresponding record $(temp', O)$.

2. Sends itself the message $(Process\_Next\_Step, O)$.

3. Removes $(temp', O)$ from B_i.

When an honest router receives a message of the form "Onion $temp'$ received" from the ideal functionality, it notifies environment Z about it and awaits instructions for when to forward the onion $temp'$ to its next destination. When instructed by Z, it sends the message "Forward_Onion $temp'$" to the ideal functionality. It is not hard to see that Z learns nothing other than pieces of paths of onions formed by the honest sender (i.e., does not learn a sub-path's position or relations among different sub-paths). Moreover, if the sender and the receiver are both honest, the adversary does not learn the message.

It may seem that, as defined in the ideal functionality, the adversary is too powerful because, for example, it is allowed to route just one onion at a time, and so can trace its entire route. In an onion routing implementation, however, the instructions for which onion to send on will not come directly from the adversary, but rather from an honest player's mixing strategy. That is, each (honest) router is notified that an onion has arrived and is given a handle $temp$ to that onion. Whenever the router decides (under mixing strategy) that the onion $temp$ should be sent on, she can notify the ideal functionality of using the handle $temp$. A good mixing strategy will limit the power of the adversary to trace onions in the ideal world, which will translate into limited capability in the real world as well. What mixing strategy is a good one depends on the network. Additionally, there is a trade-off between providing more anonymity and minimizing latency of the network.

The definition as is allows replay attacks by the adversary. The adversary controls the network and can replay any message it wishes. In particular, it can take an onion that party P_i wants to send to P_j and deliver it to P_j as many times as it wishes. However, it is straightforward to modify the security definition and the scheme so as to prevent replay attacks. For instance, it can be required that the sender inserts time stamps into all onions. A router P_i, in addition to the identity of the next router P_{i+1}, will also be given a time time and a random identifier oid_i (different for each onion and router). An onion router will drop the incoming onion when either the time $+ t_\Delta$ (where t_Δ is a parameter) has passed or it finds oid_i in its database. If an onion is not dropped, the router will store oid_i until time time $+ t_\Delta$ has passed. It is not difficult to adapt our scheme and model to reflect this. We omit details to keep this exposition focused.

Forward secrecy is a desirable property in general, and in this context in particular. The scheme can be constructed from any CCA2-secure cryptosystem, and in particular, from a forward secure one. Another desirable property of an onion routing scheme is being able to respond to a message received anonymously. We address this after presenting our construction.

A cryptographic definition of an onion routing scheme is given in [20] as follows to show why a scheme satisfying this definition is sufficient to realize the onion routing functionality described above.

Definition 13 *(Onion routing scheme I/O). A set of algorithms (G,FormOnion, ProcOnion) satisfies the I/O spec for an onion routing scheme for message space $M(1^\lambda)$ and set of router names Q if:*

- *G is a key generation algorithm, possibly taking as input some public parameters p, and a router name $P : (PK, SK) \leftarrow G(1^\lambda, p, P)$.*

- ***FormOnion*** *is a probabilistic algorithm that on input a message $m \in M(1^\lambda)$, an upper bound on the number of layers N, a set of router names $(P_1, \ldots, P_{n+1})$ (each $P_i \in Q, n \leq N$), and a set of public keys corresponding to these routers $(PK_1, \ldots, PK_{n+1})$, outputs a set of onion layers $(O_1, \ldots, O_{n+1})$. (As N is typically a system-wide parameter, it is usually omitted to give it as input to this algorithm.)*

- ***ProcOnion*** *is a deterministic algorithm that on input an onion O, identity P, and a secret key SK peel off a layer of the onion to obtain a new onion O' and a destination P' for sending it: $(O', P') \leftarrow ProcOnion(SK, O, P)$.*

Definition 14 *(Onion evolution, path, and layering). Let (G, FormOnion, ProcOnion) satisfy the onion routing I/O spec. Let p be the public parameters. Suppose that we have a set $Q, \perp \notin Q$, consisting of a polynomial number of (honest) router names. Suppose that we have a public-key infrastructure on Q, i.e., corresponding to each name $P \in Q$ there exists a key pair $(PK(P), SK(P))$, generated by running $G(1^\lambda, p, P)$. Let O be an onion received by router $P \in Q$. Let $E(O, P) = \{(O_i, P_i) : i \geq 1\}$ be the maximal ordered list of pairs such that $P_1 = P$, $O_1 = O$, and for all $i > 1$, $P_i \in Q$, and $(O_i, P_i) = ProcOnion(SK(P_{i-1}), O_{i-1}, P_{i-1})$. Then $E(O, P)$ is the evolution of onion O starting at P. Moreover, if $E(O, P) = (O_i, P_i)$ is the evolution of an onion, then $\boldsymbol{P}(O, P) = \{Pi\}$ is the path of the onion, while $L(O, P) = \{O_i\}$ is the layering of the onion.*

Onion correctness is the simple condition that if an onion is formed correctly and the correct routers process it in the correct order, the correct message is received by the last router P_{n+1}.

Definition 15 *(Onion correctness). Let (G, FormOnion, ProcOnion) satisfy the I/O spec for an onion routing scheme. Then for all settings of the public parameters p, for all $n < N$, and for all Q with a public key infrastructure as in Definition 14, for any path $\boldsymbol{P} = (P_1, \ldots, P_{n+1}), P \in Q$, for all messages $m \in M(1^\lambda)$, and for all onions O1 formed as*

$$(O_1, \ldots, O_{n+1}) \leftarrow FormOnion(m, N, (P_1, \ldots, P_{n+1}), (PK(P_1), \ldots, PK(P_{n+1})))$$

the following is true: (1) correct path: $P(O_1, P_1) = (P_1, \ldots, P_{n+1})$; (2) correct layering: $L(O_1, P_1) = (O_1, \ldots, O_{n+1})$; (3) correct decryption: $(m, \diamond) = ProcOnion(SK(P_{n+1}), O_{n+1}, P_{n+1})$.

Onion integrity requires that even for an onion created by an adversary, the path is going to be of length N at most.

Definition 16 *(Onion integrity). An onion routing scheme satisfies onion integrity if for all probabilistic polynomial time adversaries, the probability (taken over the choice of the public parameters p, the set of honest router names Q and the corresponding PKI as in Definition 14) that an adversary with adaptive access to $ProcOnion(SK(P), ., P)$ procedures for all $P \in Q$, can produce and send to a router $P_1 \in Q$ an onion O_1 such that $|P(O_1, P_1)| > N$, is negligible.*

This definition of onion security is somewhat less intuitive. Here, an adversary is launching an adaptive attack against an onion router P. It gets to send onions to this router, and see how the router reacts, i.e., obtain the output of $ProcOnion(SK(P), ., P)$. The adversarys goal is to distinguish whether a given challenge onion corresponds to a particular message and route, or a random message and null route. The unintuitive part is that the adversary can also succeed by re-wrapping an onion, i.e., by adding a layer to its challenge onion.

Definition 17 *(Onion security). Consider an adversary interacting with an onion routing challenger as follows:*

1. *The adversary receives as input a challenge public key PK, chosen by the challenger by letting $(PK, SK) \leftarrow G(1^\lambda, p)$, and the router name P.*

2. *The adversary may submit any number of onions O_i of his choice to the challenger, and obtain the output of $ProcOnion(SK, O_i, P)$.*

3. *The adversary submits n, a message m, a set of names $(P_1, \ldots, P_{n+1})$, and index j, and n key pairs $1 \leq i \leq n+1, i \neq j, (PK_i, SK_i)$. The challenger checks that the router names are valid, that the public keys correspond to the secret keys, and if so, sets $PK_j = PK$, sets bit b at random, and does the following:*

   - *If $b = 0$, let*

   $$(O_1, \ldots, O_j, \ldots, O_{n+1}) \leftarrow FormOnion(m, (P_1, \ldots, P_{n+1}),$$
   $$(PK_1, \ldots, PK_{n+1}))$$

   - *Otherwise, choose $r \leftarrow M(1^\lambda)$, and let*

   $$(O1, \ldots, Oj) \leftarrow FormOnion(r, (P_1, \ldots, P_j), (PK_1, \ldots, PK_j))$$

4. *Now the adversary is allowed to receive responses for two types of queries:*

   - *Submit any onion $O_i \neq O_j$ of his choice and obtain $ProcOnion(SK, O_i, P)$.*

- *Submit a secret key SK', an identity $P' \neq P_{j-1}$, and an onion O' such that $O_j = ProcOnion(SK', O', P')$; if P' is valid, and (SK', O', P') satisfy this condition, then the challenger responds by revealing the bit b.*

5. *The adversary then produces a guess b'.*

A scheme with onion routing I/O satisfies onion security if for all probabilistic polynomial time adversaries A of the form described above, there is a negligible function ν such that the adversary's probability of outputting $b' = b$ is at most $1/2 + \nu(\lambda)$.

This definition of security is simple enough. Yet, it turns out to be sufficient. A simulator that translates between a real-life adversary and an ideal functionality is responsible for two tasks: (1) creating some fake traffic in the real world that accounts for everything that happens in the ideal world; and (2) translating the adversary's actions in the real world into instructions for the ideal functionality.

In particular, in its capacity (1), the simulator will sometimes receive a message from the ideal functionality telling it that an onion *temp* for honest router P_j is routed through adversarial routers $(P_1, \ldots, P_{j-1})$. The simulator is going to need to make up an onion O_1 to send to the adversarial party P_1. But the simulator is not going to know the message contained in the onion, or the rest of the route. So the simulator will instead make up a random message r and compute the onion so that it decrypts to r when it reaches the honest (real) router P_j. It will form O_1 by obtaining $(O_1, \ldots, O_j) \leftarrow FormOnion(r, (P_1, \ldots, P_j), (PK_1, \ldots, PK_j))$. When the onion O_j arrives at P_j from the adversary, the simulator knows that it is time to tell the ideal functionality to deliver message *temp* to honest ideal P_j.

Now, there is a danger that this may cause errors in the simulation as far as capacity (2) is concerned: the adversary may manage to form another onion $\tilde{O}$, and send it to an honest router $\tilde{P}$ such that $(O_j, P) \in E(\tilde{O}, \tilde{P})$. The simulator will be unable to handle this situation correctly, as the simulator relies on its ability to correctly decrypt and route all real-world onions, while in this case, the simulator does not know how to decrypt and route this "fake" onion past honest router P_j. A scheme satisfying the definition above would prevent this from happening: the adversary will not be able to form an onion $O'6 \neq O_{j-1}$ sent to an honest player P' such that $(P_j, O_j) = ProcOnion(SK(P0), O', P')$.

4.3   Second Generation: Tor

The most famous practical application of onion routing is Tor [34], which is also called the second generation onion routing. Tor is actually a protocol for asynchronous, loosely federated onion routers that provides the following improvements over the old onion routing design.

- Perfect forward secrecy
  In the original onion routing design, a single hostile node could record traffic and later compromise successive nodes in the circuit and force them to decrypt it. Rather than using a single multiply encrypted data structure (an onion) to lay each circuit, Tor now uses an incremental or telescoping path-building design, where the initiator negotiates session keys with each successive hop in the circuit. Once these keys are deleted, subsequently compromised nodes cannot decrypt old traffic. As a side benefit, onion replay detection is no longer necessary, and the process of building circuits is more reliable, since the initiator knows when a hop fails and can then try extending to a new node.

- Separation of "protocol cleaning" from anonymity
  Onion routing originally required a separate "application proxy" for each supported application protocol, most of which were never written, so many applications were never supported. Tor uses the standard and near-ubiquitous SOCKS proxy interface, allowing us to support most TCP-based programs without modification. Tor now relies on the filtering features of privacy-enhancing application-level proxies such as Privoxy, without trying to duplicate those features itself.

- No mixing, padding, or traffic shaping (yet)
  Onion routing originally called for batching and reordering cells as they arrived, assumed padding between ORs, and in later designs added padding between onion proxies (users) and ORs. Tradeoffs between padding protection and cost were discussed, and traffic shaping algorithms were theorized to provide good security without expensive padding, but no concrete padding scheme was suggested. Recent research and deployment experience suggest that this level of resource use is not practical or economical; and even full link padding is still vulnerable. Thus, until a proven and convenient design for traffic shaping or low-latency mixing that improves anonymity against a realistic adversary is obtained, these strategies can only be left out.

- Many TCP streams can share one circuit
  Onion routing originally built a separate circuit for each application level request, but this required multiple public key operations for every request, and also presented a threat to anonymity from building so many circuits. Tor multiplexes multiple TCP streams along each circuit to improve efficiency and anonymity.

- Leaky-pipe circuit topology
  Through in-band signaling within the circuit, Tor initiators can direct traffic to nodes partway down the circuit. This novel approach allows traffic to exit the circuit from the middle—possibly frustrating traffic shape and volume attacks based on observing the end of the circuit. (It

also allows for long-range padding if future research shows this to be worthwhile.)

- Congestion control
  Earlier anonymity designs do not address traffic bottlenecks. Unfortunately, typical approaches to load balancing and flow control in overlay networks involve inter-node control communication and global views of traffic. Tor's decentralized congestion control uses end-to-end routing to maintain anonymity while allowing nodes at the edges of the network to detect congestion or flooding and send less data until the congestion subsides.

- Directory servers
  The earlier onion routing design planned to flood state information through the network approach that can be unreliable and complex. Tor takes a simplified view toward distributing this information. Certain more trusted nodes act as directory servers: they provide signed directories describing known routers and their current state. Users periodically download them via HTTP.

- Variable exit policies
  Tor provides a consistent mechanism for each node to advertise a policy describing the hosts and ports to which it will connect. These exit policies are critical in a volunteer-based distributed infrastructure, because each operator is comfortable with allowing different types of traffic to exit from his node.

- End-to-end integrity checking
  The original onion routing design did no integrity checking on data. Any node on the circuit could change the contents of data cells as they passed by—for example, to alter a connection request so it would connect to a different webserver, or to tag encrypted traff and look for corresponding corrupted traffic at the network edges. Tor hampers these attacks by verifying data integrity before it leaves the network.

- Rendezvous points and hidden services
  Tor provides an integrated mechanism for responder anonymity via location-protected servers. Previous onion routing designs included long-lived "reply onions" that could be used to build circuit to a hidden server, but these reply onions did not provide forward security, and became useless if any node in the path went down or rotated its keys. In Tor, clients negotiate rendezvous points to connect with hidden servers; reply onions are no longer required.

As emphasized in [34], the following considerations have directed the evolution from the initial onion routing to Tor.

- Deployability

  The design is deployed and used in the real world. Thus it must not be expensive to run (for example, by requiring more bandwidth than volunteers are willing to provide); must not place a heavy liability burden on operators (for example, by allowing attackers to implicate onion routers in illegal activities); and must not be difficult or expensive to implement (for example, by requiring kernel patches or separate proxies for every protocol). It is not supposed to be run by non-anonymous parties (such as websites).

- Usability

  A hard-to-use system has fewer users—and because anonymity systems hide users among users, a system with fewer users provides less anonymity. Usability is thus not only a convenience: it is a security requirement. Tor should therefore not require modifying familiar applications; should not introduce prohibitive delays; and should require as few configuration decisions as possible. Finally, Tor should be easily implementable on all common platforms; users are not require to change their operating systems to be anonymous. (Tor currently runs on Win32, Linux, Solaris, BSD-style Unix, MacOS X, and probably others.)

- Flexibility

  The protocol must be flexible and well specified, so Tor can serve as a test bed for future research. Many of the open problems in low-latency anonymity networks, such as generating dummy traffic or preventing Sybil attacks, may be solvable independently from the issues solved by Tor. Hopefully future systems will not need to reinvent Tor's design.

- Simple design

  The protocol's design and security parameter must be well understood. Additional features impose implementation and complexity costs; adding unproven techniques to the design threatens deployability, readability, and ease of security analysis. Tor aims to deploy a simple and stable system that integrates the best accepted approaches to protecting anonymity.

4.3.1   Design of Tor

The Tor is an overlay network; each onion router (OR) runs as a normal user-level process without any special privileges. Each onion router maintains a TLS connection to every other onion router. Each user runs local software called an onion proxy (OP) to fetch directories, establish circuits across the network, and handle connections from user applications. These onion proxies accept TCP streams and multiplex them across the circuits. The onion router on the other side of the circuit connects to the requested destinations and relays data.

Each onion router maintains a long-term identity key and a short-term onion key. The identity key is used to sign TLS certificates, to sign the OR's router descriptor (a summary of its keys, address, bandwidth, exit policy, and so on), and (by directory servers) to sign directories. The onion key is used to decrypt requests from users to set up a circuit and negotiate ephemeral keys. The TLS protocol also establishes a short term link key when communicating between ORs. Short-term keys are rotated periodically and independently, to limit the impact of key compromise.

Onion routers communicate with one another, and with users' OPs, via TLS connections with ephemeral keys. Using TLS conceals the data on the connection with perfect forward secrecy, and prevents an attacker from modifying data on the wire or impersonating an OR.

Traffic passes along these connections in fixed-size cells. Each cell is 512 bytes, and consists of a header and a payload. The header includes a circuit identifier (circID) that specifies which circuit the cell refers to (many circuits can be multiplexed over the single TLS connection), and a command to describe what to do with the cell's payload. (Circuit identifiers are connection-specific: each circuit has a different circID on each OP/OR or OR/OR connection it traverses.) Based on their command, cells are either control cells, which are always interpreted by the node that receives them, or relay cells, which carry end-to-end stream data. The control cell commands are: padding (currently used for keepalive, but also usable for link padding); create or created (used to set up a new circuit); and destroy (to tear down a circuit).

Relay cells have an additional header (the relay header) at the front of the payload, containing a streamID (stream identifier: many streams can be multiplexed over a circuit); an end-to-end checksum for integrity checking; the length of the relay payload; and a relay command. The entire contents of the relay header and the relay cell payload are encrypted or decrypted together as the relay cell moves along the circuit, using the 128-bit AES cipher in counter mode to generate a cipher stream. The relay commands are: relay data (for data flowing down the stream), relay begin (to open a stream), relay end (to close a stream cleanly), relay teardown (to close a broken stream), relay connected (to notify the OP that a relay begin has succeeded), relay extend and relay extended (to extend the circuit by a hop, and to acknowledge), relay truncate and relay truncated (to tear down only part of the circuit, and to acknowledge), relay sendme (used for congestion control), and relay drop (used to implement long-range dummies).

Onion routing originally built one circuit for each TCP stream. Because building a circuit can take several tenths of a second (due to public key cryptography and network latency), this design imposes high costs on applications like web browsing that open many TCP streams.

In Tor, each circuit can be shared by many TCP streams. To avoid delays, users construct circuits preemptively. To limit linkability among their streams, users' OPs build a new circuit periodically if the previous ones have been used, and expire old used circuits that no longer have any open streams.

OPs consider rotating to a new circuit once a minute: thus even heavy users spend negligible time building circuits, but a limited number of requests can be linked to each other through a given exit node. Also, because circuits are built in the background, OPs can recover from failed circuit creation without harming user experience.

A user's OP constructs circuits incrementally, negotiating a symmetric key with each OR on the circuit, one hop at a time. To begin creating a new circuit, the OP (call her Alice) sends a create cell to the first node in her chosen path (call him Bob). (She chooses a new circID CAB not currently used on the connection from her to Bob.) The create cell's payload contains the first half of the Diffie-Hellman handshake (g^x), encrypted to the onion key of the OR. Bob responds with a created cell containing g^y along with a hash of the negotiated key $K = g^{xy}$.

To extend the circuit further, Alice sends a relay extend cell to Bob, specifying the address of the next OR (call her Carol), and an encrypted g^{x_2} for her. Bob copies the half-handshake into a create cell, and passes it to Carol to extend the circuit. (Bob chooses a new circID CBC not currently used on the connection between him and Carol. Alice never needs to know this circID; only Bob associates CAB on his connection with Alice to CBC on his connection with Carol.) When Carol responds with a created cell, Bob wraps the payload into a relay extended cell and passes it back to Alice. Now the circuit is extended to Carol, and Alice and Carol share a common key $K_2 = g^{x_2 y_2}$.

To extend the circuit to a third node or beyond, Alice proceeds as above, always telling the last node in the circuit to extend one hop further.

This circuit-level handshake protocol achieves unilateral entity authentication (Alice knows she's handshaking with the OR, but the OR doesn't care who is opening the circuit—Alice uses no public key and remains anonymous) and unilateral key authentication (Alice and the OR agree on a key, and Alice knows only the OR learns it). It also achieves forward secrecy and key freshness. More formally, the protocol is as follows (where $E_{PK_{Bob}}(.)$ is encryption with Bob's public key, H is a secure hash function, and $|$ is concatenation):

$$Alice \rightarrow Bob : E_{PKBob}(g^x)$$
$$Bob \rightarrow Alice : g^y, H(K|\text{``handshake''})$$

In the second step, Bob proves that it was he who received g^x, and who chose y. We use PK encryption in the first step (rather than, say, using the first two steps of STS, which has a signature in the second step) because a single cell is too small to hold both a public key and a signature. Preliminary analysis with the NRL protocol analyzer shows this protocol to be secure (including perfect forward secrecy) under the traditional Dolev-Yao model.

Once Alice has established the circuit (so she shares keys with each OR on the circuit), she can send relay cells. Upon receiving a relay cell, an OR looks up the corresponding circuit, and decrypts the relay header and payload with the session key for that circuit. If the cell is headed away from Alice, the OR then checks whether the decrypted cell has a valid digest (as an optimization, the first two bytes of the integrity check are zero, so in most cases we can avoid computing the hash). If valid, it accepts the relay cell and processes it as described below. Otherwise, the OR looks up the circID and OR for the next step in the circuit, replaces the circID as appropriate, and sends the decrypted relay cell to the next OR. (If the OR at the end of the circuit receives an unrecognized relay cell, an error has occurred, and the circuit is torn down.)

OPs treat incoming relay cells similarly: they iteratively unwrap the relay header and payload with the session keys shared with each OR on the circuit, from the closest to farthest. If at any stage the digest is valid, the cell must have originated at the OR whose encryption has just been removed.

To construct a relay cell addressed to a given OR, Alice assigns the digest, and then iteratively encrypts the cell payload (that is, the relay header and payload) with the symmetric key of each hop up to that OR. Because the digest is encrypted to a different value at each step, only at the targeted OR will it have a meaningful value. This leaky pipe circuit topology allows Alice's streams to exit at different ORs on a single circuit. Alice may choose different exit points because of their exit policies or to keep the ORs from knowing that two streams originate from the same person.

When an OR later replies to Alice with a relay cell, it encrypts the cell's relay header and payload with the single key it shares with Alice, and sends the cell back toward Alice along the circuit. Subsequent ORs add further layers of encryption as they relay the cell back to Alice.

To tear down a circuit, Alice sends a destroy control cell. Each OR in the circuit receives the destroy cell, closes all streams on that circuit, and passes a new destroy cell forward. But just as circuits are built incrementally, they can also be torn down incrementally. Alice can send a relay truncate cell to a single OR on a circuit. That OR then sends a destroy cell forward, and acknowledges with a relay truncated cell. Alice can then extend the circuit to different nodes, without signaling to the intermediate nodes (or a limited observer) that she has changed her circuit. Similarly, if a node on the circuit goes down, the adjacent node can send a relay truncated cell back to Alice. Thus the "break a node and see which circuit go down" attack is weakened.

When Alice's application wants a TCP connection to a given address and port, it asks the OP (via SOCKS) to make the connection. The OP chooses the newest open circuit (or creates one if needed), and chooses a suitable OR on that circuit to be the exit node (usually the last node, but may be others due to exit policy conflicts) The OP then opens the stream by sending a relay begin cell to the exit node, using a new random streamID. Once the exit node connects to the remote host, it responds with a relay connected cell. Upon receipt, the OP sends a SOCKS reply to notify the application of its success. The OP now accepts data from the application's TCP stream, packaging it into relay data cells and sending those cells along the circuit to the chosen OR.

There is a catch to using SOCKS, however—some applications pass the alphanumeric host name to the Tor client, while others resolve it into an IP address first and then pass the IP address to the Tor client. If the application does DNS resolution first, Alice thereby reveals her destination to the remote DNS server, rather than sending the host name through the Tor network to be resolved at the far end. Common applications like Mozilla and SSH have this flaw.

With Mozilla, the flaw is easy to address: the filtering HTTP proxy called Privoxy gives a host name to the Tor client, so Alice's computer never does DNS resolution. But a portable general solution, such as is needed for SSH, is an open problem. Modifying or replacing the local name server can be invasive, brittle, and unportable. Forcing the resolver library to prefer TCP rather than UDP is hard, and also has portability problems. Dynamically intercepting system calls to the resolver library seems a promising direction. Altough a tool similar to dig can be provided to perform a private lookup through the Tor network, it is recommended in [34] to use privacy-aware proxies like Privoxy wherever possible.

Closing a Tor stream is analogous to closing a TCP stream: it uses a two-step handshake for normal operation, or a one-step handshake for errors. If the stream closes abnormally, the adjacent node simply sends a relay teardown cell. If the stream closes normally, the node sends a relay end cell down the circuit, and the other side responds with its own relay end cell. Because all relay cells use layered encryption, only the destination OR knows that a given relay cell is a request to close a stream. This two-step handshake allows Tor to support TCP-based applications that use half-closed connections.

Because the old onion routing design used a stream cipher without integrity checking, traffic was vulnerable to a malleability attack: though the attacker could not decrypt cells, any changes to encrypted data would create corresponding changes to the data leaving the network. This weakness allowed an adversary who could guess the encrypted content to change a padding cell to a destroy cell; change the destination address in a relay begin cell to the adversary's webserver; or change an FTP command from dir to rm *. (Even an external adversary could do this, because the link encryption similarly used a stream cipher.)

Because Tor uses TLS on its links, external adversaries cannot modify data. Addressing the insider malleability attack, however, is more complex. Integrity is only checked at the edges of each stream. (Remember that in our leaky-pipe circuit topology, a stream's edge could be any hop in the circuit.) When Alice negotiates a key with a new hop, they each initialize a SHA-1 digest with a derivative of that key, thus beginning with randomness that only the two of them know. Then they each incrementally add to the SHA-1 digest the contents of all relay cells they create, and include with each relay cell the first four bytes of the current digest. Each also keeps a SHA-1 digest of data received, to verify that the received hashes are correct.

Volunteers are more willing to run services that can limit their bandwidth usage. To accommodate them, Tor servers use a token bucket approach to enforce a long-term average rate of incoming bytes, while still permitting short-term bursts above the allowed bandwidth.

Because the Tor protocol outputs about the same number of bytes as it takes in, it is sufficient in practice to limit only incoming bytes. With TCP streams, however, the correspondence is not one-to-one: relaying a single incoming byte can require an entire 512-byte cell. (We cannot just wait for more bytes, because the local application may be awaiting a reply.) Therefore, we treat this case as if the entire cell size had been read, regardless of the cell's fullness

Further, a circuit's edges can heuristically distinguish interactive streams from bulk streams by comparing the frequency with which they supply cells. Tor can provide good latency for interactive streams by giving them preferential service, while still giving good overall throughput to the bulk streams. Such preferential treatment presents a possible end-to-end attack, but an adversary observing both ends of the stream can already learn this information through timing attacks.

Even with bandwidth rate limiting, there is still a worry about congestion, either accidental or intentional. If enough users choose the same OR-to-OR connection for their circuits, that connection can become saturated. For example, an attacker could send a large file through the Tor network to a webserver he runs, and then refuse to read any of the bytes at the webserver end of the circuit. Without some congestion control mechanism, these bottlenecks can propagate back through the entire network. We do not need to reimplement-full TCP windows (with sequence numbers, the ability to drop cells when we are full and retransmit later, and so on), because TCP already guarantees in-order delivery of each cell.

To control a circuit's bandwidth usage, each OR keeps track of two windows. The packaging window tracks how many relay data cells the OR is allowed to package (from incoming TCP streams) for transmission back to the OP, and the delivery window tracks how many relay data cells it is willing to deliver to TCP streams outside the network. Each window is initialized (say, to 1000 data cells). When a data cell is packaged or delivered, the appropriate window is decremented. When an OR has received enough data cells (currently 100), it sends a relay sendme cell toward the OP, with streamID zero. When an OR receives a relay sendme cell with streamID zero, it increments its packaging window. Either of these cells increments the corresponding window by 100. If the packaging window reaches 0, the OR stops reading from TCP connections for all streams on the corresponding circuit, and sends no more relay data cells until receiving a relay sendme cell.

The OP behaves identically, except that it must track a packaging window and a delivery window for every OR in the circuit. If a packaging window reaches 0, it stops reading from streams destined for that OR. The stream-level congestion control mechanism is similar to the circuit-level mechanism.

ORs and OPs use relay sendme cells to implement end-to-end flow control for individual streams across circuits. Each stream begins with a packaging window (currently 500 cells), and increments the window by a fixed value (50) upon receiving a relay sendme cell. Rather than always returning a relay sendme cell as soon as enough cells have arrived, the stream-level congestion control also has to check whether data has been successfully flushed onto the TCP stream; it sends the relay sendme cell only when the number of bytes pending to be flushed is under some threshold (currently 10 cells' worth).

4.3.2 Application of Symmetric Cipher and Diffie-Hellman Key Exchange in Tor: Efficiency Improvement

The suggestion to employ symmetric cipher and Diffie-Hellman key exchange in Tor [34] is quite simple. To precisely assess its cost, we need to specify it in detail. For simplicity of description, our specification focuses on efficiency improvement through symmetric cipher and Diffie-Hellman key exchange, while the other optimisations of onion routing in Tor are ignored and the following symbols are used .

- p and q are large primes and q is a factor of $p-1$. G is the cyclic subgroup with order q in Z_p^* and g is a generator of G.

- Encryption of m using key k is denoted as $E_k(m)$ where block cipher (e.g., AES) is employed.

- Encryption chain of m using block cipher and key $k_1, k_2, \ldots, k_i$ is denoted as $E_{k_1,k_2,\ldots,k_i}(m)$. The encryptions are performed layer by layer. k_1 is the the key used in the most outer layer; k_2 is the the key used in the second most outer layer; $\ldots$; k_i is the the key used in the most inner layer.

- In onion routing, the routers are $P_1, P_2, \ldots, P_n$ and the receiver is denoted as the last router P_{n+1}.

- The private key of P_i is x_i, which is randomly chosen from Z_q. The corresponding public keys are $y_1, y_2, \ldots, y_n$ where $y_i = g^{x_i} \bmod p$ for $i = 1, 2, \ldots, n$.

Symmetric ciphers like block ciphers are very efficient. However, unlike asymmetric ciphers, they depend on key exchange protocols to distribute keys. The most common is Diffie-Hellman key exchange protocol. Two parties A and B can cooperate to generate a session key as follows.

1. A randomly chooses α from Z_q and sends his key base $\mu = g^\alpha \bmod p$ to B.

2. B randomly chooses β from Z_q and sends his key base $\nu = g^\beta \bmod p$ to A.

3. A can calculate the key $k = \nu^\alpha \bmod p$, while B can calculate the key $k = \mu^\beta \bmod p$.

The famous Diffie-Hellman problem is as follows.

Definition 18 *(Diffie-Hellman problem) Given μ and ν, it is difficult to calculate k if the discrete logarithm problem is hard.*

The suggested efficiency improvement in Tor is specified in details as follows where a message m is sent by a sender through n routers $P_1, P_2, \ldots, P_n$ to a receiver P_{n+1}.

1. For the receiver and each router P_i where $1 \le i \le n + 1$, the sender randomly chooses an integer s_i from Z_q and calculates $\hat{k}_i = g^{s_i} \bmod p$.

2. The sender sends $\hat{k}_1$ to P_1, which returns $\hat{k}'_1 = g^{s'_1} \bmod p$ where s'_1 is randomly chosen from Z_q. Both the sender and P_1 obtains their session key $k_1 = g^{s_1 s'_1} \bmod p$.

3. The sender sends $E_{k_1}(P_2)$ and $E_{k_1}(\hat{k}_2)$ to P_1, who decrypts the two ciphertexts using his session key and then sends $\hat{k}_2$ and $\hat{k}'_1$ to P_2.

4. P_2 randomly chooses s'_2 from Z_q and obtains his session key with the sender $k_2 = \hat{k}_2^{s'_2} = g^{s_2 s'_2}$ and his session key with P_1, $K_{1,2} = K_{1,2}\hat{k}'^{s'_2}_1$. He sends $g^{s'_2}$ to P_1 and the sender such that session keys are established between P_2 and the previous nodes. The following routers perform the same operations and finally every P_i obtains his session key $k_i = g^{s_1 s'_i}$ where s'_i is randomly chosen by P_i.

5. The sender encrypts the message m, the key base list $g^{s_1}, g^{s_2}, \ldots, g^{s_{n+1}}$ and the route list $p_1, p_2, \ldots, p_{n+1}$ as follows.

   (a) He calculates $e = E_{k_1, k_2, \ldots, k_{n+1}}(m)$.

   (b) He calculates $K_i = E_{k_1, k_2, \ldots, k_{i-1}}(g^{s_i})$ for $i = 1, 2, \ldots, n + 1$.

   (c) He calculates $p_i = E_{k_1, k_2, \ldots, k_i}(P_{i+1})$ for $i = 1, 2, \ldots, n + 1$ where $P_{n+2} = P_{n+1}$.

   (d) He sends out the initial onion

$$O_1 = (a_1, b_{1,1}, b_{1,2}, \ldots, b_{1,n+1},$$
$$c_{1,1}, c_{1,2}, \ldots, c_{1,n+1})$$
$$= (e, K_1, K_2, \ldots, K_{n+1}, p_1, p_2, \ldots, p_{n+1})$$

   to P_1.

6. Each router P_i routes the onion as follows where the onion is in the form $O_i = (a_i, b_{i,1}, b_{i,2}, \ldots, b_{i,n+1}, c_{i,1}, c_{i,2}, \ldots, c_{i,n+1})$ when it is sent to P_i.

   (a) P_i generates his session key $k_i = b_{i,1}^{x_i} \bmod p$.

   (b) P_i uses k_i to decrypt $c_{i,j}$ for $j = 1, 2, \ldots, n+1$ and obtains $P_{i+1} = D_{k_i}(c_{i,1})$.

   (c) P_i uses k_i to decrypt a_i and obtains $a_{i+1} = D_{k_i}(a_i)$.

   (d) Finally, P_i sends

$$O_{i+1} = (a_{i+1}, b_{i+1,1}, b_{i+1,2}, \ldots,$$
$$b_{i+1,n+1}, c_{i+1,1}, c_{i+1,2}, \ldots, c_{i+1,n+1})$$

   to P_{i+1} where $b_{i+1,j} = D_{k_i}(b_{i,j+1})$ and $c_{i+1,j} = D_{k_i}(c_{i,j+1})$ for $j = 1, 2, \ldots, n$ and $b_{i+1,n+1}$ and $c_{i+1,n+1}$ are two random integers in the ciphertext space of the employed symmetric encryption algorithm.

7. At last, P_{n+1} receives

$$O_{n+1} = (a_{n+1}, b_{n+1,1}, b_{n+1,2}, \ldots,$$
$$b_{n+1,n+1}, c_{n+1,1}, c_{n+1,2}, \ldots, c_{n+1,n+1})$$

and operates as follows.

   (a) P_{n+1} generates his session key $k_{n+1} = b_{n+1,1}^{x_{n+1}} \bmod p$.

   (b) P_{n+1} uses k_{n+1} to decrypt $c_{n+1,j}$ and obtains $P_{n+1} = D_{k_{n+1}}(c_{n+1,1})$.

   (c) P_{n+1} knows that he is the receiver as P_{n+1} is his own identity.

   (d) P_{n+1} uses k_{n+1} to decrypt a_{n+1} and obtains $m = D_{k_{n+1}}(a_{n+1})$.

Chapter 5

Optimisation and Practical Application of Onion Routing

Various applications of onion routing have their special practical requirements. When stronger anonymity is required and more routers are employed, efficiency becomes critical and the intensive operations (especially those asymmetric cipher operations) need to be reduced. When applied to verifiable applications, onion routing should provide verification of its routing operations to guarantee that the routed message is not lost or tampered with. Sometimes, two parties need to interactively communicate with each other and two-way anonymous communciation must be supported, so the normal one-way onion routing needs to be extended to run in a two-way manner.

5.1 Verifiable TOR: a Verifiable Application of Onion Routing

An obvious advantage of onion routing over other specifications of anonymous communication network (e.g., mix networks [42, 74, 52, 75, 41, 93, 90, 51], which send multiple messages from a unique sender to a unique receiver through a unique path) is that each of the multiple senders can send his message to any of multiple receivers and freely choose a dynamic routing path and so higher flexibility and applicability are achieved. Another advantage of onion routing is that Tor, its second generation, gets rid of costly asymmetric encryptions and decryptions, which are inevitable in other anonymous communication systems like mix networks.

In this section, verifiable onion routing is designed. More precisely, its advanced and practical variant, Tor, is optimised to achieve verifiability. Firstly, a verification mechanism is designed. After a receiver receives a message, the onion packet of the message goes through some additional routing and finally goes back to the sender. It carries a receipt from the receiver to the sender. The sender can check the receipt to verify reception of his message by the receiver without tampering. Although this extended routing doubles the cost and exposes more transactions to the attacks based on traffic monitoring, it fills a gap and extends applicability of onion routing. Moreover, as suggested in Section 5.1.2, choice of the length and routers of the inbound routing can be made as random as possible (e.g., with the possibility to employ a couple of routers on the outbound route).

5.1.1   Preliminaries

Symbol denotions and background knowledge to be used are introduced in this section.

- p and q are large primes and q is a factor of $p-1$. G is the cyclic subgroup with order q in Z_p^*. g is a generator of G.

- Encryption of m using key k is denoted as $E_k(m)$ where a block cipher (e.g., AES) is employed.

- Encryption chain of m using block cipher and key $k_1, k_2, \ldots, k_i$ is denoted as $E_{k_1, k_2, \ldots, k_i}(m)$. The encryptions are performed layer by layer. k_1 is the the key used in the outer most layer; k_2 is the the key used in the second outer most layer; $\ldots$; k_i is the the key used in the inner most layer.

- In onion routing, the routers and receiver are denoted as $P_1, P_2, \ldots,$.

- The private key of P_i is x_i, which is randomly chosen from Z_q. The corresponding public key is $y_i = g^{x_i} \bmod p$.

Symmetric ciphers like block ciphers are very efficient in encryption and decryption. However, unlike asymmetric ciphers, they depend on key exchange protocols to distribute keys. The most common is Diffie-Hellman key exchange protocol. Two parties A and B can cooperate to generate a session key as follows.

1. A randomly chooses α from Z_q and sends his key base $\mu = g^\alpha \bmod p$ to B.

2. B randomly chooses β from Z_q and sends his key base $\nu = g^\beta \bmod p$ to A.

3. A can calculate the session key $k = \nu^\alpha \bmod p$, while B can calculate the session key $k = \mu^\beta \bmod p$.

Security of this key exchange protocol depends on hardness of the famous Diffie-Hellman problem as recalled in the following.

Definition 19 *(Diffie-Hellman problem defined in Page 28 of Chapter 3 of [71]) Given μ and ν, it is difficult to calculate k if the discrete logarithm problem is hard.*

5.1.2 Advanced Tor with a Verification Mechanism

The advanced Tor protocol adopts two simple ideas. Firstly, an onion packet obtains a receipt from its receiver and is then routed back to its sender. Secondly, symmetric cipher is employed in encryption and decryption of the onion layers, while every router's secret session key is distributed by the sender using a separate Diffie-Hellman handshake. This protocol is useful in three aspects. Firstly, it is the first verifiable onion routing protocol. Secondly, it is the first detailed implementation of symmetric cipher and supporting key distribution mechanism in onion routing as a key distribution for symmetric cipher is not implemented in detail in the description of Tor in [34].

In the verifiable Tor protocol, a message m is sent by a sender S through n routers $P_1, P_2, \ldots, P_n$ to a receiver P_{n+1}. Encryption of the message may actually contain multiple symmetric ciphertext blocks as the message may be long and is divided into multiple blocks when encrypted. For convenience of description, encryption of the message is still denoted as a single variable and the readers should be aware that it is the encryption of the whole message and may contain multiple blocks. Although a different number of routers can be chosen to route the receipt back to the sender, for simplicity of description and efficiency comparison (in Section 5.3.4), we suppose that it is sent by the receiver back to the sender through n routers $P_{n+2}, P_{n+3}, \ldots, P_{2n+1}$. In practice it is very probable that the number of routers to transfer the receipt is different from the number of routers to transfer the message. The two sets of routers do not have to be completely different and some routers may be employed in both transfers. Moreover, the same tagging mechanism in the protocol is employed in the optimisation to add random ciphertexts to the end of the onion packet to keep its length unchanged. The protocol is described as follows.

1. For the receiver and the routers P_i for $1 \leq i \leq 2n + 1$, the sender randomly chooses an integer s_i from Z_q and generates a session key $k_i = y_i^{s_i}$.

2. The sender encrypts the message m, the key base list $g^{s_1}, g^{s_2}, \ldots, g^{s_{2n+1}}$ and the route list $p_1, p_2, \ldots, p_{2n+1}, S$ as follows.

   (a) He calculates $e = E_{k_1, k_2, \ldots, k_{n+1}}(P_{n+1}, m)$.

   (b) He calculates $K_i = E_{k_1, k_2, \ldots, k_{i-1}}(g^{s_i})$ for $i = 2, 3, \ldots, 2n + 1$.

(c) He calculates $p_i = E_{k_1,k_2,\ldots,k_i}(P_{i+1})$ for $i = 1, 2, \ldots, 2n + 1$ where $P_{2n+2} = S$.

(d) He sends out the initial onion packet

$$O_1 = (a_1, b_{1,1}, b_{1,2}, \ldots, b_{1,2n+1}, c_{1,1}, c_{1,2}, \ldots, c_{1,2n+1})$$
$$= (e, K_1, K_2, \ldots, K_{2n+1}, p_1, p_2, \ldots, p_{2n+1})$$

to P_1 where $K_1 = g^{s_1} \bmod p$.

3. For $i = 1, 2, \ldots, n$ each router P_i routes the onion packet as follows where the onion he receives is in the form $O_i = (a_i, b_{i,1}, b_{i,2}, \ldots, b_{i,2n+1}, c_{i,1}, c_{i,2}, \ldots, c_{i,2n+1})$.

(a) P_i generates his session key $k_i = b_{i,1}^{x_i} \bmod p$.

(b) P_i uses k_i to decrypt $c_{i,1}$ and obtains $P_{i+1} = D_{k_i}(c_{i,1})$.

(c) P_i sends

$$O_{i+1} = (a_{i+1}, b_{i+1,1}, b_{i+1,2}, \ldots, b_{i+1,2n+1}, c_{i+1,1}, c_{i+1,2}, \ldots, c_{i+1,2n+1})$$

to P_{i+1} where $a_{i+1} = D_{k_i}(a_i)$, $b_{i+1,j} = D_{k_i}(b_{i,j+1})$ and $c_{i+1,j} = D_{k_i}(c_{i,j+1})$ for $j = 1, 2, \ldots, 2n$ and $b_{i+1,2n+1}$ and $c_{i+1,2n+1}$ are two random ciphertexts in the ciphertext space of the employed symmetric encryption algorithm.

4. After the routing by $P_1, P_2, \ldots, P_n$, the receiver P_{n+1} receives

$$O_{n+1} = (a_{n+1}, b_{n+1,1}, b_{n+1,2}, \ldots, b_{n+1,2n+1}, c_{n+1,1}, c_{n+1,2}, \ldots,$$
$$c_{n+1,2n+1})$$

and operates as follows.

(a) P_{n+1} generates his session key $k_{n+1} = b_{n+1,1}^{x_{n+1}} \bmod p$.

(b) P_{n+1} uses k_{n+1} to decrypt $c_{n+1,1}$ and obtains P_{n+2}.

(c) P_{n+1} uses k_{n+1} to decrypt a_{n+1} and obtains the message m and his own identity P_{n+1}. He knows that he is the receiver as P_{n+1} is his own identity. So he generates $a_{n+2} = H(m)$ where $H()$ is a one-way and collision-free hash function.

(d) P_{n+1} sends

$$O_{n+2} = (a_{n+2}, b_{n+2,1}, b_{n+2,2}, \ldots, b_{n+2,2n+1}, c_{n+2,1}, c_{n+2,2}, \ldots,$$
$$c_{n+2,2n+1})$$

to P_{n+2} where $b_{n+2,j} = D_{k_{n+1}}(b_{n+1,j+1})$ and $c_{n+2,j} = D_{k_{n+1}}(c_{n+1,j+1})$ for $j = 1, 2, \ldots, 2n$ and $b_{n+2,2n+1}$ and $c_{n+2,2n+1}$ are two random ciphertexts in the ciphertext space of the employed symmetric encryption algorithm.

5. For $i = n+2, n+3, \ldots, 2n+1$ each router P_i routes the onion packet as follows where the onion he receives is in the form $O_i = (a_i, b_{i,1}, b_{i,2}, \ldots, b_{i,2n+1}, c_{i,1}, c_{i,2}, \ldots, c_{i,2n+1})$.

   (a) P_i generates his session key $k_i = b_{i,1}^{x_i} \bmod p$.

   (b) P_i uses k_i to decrypt $c_{i,1}$ and obtains $P_{i+1} = D_{k_i}(c_{i,1})$.

   (c) P_i sends

$$O_{i+1} = (a_{i+1}, b_{i+1,1}, b_{i+1,2}, \ldots, b_{i+1,2n+1}, c_{i+1,1}, c_{i+1,2}, \ldots,$$
$$c_{i+1,2n+1})$$

   to P_{i+1} where $a_{i+1} = D_{k_i}(a_i)$, $b_{i+1,j} = D_{k_i}(b_{i,j+1})$ and $c_{i+1,j} = D_{k_i}(c_{i,j+1})$ for $j = 1, 2, \ldots, 2n$ and $b_{i+1,2n+1}$ and $c_{i+1,2n+1}$ are two random ciphertexts in the ciphertext space of the employed symmetric encryption algorithm.

6. After the routing by $P_{n+2}, P_{n+3}, \ldots, P_{2n+1}$, the sender S receives

$$O_{2n+2} = (a_{2n+2}, b_{2n+2,1}, b_{2n+2,2}, \ldots, b_{2n+2,2n+1},$$
$$c_{2n+2,1}, c_{2n+2,2}, \ldots, c_{2n+2,2n+1})$$

   and operates as follows.

   (a) S calculates $k = b_{2n+2,1}^{x} \bmod p$ where x is his own private key.

   (b) S tries to use k to decrypt $c_{2n+2,1}$ but does not obtain a legal identity in its correct format.[1] He knows that he is not a router or receiver of the onion packet. The only possibility is that his own onion packet is returned by the receiver.

   (c) S calculates $h = E_{k_{n+2}, k_{n+3}, \ldots, k_{2n+1}}(a_{2n+2})$. If $h = H(m)$, he is ensured that P_{n+1} receives m. Otherwise, he can tell that routing of his message m fails and he will resend it.

Note that although the encryption chain for the next router's identity is completely decrypted and discarded by each router, the length of the encrypted route list is kept unchanged in the advanced Tor protocol for the sake of untraceability. If an onion packet becomes shorter after each router's routing, its change in length can be observed and exploited to trace it. So we keep the length of the encrypted route list constant to maintain the size of an onion packet. This is implemented in the protocol by inserting a random tag into the onion packet after an encryption chain is discarded. This verifiable Tor protocol only employs symmetric cipher in encryption and decryption operations. The only public key cryptographic operations in it are $2n+1$ instances of Diffie-Hellman key exchange. Although needing more encryption and decryption operations than traditional onion routing, it is still more efficient in computation than the latter.

---

[1] The concrete format of a legal participant's identity depends on the concrete application and can be regulated by the organizer.

5.2   Efficiency Improvment Using Diffie-Hellman Chain

The key technique in onion routing is encryption chain, in which a message is successively encrypted with multiple keys. More precisely, multiple keys form a chain and are employed one by one to encrypt a message. Along with the message, each of the identities of all the routers on its routing path is encrypted in an encryption chain using the encryption keys of all the routers before it. When an onion packet is routed by a router, the router partially unwraps it by removing one layer of encryption from each of its encryption chains. At the same time the router recovers the identity of the next router and then forwards the partially decrypted packet to it. In onion routing, the encryption chains are originally implemented through asymmetric cipher. Namely, the messages and identities of the routers are encrypted using the routers' public keys and the routers unwrap the onion packet using their private keys. An advantage of using asymmetric cipher is that with the support of PKI or ID-based public key system no special key exchange operation is needed. As in an n-router onion routing, there are $n + 1$ encryption chains (one for the message and the others for the routers and the receiver) and $O(n^2)$ encryption and decryption operations, so that an implementation through an asymmetric cipher is inefficient.

Tor [34] as the second generation of onion routing proposes a few optimisations. A suggested optimisation in Tor is to replace an asymmetric cipher with a much more efficient symmetric cipher to improve efficiency of onion routing. It is common sense that a symmetric cipher is much more efficient than an asymmetric cipher. The key point in using symmetric cipher is how to distribute the session keys using public key operations, while a simple solution to the key-exchange problem in application of symmetric cipher is the Diffie-Hellman key exchange protocol. It is suggested in Tor [34] to employ Diffie-Hellman handshake to implement key changes and generate session keys for the routers. However the detailed study of the key exchange mechanism in Section 4.3.2 illustrates that although improving computational efficiency of the routers, the suggested efficiency improvement in Tor [34] is not very satisfactory. Firstly, it greatly increases communicational cost. Secondly, the sender's computational cost is still high.

The symmetric cipher-based key chain in Tor [34] is optimised in this section. Firstly, the Diffie-Hellman handshake is optimised and the number of communication rounds is reduced in Tor to obtain a simple optimisation. As it is still a direct application of Diffie-Hellman key exchange, its efficiency improvement is still not satisfactory. The Diffie-Hellman key exchange is then extended and adapted for onion routing in a more advanced way such that a sender can efficiently distribute the sysmmetric sessions keys to the routers through the onion packet. The new key exchange technique is called Diffie-Hellman chain, which chains up the Diffie-Hellman handshakes for the routers and receiver such that they are much more efficient then separate Diffie-Hellman handshakes. An efficient onion routing protocol is designed in Section 5.2.2. It employs Diffie-Hellman chain and block cipher encryption chain to improve computational and communicational efficiency of Tor. The new onion routing protocol is more appliable than most onion routing implementations including Tor. Networks with smaller bandwidth and lower-power routers can employ them to achieve anonymity.

5.2.1 A Simple Optimisation of Tor and its Drawback: Simpler but Still Direct Application of Diffie-Hellman Key Exchange

A simple optimisation of Tor is proposed in this section. As in the original onion routing (and many other cryptographic protocols), it assumes that every router and the receiver have discrete-logarithm-based public key encryption algorithms (e.g., El Gamal encryption) and already set up their public keys so that half of preparation work in Diffie-Hellman key exchange can be saved. Moreover, multiple rounds of communication between each pair of participants are combined to improve communication efficiency. It still employs Diffie-Hellman handshakes in the staightforward way and is described as follows.

1. For the receiver and each router P_i where $1 \leq i \leq n+1$, the sender randomly chooses an integer s_i from Z_q and generates a session key $k_i = y_i^{s_i}$.

2. The sender encrypts the message m, the key base list $g^{s_1}, g^{s_2}, \ldots, g^{s_{n+1}}$ and the route list $p_1, p_2, \ldots, p_{n+1}$ as follows.

   (a) He calculates $e = E_{k_1, k_2, \ldots, k_{n+1}}(m)$.
   (b) He calculates $K_i = E_{k_1, k_2, \ldots, k_{i-1}}(g^{s_i})$ for $i = 1, 2, \ldots, n+1$.
   (c) He calculates $p_i = E_{k_1, k_2, \ldots, k_i}(P_{i+1})$ for $i = 1, 2, \ldots, n+1$ where $P_{n+2} = P_{n+1}$.
   (d) He sends out the initial onion

   $$O_1 = (a_1, b_{1,1}, b_{1,2}, \ldots, b_{1,n+1},$$
   $$c_{1,1}, c_{1,2}, \ldots, c_{1,n+1})$$
   $$= (e, K_1, K_2, \ldots, K_{n+1}, p_1, p_2, \ldots, p_{n+1})$$

   to P_1.

3. Each router P_i routes the onion as follows where the onion is in the form $O_i = (a_i, b_{i,1}, b_{i,2}, \ldots, b_{i,n+1}, c_{i,1}, c_{i,2}, \ldots, c_{i,n+1})$ when it is sent to P_i.

   (a) P_i generates his session key $k_i = b_{i,1}^{x_i} \mod p$.
   (b) P_i uses k_i to decrypt $c_{i,j}$ for $j = 1, 2, \ldots, n+1$ and obtains $P_{i+1} = D_{k_i}(c_{i,1})$.

(c) P_i uses k_i to decrypt a_i and obtains $a_{i+1} = D_{k_i}(a_i)$.

(d) Finally, P_i sends

$$O_{i+1} = (a_{i+1}, b_{i+1,1}, b_{i+1,2}, \ldots,$$
$$b_{i+1,n+1}, c_{i+1,1}, c_{i+1,2}, \ldots, c_{i+1,n+1})$$

to P_{i+1} where $b_{i+1,j} = D_{k_i}(b_{i,j+1})$ and $c_{i+1,j} = D_{k_i}(c_{i,j+1})$ for $j = 1, 2, \ldots, n$ and $b_{i+1,n+1}$ and $c_{i+1,n+1}$ are two random integers in the ciphertext space of the employed symmetric encryption algorithm.

4. At last, P_{n+1} receives

$$O_{n+1} = (a_{n+1}, b_{n+1,1}, b_{n+1,2}, \ldots,$$
$$b_{n+1,n+1}, c_{n+1,1}, c_{n+1,2}, \ldots, c_{n+1,n+1})$$

and operates as follows.

(a) P_{n+1} generates his session key $k_{n+1} = b_{n+1,1}^{x_{n+1}} \bmod p$.

(b) P_{n+1} uses k_{n+1} to decrypt $c_{n+1,j}$ and obtains $P_{n+1} = D_{k_{n+1}}(c_{n+1,1})$.

(c) P_{n+1} knows that itself is the receiver as P_{n+1} is its own identity.

(d) P_{n+1} uses k_{n+1} to decrypt a_{n+1} and obtains $m = D_{k_{n+1}}(a_{n+1})$.

This modified Tor protocol only employs symmetric cipher in encryption and decryption operations. The only public key operations in it are $n + 1$ instances of Diffie-Hellman key exchange. Although more encryption and decryption operations are needed than in traditional onion routing, it is still more efficient in computation. However, it is less efficient in communication than traditional onion routing as its onion packet contains additional encrypted key bases $b_{i,1}, b_{i,2}, \ldots, b_{i,n+1}$. So its advantage in efficiency is not obvious. Therefore, it is only a prototype, while our final proposal is based on it but has higher requirements on efficiency: only using symmetric ciphers in encryption and decryption in comparison with traditional onion routing

- very little additional communication (e.g., one more integer) is needed;

- no more additional encryption or decryption operation is needed.

5.2.2 A New and More Advanced Technique: Diffie-Hellman Chain

The simple optimisation protocol in Section 5.2.1 has demonstrated that direct application of Diffie-Hellman key exchange to onion routing (including original onion routing and Tor) cannot achieve satisfactory advantages in efficiency. To reduce additional communication and encryption and decryption operations, a novel technique, Diffie-Hellman chain, is designed. The Diffie-Hellman key bases for all the routers and the receiver are sealed in the Diffie-Hellman chain, which appears in each onion packet in the form of a single integer. For each router to generate his session key, he needs his private key and a key base initially sealed in the Diffie-Hellman chain by the sender and then recovered by cooperation of all the previous routers in the course of routing. As only one single integer is needed in each onion packet to represent the Diffie-Hellman chain and commit to all the Diffie-Hellman key bases, a very small amount of additional communication is employed and no more encryption (decryption) operation is needed in comparison with traditional onion routing.

A new protocol, called compressed onion routing, is proposed. A packet (onion) consists of three parts: message, route list and key base. Route list contains the identities of all the nodes on the route. Key base is the base to generate the session keys (symmetric keys) distributed to the nodes. The message part in compressed onion routing is similar to that in most onion routing schemes. The message is encrypted in an encryption chain using the sessions keys of all the nodes. The readers only need to note that efficient block cipher is employed in the encryption chain. In compressed onion routing, the route list is the same as in other onion routing schemes. It consists of all the routers' identities. One encryption chain is used to seal each router's identity using the session keys of all the routers before it. The readers only need to note that efficient block cipher is employed in the encryption chains for the route list.

The most important novel technique is generation and update of the key base, which enables key exchange. Each router builds his session key on the base of the key base using his private key and update the key base for the next router. The key generation function is similar to Diffie-Hellman key generation, but we do not employ separate Diffie-Hellman key exchange protocols to distribute the session keys to the routers. Instead the key base updating mechanism actually generates a key base chain and so all the session keys and their generation functions are linked in a chain structure. The key exchange technique is called Diffie-Hellman chain. After obtaining his session key, each router can extract the identity of the next router from the route list using his session key, remove one layer of encryption from the message using his session key and then forward the onion to the next router. The Diffie-Hellman chain only needs the bandwidth of one integer, and thus is much more efficient than separate key distribution in communication. Novelty of the new compressed onion routing protocol is that distribution of the sessions keys and encryption of the routers' identities are compressed such that fewer computationally costly public key operations and communicationally costly encryption chains are needed.

Suppose a message m is sent by a sender through n routers $P_1, P_2, \ldots, P_n$ to the receiver P_{n+1}. Firstly, the sender generates the session keys $k_1, k_2, \ldots, k_{n+1}$ respectively for $P_1, P_2, \ldots, P_{n+1}$ as follows.

1. The sender randomly chooses an integer s_1 from Z_q.

2. The sender calculates P_1's session key $k_1 = y_1^{s_1} \bmod p$.

3. The sender calculates $s_2 = s_1 + k_1 \bmod q$.

4. The sender calculates P_2's session key $k_2 = y_2^{s_2} \bmod p$.

5. ......

6. ......

7. The sender calculates $s_{n+1} = s_n + k_n \bmod q$.

8. The sender calculates P_{n+1}'s session key $k_{n+1} = y_{n+1}^{s_{n+1}} \bmod p$.

Generally speaking, for $i = 1, 2, \ldots, n+1$,

1. If $i > 1$ the sender calculates $s_i = s_{i-1} + k_{i-1} \bmod q$ as his secret seed in the Diffie-Hellman chain for generation of k_i.

2. The sender calculates $k_i = y_i^{s_i}$ where s_1 is randomly chosen from Z_q.

In summary, the sender uses the sum of the previous node's session key and his secret seed in the Diffie-Hellman generation of the previous node's session key as his secret seed to generate a node's Diffie-Hellman session key. The other secret seed to generate the node's session key is the node's private key.

The route list consists of $p_1, p_2, \ldots, p_{n+1}$ where $p_i = E_{k_1, k_2, \ldots, k_i}(P_{i+1})$ and $P_{n+2} = P_{n+1}$. The message is encrypted into $e = E_{k_1, k_2, \ldots, k_{n+1}}(m)$. The onion is in the form of $O_i = (a_i, b_i, c_{i,1}, c_{i,2}, \ldots, c_{i,n+1})$ when it reaches P_i where a_i is the encrypted message, b_i is the key base, and $c_{i,1}, c_{i,2}, \ldots, c_{i,n+1}$ is the encrypted route list. Note that although the encryption chain for the next router's identity is completely decrypted and discarded by each router, the length of the encrypted route list is kept unchanged for the sake of untraceability. If an onion packet becomes shorter after each router's routing, its change in length can be observed and exploited to trace it. So we keep the length of each encrypted route list constant to maintain the size of onion packets. This can be implemented by inserting a random tag into the onion packets after they discard an encryption chain. The initial onion $O_1 = (a_1, b_1, c_{1,1}, c_{1,2}, \ldots, c_{1,n+1}) = (e, g^{s_1}, p_1, p_2, \ldots, p_{n+1})$. Note that e may actually contain multiple symmetric ciphertext blocks as the message may be long and is divided into multiple blocks when being encrypted. For convenience of description, encryption of the message is still denoted as a single variable and the readers should be aware that it is the encryption of the whole message and may contain multiple blocks.

P_1 receives $O_1 = (a_1, b_1, c_{1,1}, c_{1,2}, \ldots, c_{1,n+1})$ from the sender and then operates as follows.

1. P_1 generates his session key $k_1 = b_1^{x_1} \bmod p$.

2. P_1 uses k_1 to decrypt $c_{1,j}$ for $j = 1, 2, \ldots, n+1$ and obtains $P_2 = D_{k_1}(c_{1,1})$.

3. P_1 uses k_1 to decrypt a_1 and obtains $a_2 = D_{k_1}(a_1)$.

4. P_1 calculates the new key base $b_2 = b_1 g^{k_1} \bmod p$.

Finally, P_1 sends $O_2 = (a_2, b_2, c_{2,1}, c_{2,2}, \ldots, c_{2,n+1})$ to P_2 where $c_{2,i} = D_{k_1}(c_{1,i+1})$ for $i = 1, 2, \ldots, n$ and $c_{2,n+1}$ is a random integer in the ciphertext space of the employed block encryption algorithm.

More generally, for $i = 1, 2, \ldots, n$ each P_i receives $O_i = (a_i, b_i, c_{i,1}, c_{i,2}, \ldots, c_{i,n+1})$ and operates as follows.

1. P_i generates his session key $k_i = b_i^{x_i} \bmod p$.

2. P_i uses k_i to decrypt $c_{i,j}$ for $j = 1, 2, \ldots, n + 1$ and obtains $P_{i+1} = D_{k_i}(c_{i,1})$.

3. P_i uses k_i to decrypt a_i and obtains $a_{i+1} = D_{k_i}(a_i)$.

4. P_i calculates the new key base $b_{i+1} = b_i g^{k_i} \bmod p$.

Finally, P_i sends $O_{i+1} = (a_{i+1}, b_{i+1}, c_{i+1,1}, c_{i+1,2}, \ldots, c_{i+1,n+1})$ to P_{i+1} where $c_{i+1,j} = D_{k_i}(c_{i,j+1})$ for $j = 1, 2, \ldots, n$ and $c_{i+1,n+1}$ is a random integer in the ciphertext space of the employed symmetric encryption algorithm.

At last, P_{n+1} receives $O_{n+1} = (a_{n+1}, b_{n+1}, c_{n+1,1}, c_{n+1,2}, \ldots, c_{n+1,n+1})$ and operates as follows.

1. P_{n+1} generates his session key $k_{n+1} = b_{n+1}^{x_{n+1}} \bmod p$.

2. P_{n+1} uses k_{n+1} to decrypt $c_{n+1,j}$ and obtains $P_{n+1} = D_{k_{n+1}}(c_{n+1,1})$.

3. P_{n+1} knows that itself is the receiver as P_{n+1} is its own identity.

4. P_{n+1} uses k_{n+1} to decrypt a_{n+1} and obtains $m = D_{k_{n+1}}(a_{n+1})$.

5.2.3 Analysis and Comparison

Security of the compressed onion routing scheme depends on hardness of Diffie-Hellman problem as its key exchange mechanism is an extension of Diffie-Hellman key exchange. Its main trick is combining key exchange with encryption chain such that every router can obtain his session key with the help of the previous router. As security of Diffie-Hellman key exchange has been formally proved and hardness of the Diffie-Hellman problem is widely accepted, no further proof of security is needed except for Theorem 21, which shows that the session keys can be correctly exchanged.

Theorem 21 *For $j = 1, 2, \ldots, n + 1$, the same session key k_i is generated, respectively by the sender as $k_i = y_i^{s_i} \bmod p$ and by P_i as $k_i = b_i^{x_i} \bmod p$.*

To prove Theorem 21, a lemma has to be proved first.

Lemma 12 *For $j = 1, 2, \ldots, n + 1$, $b_i = g^{s_i} \bmod p$.*

Proof: Mathematical induction is used.

1. When $i = 1$, $b_1 = g^{s_1} \bmod p$.

2. When $i = j$, suppose $b_j = g^{s_j} \bmod p$. Then a deduction can be made in next step.

3. When $i = j + 1$, $b_{j+1} = b_j g^{k_j} = g^{s_j} g^{k_j} \bmod p$ as supposed in the last step that $b_i = g^{s_i}$ when $i = j$. So

$$b_{j+1} = g^{s_j} g^{k_j} = g^{s_j + k_j} = g^{s_{j+1}} \bmod p$$

Therefore, $b_i = g^{s_i} \bmod p$ for $j = 1, 2, \ldots, n + 1$ as a result of mathematical induction. $\square$

Proof of Theorem 21:
According to Lemma 12,

$$y_i^{s_i} = g^{x_i s_i} = b_i^{x_i} \bmod p$$

for $j = 1, 2, \ldots, n + 1$. $\square$

Efficiency comparison between our new onion routing protocol and the existing anonymous communication channels is given in Table 5.1, Table 5.2, Table 5.3 and Table 5.4 where AOR stands for asymmetric cipher-based onion routing and COR stands for compressed onion routing. The first table shows the advantage of our new technique over the existing anonymous communication channels including onion routing and mix networks. The last three tables show our optimisation of onion routing. It is assumed that the employed block cipher is 256-bit AES. For simplicity, it is assumed that the message is one block long, while the size of one block of the employed block cipher should be large enough for a router's identity. All the ciphertexts are one block long in our analysis, which does not lose generality and can be extended to long message cases in a straightforward way. As for asymmetric ciphers in AOR, it is supposed that El Gamal encryption, which is the most popular with onion routing, is employed. More precisely, it is assumed that the El Gamal encryption algorithm uses 1024-bit integers. Comparison in the four tables illustrates that great efficiency improvement is achieved in the two compressed onion routing protocols.

Compressed onion routing greatly improves efficiency by using symmetric ciphers and Diffie-Hellman chains. It needs smaller packet size and less computation than the existing onion routing schemes including TOR.

5.2.4   Further Optimisation: Small Compressed Onion Routing

Although compressed onion routing greatly improves computational efficiency, it is still not efficient enough in communication. It employs $n + 2$ encryption

Table 5.1: Comparison of anonymous communication channels

Scheme	Public key exponentiation	Flexibility and applicability
Mix network	$\geq 6n + 4$	No
AOS	$2(n + 1)(n + 4)$	Yes
Tor	$2(2n - 1)$	Yes
COR	$3(n + 1)$	Yes

Table 5.2: Computational efficiency comparison for sender

Scheme	Public key exponentiation	Block cipher encryption
AOS	$(n + 1)(n + 4)$	0
Tor	$n + 1$	$(n + 1)(1 + (3n + 2)/2)$
COR	$n + 1$	$(n + 1)(1 + (n + 2)/2)$

Table 5.3: Computational efficiency comparison for router (receiver)

Scheme	Average public key exponentiation	Average block cipher decryption
AOS	$n + 4$	0
Tor	3	$2(n + 1)$
COR	2	$(n + 4)/2$

Table 5.4: Communicational efficiency comparison

Scheme	Number of bits in onion packet	Rounds
AOS	$2048(n + 2)$	$n + 1$
Tor	$256(n + 2)$	$(n + 1)(n + 3)$
COR	$256(n + 2) + 1024$	$n + 1$

chains, so its packet contains $n + 2$ ciphertexts. To improve communication efficiency, we can compress the whole route list into one encryption chain to design a further improved onion routing protocol called small compressed onion routing. To support this improvement on the size of onion packets, an on-line index table is needed. It can be set up on a server and any one can look it up. The message encryption and session key exchange in small compressed onion routing are unchanged, but only one encryption chain in the form of one ciphertext is needed for the route list. Using this mechanism, not only the size of an onion packet is much smaller but also the number of decryptions is greatly reduced. Its detailed specification is described as follows.

1. The sender calculates $c_i = E_{k_i, k_{i+1}, \ldots, k_{n+1}}(P_{n+1})$ for $i = 1, 2, \ldots, n + 1$.

2. The sender calculates $d_i = c_i \oplus P_{i-1}$ for $i = 2, 3, \ldots, n$ and inserts (d_i, P_i) for $i = 2, 3, \ldots, n$ into the index table. The data in the index table are listed in increasing order of d_i.

The initial onion is $O_1 = (a_1, b_1, c_1)$. P_1 receives $O_1 = (a_1, b_1, c_1)$ from the sender and then operates as follows.

1. P_1 generates his session key $k_1 = b_1^{x_1} \bmod p$.

2. P_1 uses k_1 to decrypt c_1 and obtains $c_2 = D_{k_1}(c_1)$.

3. P_1 calculates $d = c_2 \oplus P_1$.

4. P_1 looks up d in the index table and finds the identity stored together with it, namely the identity of the next router P_2.

5. P_1 uses k_1 to decrypt a_1 and obtains $a_2 = D_{k_1}(a_1)$.

6. P_1 calculates the new key base $b_2 = b_1 g^{k_1} \bmod p$.

7. P_1 sends $O_2 = (a_2, b_2, c_2)$ to P_2.

More generally, for $i = 1, 2, \ldots, n$ each P_i receives $O_i = (a_i, b_i, c_i)$ and operates as follows.

1. P_i generates his session key $k_i = b_i^{x_i} \bmod p$.

2. P_i uses k_i to decrypt c_i and obtains $c_{i+1} = D_{k_i}(c_i)$.

3. P_i calculates $d = c_{i+1} \oplus P_i$.

4. P_1 looks up d in the index table and finds the identity stored together with it, namely the identity of the next router P_{i+1}.

5. P_i uses k_i to decrypt a_i and obtains $a_{i+1} = D_{k_i}(a_i)$.

6. P_i calculates the new key base $b_{i+1} = b_i g^{k_i} \bmod p$.

7. P_i sends $O_{i+1} = (a_{i+1}, b_{i+1}, c_{i+1})$ to P_{i+1}.

At last, P_{n+1} receives $O_{n+1} = (a_{n+1}, b_{n+1}, c_{n+1})$ and operates as follows.

1. P_{n+1} generates his session key $k_{n+1} = b_{n+1}^{x_{n+1}} \bmod p$.

2. P_{n+1} uses k_{n+1} to decrypt c_{n+1} and obtains $P_{n+1} = D_{k_{n+1}}(c_{n+1})$.

3. P_{n+1} knows that he is the receiver as P_{n+1} is his own identity.

4. P_{n+1} uses k_{n+1} to decrypt a_{n+1} and obtains $m = D_{k_{n+1}}(a_{n+1})$.

5.3 A Practical Application: Paid and Anonymous Use of Cloud Softwares

In the era of cloud computing, it is very popular for software users to rent the softwares they need and use them on-line instead of buying them and installing them locally. After paying the renting cost to a software provider, a user can use the rent cloud software on-line in two steps. Firstly, he sends the software provider his input to the software. Then, the software provider runs the software with the input and returns the output to the user. Software renting in the cloud has some obvious advantages as the user does not need to care about the software except knowing that it runs in the cloud. Renting a software is cheaper than buying it. Secondly, the users do not need to provide local hardware to run the software. Thirdly, the users do not need to worry about system maintenance and software updates. Fourthly, the software provider does not need to worry about copyright violation. However, this new trend raises some security concerns. One of them is privacy of the users as both their inputs to the softwares and the softwares' outputs to them are transmitted on-line between the users and the software providers. Many users do not want to reveal their inputs to some softwares and the returned outputs to other parties as they may contain sensitive information. For example, users of financial management softwares will not reveal their financial data and users of market analysis softwares will not reveal the analysis result. Privacy of users of cloud rent softwares has the following two requirements.

- Their inputs to the softwares and the softwares' outputs to them are confidential when transmitted on the Internet.

- Their inputs to the softwares and the softwares' outputs to them are confidential to the software providers. At least the software providers cannot link the identities of the users to their inputs and outputs. Even if a software provider receives an input and runs it to obtain an output, he has no idea to which user they belong.

The first requirement is not hard to satisfy: encrypting the inputs and outputs when they are transmitted on the Internet is enough. Of course, key exchange between the software users and software providers is needed. The second requirement is harder to satisfy. A software user has to inject an input into the software and extract an output from it. The only way to hide the input and the output from the software provider is to design a software able to process encrypted input and returns an encrypted output. Although in theory secure computation techniques [29, 58, 61] can process secret inputs and calculate their functions, in practice there are some difficulties in applying them to private usage of cloud softwares. Firstly, practical softwares usually employ complex computations and implement them through secure computation is complex and costly, especially when the software provider is a single party and cannot employ multi-party secure computation techniques [13, 32, 14, 31]. Secondly, different software users employ different encryption keys and no existing secure computation techniques can process inputs encrypted with different keys. So, to the best of our knowledge, there is no practical software accepting an encrypted input and returning an encrypted output.

A practical solution to private usage of cloud software is anonymizing the users. Namely, although a software provider receives an input from a user, runs it on the software and returns an output to the user, he cannot link the input and the output to the user as the user is anonymous. More precisely, although the software provider knows the input and the output in plaintext, he cannot link them to users who access the software service anonymously. Anonymity of the software users raises another question: how to authenticate the anonymous users and guarantee that only qualified users can access the software. An obvious solution for anonymous authentication is pseudonym. In private usage of cloud software, pseudonym technique must cooperate with a billing system as very often paid usage to a cloud software is not permanent. A legal user usually buys a certain time of usage of a software such that his access to the software is permitted until his time of usage runs out. Therefore, anonymous authentication for a limited number of times must be supported.

After anonymous authentication for a limited number of times is implemented, there is another practical consideration: the software users' network connection to the software providers must be anonymous and not traceable. Otherwise, even if a user uses a pseudonym to access a software, he can still be traced through his network connection (e.g., his IP address). An anonymous communication network is needed. The most common anonymous communication network is onion routing [44, 45, 20], whose most popular real-world version is Tor [34]. However, application of onion routing to private usage of cloud software faces a challenge: onion routing is usually one-way and only deals with a transmit from a sender to a receiver where the receiver does not respond to the sender. More precisely, although a software user can submit his pseudonym and input to a software provider through onion routing, the software provider still needs additional support to return the output of the software to the software user as the user is anonymous and his location is unknown. Therefore, a two-way anonymous communication network is needed.

In this section, onion routing is optimised to support anonymous usage of cloud software. Firstly, an anonymous token technique is proposed to enable the software users to buy tokens from the software providers and use them anonymously. A token from a software provider permits a software user to use the software of the provider once. A special mechanism prevents the users from tampering with their tokens or reusing them. Secondly and more importantly, a two-way onion routing technique is proposed to support two-way anonymous communication between the software providers and the software users. As efficiency of onion routing deteriorates after extension to two-way use, an efficiency improvement mechanism is applied to it to prevent its high efficiency from being compromised.

5.3.1 How to Obtain Anonymous Usage Permit of a Cloud Software: Anonymous Token

If a software provider wants to sell online usage of cloud software, he can act as follows.

- He publishes detailed information about the software such as its functionality and performance. He publishes the price of online usage of the software as well.

- He chooses an RSA composite $N = pq$ where p and q are large primes. He chooses his RSA private key d and publishes his public key $e = d^{-1} \bmod N$.

A user wanting to buy the usage of the cloud software can buy an anonymous token as his access privilege to the software as follows.

1. He employs a one-way and collision-resistant hash function $H()$ from Z_l to Z_N where l is a security parameter.

2. He randomly chooses an integer t from Z_l and calculates $t' = H(t)$.

3. He randomly chooses another integer r from Z_N and calculates $T = t'r^e \bmod N$.

4. He pays the price for the software to the provider and asks the provider to sign T.

5. The provider receives the money and returns the user $T' = T^d \bmod N$.

The user can extract an anonymous token from T' and employ it to use the cloud software anonymously as follows.

1. He calculates $\kappa = T'/r \bmod N$.

2. When he wants to use the cloud software, he submits (t, κ) as his anonymous token to the software provider together with his input to the software.

3. The software provider verifies validity of the token as follows.

   (a) He first checks his database that stores the used tokens. The received token cannot exist in the database.

   (b) He verifies $\kappa = h(t)^d \bmod N$, which must be satisfied.

   If and only if both verifications are passed, the user has the access privilege to the software. When the verifications are passed, the software provider runs the software with the user's input and sends the output of the software to the user. Otherwise, the user's request is rejected.

4. The software provider inserts the used token into his database and it cannot be used again.

The difficulty of factorizing N and thus finding d given e and the one-way nature and collision-resistance of the employed hash function guarantee that anonymous tokens cannot be forged or malleated. This security assumption is similar to the popular security assumption for the hash-and-sign technology in digital signature (Chapter 11 of [71]), which assumes that when a digital signature is the hash function of the message to sign raised to the power of an RSA private key, it cannot be forged if RSA assumption is solid and the employed hash function is one-way and collision-resistant. Under the security assumption, no polynomial adversary can forge an anonymous token or malleate a used token into a new token. Moreover, as a random integer r is involved in generation of T and its influence is removed when the anonymous token, (t, κ), is extracted, the software provider cannot link the anonymous token (t, κ) to the corresponding T he signs earlier and the anonymity of the software user is achieved.

Any user can buy multiple tokens for multiple-time usage of cloud software. A software provider can sell a permanent token to users frequently using a software. When buying a permanent token, the software user and the software provider use a special public/private key pair different from (e, d). When a permanent token is used, the software user and the software provider employ the special public/private key pair to generate and verify the token and there is no database to record the used tokens.

So far we have not discussed how the software users and the software providers communicate to each other when purchasing and consuming anonymous tokens. When a software user buys an anonymous token, he can visit the software provider in person and make the payment in the normal way. Alternatively, the software user can buy the token online using credit card or e-cash [26, 24]. Choice of the employed communication network for the purchase communication depends on whether the software user wants to hide his identity completely. If a software user wants to buy a token using his real identity and use it anonymously later, he can buy it through normal network connections. If a software user does not want to reveal his identity when buying a token, he needs to employ the anonymous communication network proposed in Section 5.3.3 to communicate with the software provider and pay by anonymous e-cash [26, 24]. Communication network for the software accessing communication must be anonymous and so must employ the anonymous communication network proposed in Section 5.3.3.

A main difference of our anonymous token from anonymous e-coin (e-cash) is that the receiver of any anonymous token is unique, while an e-coin is issued by a finance institute (e.g. bank) and may be received by any vendor. So the database of used e-coins is maintained by their issuing bank and needed to be checked by any vendor. Therefore, to detect invalid e-coins in real time a vendor needs to have a real-time network connection to the bank. In our design of anonymous tokens, every software provider can maintain his own database and does not need help from any third party. Another difference is that our anonymous token is simpler than e-coin as it does not need to contain information like issuing party and value.

As mentioned before, even if a software user uses an anonymous token to access cloud software he still needs an anonymous communication network to communicate with the software provider. As the most popular anonymous communication network, onion routing, usually only supports one-way anonymous communication, it is extended to support two-way anonymous communication in this section. Moreover, its efficiency is optimised by employing a more efficient key exchange mechanism than that in Tor.

5.3.2 Two-Way Onion Routing to Support Anonymous Usage of Cloud Software

The new design adopts two ideas. Firstly, two-way onion routing is implemented such that the initial sender of an onion packet can fetch some information from a receiver of the onion. More precisely, an onion packet is routed back to its initial sender after obtaining some information from the router at the end of its route. Secondly, as in Tor, a symmetric cipher is employed in encryption and decryption of the onion layers, while every router's secret session key is distributed by the sender using a separate Diffie-Hellman handshake. The new protocol describes a more detailed implementation of symmetric cipher operations and the supporting key distribution mechanism in onion routing as key distribution for symmetric cipher is not implemented in detail in the description of Tor in [34].

Suppose an inquiry package m (which contains at least the input to cloud software and an anonymous token enabling the user to use the software) is sent by the user S through n routers $P_1, P_2, \ldots, P_n$ to a software provider P_{n+1}. Encryption of the inquiry package may actually contain multiple symmetric ciphertext blocks as the inquiry package may be long and is divided into multiple blocks when being encrypted. For convenience of description, encryption of the inquiry package is still denoted as a single variable and the readers should be aware that it is the encryption of the whole inquiry package and may contain multiple blocks. Although a different number of routers can be chosen to route the inquiry result (output of the software) back to the software user, for simplicity of description, we suppose that it is sent by the software provider back to the software user through n routers $P_{n+2}, P_{n+3}, \ldots, P_{2n+1}$. In practice it is very probable that the number of routers to transfer the inquiry result is different from the number of routers to transfer the inquiry package. The two sets of routers do not have to be completely different and some routers may be employed in both transfers. The two-way onion routing protocol is described as follows.

1. For the software provider and the routers P_i for $1 \leq i \leq 2n + 1$, the software user randomly chooses an integer s_i from Z_q and generates a session key $k_i = y_i^{s_i}$.

2. The software user encrypts the inquiry package m, the key base list $g^{s_1}, g^{s_2}, \ldots, g^{s_{2n+1}}$ and the route list $p_1, p_2, \ldots, p_{2n+1}, S$ as follows.

   (a) He calculates $e = E_{k_1, k_2, \ldots, k_{n+1}}(P_{n+1}, m)$.

   (b) He calculates $K_i = E_{k_1, k_2, \ldots, k_{i-1}}(g^{s_i})$ for $i = 2, 3, \ldots, 2n + 1$.

   (c) He calculates $p_i = E_{k_1, k_2, \ldots, k_i}(P_{i+1})$ for $i = 1, 2, \ldots, 2n + 1$ where $P_{2n+2} = S$.

   (d) He sends out the initial onion packet

   $$O_1 = (a_1, b_{1,1}, b_{1,2}, \ldots, b_{1,2n+1}, c_{1,1}, c_{1,2}, \ldots, c_{1,2n+1})$$
   $$= (e, K_1, K_2, \ldots, K_{2n+1}, p_1, p_2, \ldots, p_{2n+1})$$

   to P_1 where $K_1 = g^{s_1} \bmod p$.

3. For $i = 1, 2, \ldots, n$ each router P_i routes the onion packet as follows where the onion he receives is in the form $O_i = (a_i, b_{i,1}, b_{i,2}, \ldots, b_{i,2n+1}, c_{i,1}, c_{i,2}, \ldots, c_{i,2n+1})$.

   (a) P_i generates his session key $k_i = b_{i,1}^{x_i} \bmod p$.

   (b) P_i uses k_i to decrypt $c_{i,1}$ and obtains $P_{i+1} = D_{k_i}(c_{i,1})$.

   (c) P_i sends

   $$O_{i+1} = (a_{i+1}, b_{i+1,1}, b_{i+1,2}, \ldots, b_{i+1,2n+1}, c_{i+1,1}, c_{i+1,2}, \ldots, c_{i+1,2n+1})$$

   to P_{i+1} where $a_{i+1} = D_{k_i}(a_i)$, $b_{i+1,j} = D_{k_i}(b_{i,j+1})$ and $c_{i+1,j} = D_{k_i}(c_{i,j+1})$ for $j = 1, 2, \ldots, 2n$ and $b_{i+1,2n+1}$ and $c_{i+1,2n+1}$ are two random ciphertexts in the ciphertext space of the employed symmetric encryption algorithm.

4. After the routing by $P_1, P_2, \ldots, P_n$, the software provider P_{n+1} receives

   $$O_{n+1} = (a_{n+1}, b_{n+1,1}, b_{n+1,2}, \ldots, b_{n+1,2n+1}, c_{n+1,1}, c_{n+1,2}, \ldots, c_{n+1,2n+1})$$

   and operates as follows.

(a) P_{n+1} generates his session key $k_{n+1} = b_{n+1,1}^{x_{n+1}} \bmod p$.

(b) P_{n+1} uses k_{n+1} to decrypt $c_{n+1,1}$ and obtains P_{n+2}.

(c) P_{n+1} uses k_{n+1} to decrypt a_{n+1} and obtains the inquiry package m and his own identity P_{n+1}. He knows that he is the software provider as P_{n+1} is his own identity. He verifies validity of the anonymous token, runs the software using the input in m, obtains an output R, and generates $a_{n+2} = (E_m(R), H(m))$ where $E_m()$ denotes symmetric encryption using key m and $H()$ is a one-way and collision-free hash function.

(d) P_{n+1} sends

$$O_{n+2} = (a_{n+2}, b_{n+2,1}, b_{n+2,2}, \ldots, b_{n+2,2n+1}, c_{n+2,1}, c_{n+2,2}, \ldots, \\ c_{n+2,2n+1})$$

to P_{n+2} where $b_{n+2,j} = D_{k_{n+1}}(b_{n+1,j+1})$ and $c_{n+2,j} = D_{k_{n+1}}(c_{n+1,j+1})$ for $j = 1, 2, \ldots, 2n$ and $b_{n+2,2n+1}$ and $c_{n+2,2n+1}$ are two random ciphertexts in the ciphertext space of the employed symmetric encryption algorithm.

5. For $i = n+2, n+3, \ldots, 2n+1$, each router P_i routes the onion packet as follows where the onion he receives is in the form $O_i = (a_i, b_{i,1}, b_{i,2}, \ldots, b_{i,2n+1}, c_{i,1}, c_{i,2}, \ldots, c_{i,2n+1})$.

(a) P_i generates his session key $k_i = b_{i,1}^{x_i} \bmod p$.

(b) P_i uses k_i to decrypt $c_{i,1}$ and obtains $P_{i+1} = D_{k_i}(c_{i,1})$.

(c) P_i sends

$$O_{i+1} = (a_{i+1}, b_{i+1,1}, b_{i+1,2}, \ldots, b_{i+1,2n+1}, c_{i+1,1}, c_{i+1,2}, \ldots, c_{i+1,2n+1})$$

to P_{i+1} where $a_{i+1} = D_{k_i}(a_i)$, $b_{i+1,j} = D_{k_i}(b_{i,j+1})$ and $c_{i+1,j} = D_{k_i}(c_{i,j+1})$ for $j = 1, 2, \ldots, 2n$ and $b_{i+1,2n+1}$ and $c_{i+1,2n+1}$ are two random ciphertexts in the ciphertext space of the employed symmetric encryption algorithm.

6. After the routing by $P_{n+2}, P_{n+3}, \ldots, P_{2n+1}$, the software user S receives

$$O_{2n+2} = (a_{2n+2}, b_{2n+2,1}, b_{2n+2,2}, \ldots, b_{2n+2,2n+1}, \\ c_{2n+2,1}, c_{2n+2,2}, \ldots, c_{2n+2,2n+1})$$

and operates as follows.

(a) S calculates $k = b_{2n+2,1}^x \bmod p$ where x is his own private key.

(b) S tries to use k to decrypt $c_{2n+2,1}$ but does not obtain a legal identity in its correct format.[2] He knows that he is not a router or software provider. The only possibility is that his own onion packet is returned by the software provider.

---

[2] The concrete format of a legal participant's identity depends on the concrete application.

(c) S calculates $(\rho, \tau) = E_{k_{n+2}, k_{n+3}, \ldots, k_{2n+1}}(a_{2n+2})$. If $\tau = H(m)$, he is
ensured that the software provider P_{n+1} returns him an encrypted
inquiry result. He can extract the inquiry result as $R = D_m(\rho)$
where $D_m()$ denotes symmetric decryption using key m.

Note that although the encryption chain for the next router's identity
is completely decrypted and discarded by each router, the length of the encrypted route list is kept unchanged in the routing protocol for the sake of
untraceability. If an onion packet becomes shorter after each router's routing,
its change in length can be observed and exploited to trace it. We keep the
length of the encrypted route list constant to maintain the size of an onion
packet. This is implemented in the routing protocol by inserting a random
tag into the onion packet after an encryption chain is discarded. This routing
protocol only employs symmetric cipher in encryption and decryption operations. The only public key cryptographic operations in it are $2n + 1$ instances
of Diffie-Hellman key exchange. Although needing more encryption and decryption operations than traditional onion routing, it is still more efficient in
computation than the latter. However, it is not efficient in communication as
its onion packet contains additional encrypted key bases $b_{i,1}, b_{i,2}, \ldots, b_{i,2n+1}$,
which are large integers used in public key crypto.[3] So its efficiency still needs
improving and our final proposal will be presented in Section 5.3.3 to achieve
higher efficiency.

5.3.3   Efficiency Optimisation: Two-Way Onion Routing with Compact Diffie-Hellman Handshakes

The routing protocol in Section 5.3.2 has demonstrated that direct application
of Diffie-Hellman key exchange in multiple separate instances to onion routing
cannot achieve satisfactory advantage in efficiency. To reduce the additional
communication cost and additional encryption and decryption operations, a
novel technique, compact Diffie-Hellman handshakes, is designed. It seals the
Diffie-Hellman key bases for all the routers and the software provider in a single integer. For each router, to generate his session key, he needs his private
key and a key base initially sealed by the software user and then recovered by
cooperation of all the previous routers in the course of routing. As only one single integer is needed in each onion packet to commit to all the Diffie-Hellman
key bases, a very small amount of additional communication is employed and
very few additional encryption (decryption) operations are needed.

In the optimised two-way onion routing, an onion packet consists of three
parts: message, route list and key base. Route list contains the identities of
all the nodes on the route. Key base is the base to generate the session keys
(symmetric keys) distributed to the routers. The message part in the optimised
two-way onion routing is similar to that in most onion routing schemes. The

---

[3]The integers used in public key crypto (except for elliptic curve) are usually much larger
than the integers employed in block cipher.

message is encrypted in a chain using the sessions keys of all the routers. Like in the routing protocol in Section 5.3.2 an efficient block cipher is employed in the encryption chain. In the optimised two-way onion routing, the route list is similar to that in other onion routing schemes. It consists of all the routers' identities. One block cipher encryption chain is used to seal each router's identity using the session keys of the all the routers before it.

The most important novel technique in the optimisation is generation and update of the key base, which enables key exchanges for all the routers' session keys. Each router builds his session key on the base of the key base using his private key and updates the key base for the next router. The key generation function employs the principle of Diffie-Hellman assumption, but it does not employ separate Diffie-Hellman handshakes to distribute the session keys to the routers. Instead the key base updating mechanism actually generates a key base chain and so all the session keys and their generation functions are linked in a compact chain structure. The technique is called the compact Diffie-Hellman key exchange. After obtaining his session key, each router extracts the identity of the next router from the route list using his session key, removes one layer of encryption from the message and the route list using his session key and then forwards the onion packet to the next router. Compact Diffie-Hellman key exchange only needs the bandwidth of one integer, and thus is much more efficient than separate key exchanges in communication.

As in the routing protocol in Section 5.3.2, for simplicity, in description of the optimised two-way onion routing protocol, simple denotations are employed. We suppose that an inquiry package m is sent by a software user through n routers $P_1, P_2, \ldots, P_n$ to the software provider P_{n+1} and then through routers $P_{n+2}, P_{n+3}, \ldots, P_{2n+1}$ back to himself with an inquiry result from the software provider although the two sets of routers may actually differ in quantity and share some routers. The optimised two-way onion routing protocol is as follows.

1. Firstly, the software user generates the session keys $k_1, k_2, \ldots, k_{2n+1}$ respectively for $P_1, P_2, \ldots, P_{2n+1}$ as follows.

    (a) The software user randomly chooses an integer s_1 from Z_q.

    (b) The software user calculates P_1's session key $k_1 = y_1^{s_1} \bmod p$.

    (c) The software user calculates $s_2 = s_1 + k_1 \bmod q$.

    (d) The software user calculates P_2's session key $k_2 = y_2^{s_2} \bmod p$.

    $\ldots \ldots$

    $\ldots \ldots$

    (e) The software user calculates $s_{2n+1} = s_{2n} + k_{2n} \bmod q$.

    (f) The software user calculates P_{2n+1}'s session key $k_{2n+1} = y_{2n+1}^{s_{2n+1}} \bmod p$.

Generally speaking, for $i = 1, 2, \ldots, 2n + 1$,

(a) If $i > 1$ the software user calculates $s_i = s_{i-1} + k_{i-1} \bmod q$ as his secret seed to generate k_i.

(b) He then calculates $k_i = y_i^{s_i} \bmod p$ where s_1 is randomly chosen from Z_q.

In summary, the software user uses the sum of the previous router's session key and his secret seed in generating the previous router's session key as his secret seed to generate a router's session key. The other secret seed to generate the router's session key is the router's own private key.

2. The software user generates an onion packet containing an inquiry package, a key base and a route list. The inquiry package m contains at least the input to a cloud software and an anonymous token enabling him to use the software and is encrypted into $e = E_{k_1, k_2, \ldots, k_{n+1}}(P_{n+1}, m)$. The key base is g^{s_1}. The route list consists of $p_1, p_2, \ldots, p_{2n+2}$ where $p_i = E_{k_1, k_2, \ldots, k_i}(P_{i+1})$ for $i = 1, 2, \ldots, 2n+1$ and $P_{n+2} = S$. The initial onion

$$O_1 = (a_1, b_1, c_{1,1}, c_{1,2}, \ldots, c_{1,2n+1}) = (e, g^{s_1}, p_1, p_2, \ldots, p_{2n+1})$$

is sent to P_1.

3. P_1 receives O_1 from the software user and then operates as follows.

(a) P_1 generates his session key $k_1 = b_1^{x_1} \bmod p$.

(b) P_1 uses k_1 to decrypt $c_{1,1}$ and obtains $P_2 = D_{k_1}(c_{1,1})$.

(c) P_1 calculates the new key base $b_2 = b_1 g^{k_1} \bmod p$.

Finally, P_1 sends

$$O_2 = (a_2, b_2, c_{2,1}, c_{2,2}, \ldots, c_{2,2n+1})$$

to P_2 where $a_2 = D_{k_1}(a_1)$ and $c_{2,i} = D_{k_1}(c_{1,i+1})$ for $i = 1, 2, \ldots, 2n$ and $c_{2,2n+1}$ is a random ciphertext in the ciphertext space of the employed block encryption algorithm.

4. More generally, for $i = 2, 3, \ldots, n$ each P_i receives $O_i = (a_i, b_i, c_{i,1}, c_{i,2}, \ldots c_{i,2n+1})$ and operates as follows.

(a) P_i generates his session key $k_i = b_i^{x_i} \bmod p$.

(b) P_i uses k_i to decrypt $c_{i,1}$ and obtains $P_{i+1} = D_{k_i}(c_{i,1})$.

(c) P_i calculates the new key base $b_{i+1} = b_i g^{k_i} \bmod p$.

Finally, P_i sends

$$O_{i+1} = (a_{i+1}, b_{i+1}, c_{i+1,1}, c_{i+1,2}, \ldots, c_{i+1,2n+1})$$

to P_{i+1} where $a_{i+1} = D_{k_i}(a_i)$ and $c_{i+1,j} = D_{k_i}(c_{i,j+1})$ for $j = 1, 2, \ldots, 2n$ and $c_{i+1,2n+1}$ is a random ciphertext in the ciphertext space of the employed symmetric encryption algorithm.

5. After the routing by $P_1, P_2, \ldots, P_n$, the software provider P_{n+1} receives

$$O_{n+1} = (a_{n+1}, b_{n+1}, c_{n+1,1}, c_{n+1,2}, \ldots, c_{n+1,2n+1})$$

and operates as follows.

(a) P_{n+1} generates his session key $k_{n+1} = b_{n+1}^{x_{n+1}} \bmod p$.

(b) P_{n+1} uses k_{n+1} to decrypt $c_{n+1,1}$ and obtains P_{n+2}.

(c) P_{n+1} uses k_{n+1} to decrypt a_{n+1} and obtains the inquiry package m and his own identity P_{n+1}. He knows that he is the software provider as P_{n+1} is his own identity. He verifies validity of the anonymous token, runs the software using the input in m, obtains an output R, and generates $a_{n+2} = (E_m(R), H(m))$ where $E_m()$ denotes symmetric encryption using key m and $H()$ is a one-way and collision-free hash function.

(d) P_{n+1} sends

$$O_{n+2} = (a_{n+2}, b_{n+2}, c_{n+2,1}, c_{n+2,2}, \ldots, c_{n+2,2n+1})$$

to P_{n+2} where $b_{n+2} = b_{n+1} g^{k_{n+1}} \bmod p$ and $c_{n+2,j} = D_{k_{n+1}}(c_{n+1,j+1})$ for $j = 1, 2, \ldots, 2n$ and $c_{n+2,2n+1}$ is a random ciphertext in the ciphertext space of the employed symmetric encryption algorithm.

6. For $i = n+2, n+3, \ldots, 2n+1$ each router P_i routes the onion packet as follows where the onion he receives is in the form $O_i = (a_i, b_i, c_{i,1}, c_{i,2}, \ldots, c_{i,2n+1})$.

(a) P_i generates his session key $k_i = b_i^{x_i} \bmod p$.

(b) P_i uses k_i to decrypt $c_{i,1}$ and obtains $P_{i+1} = D_{k_i}(c_{i,1})$.

(c) P_i calculates the new key base $b_{i+1} = b_i g^{k_i} \bmod p$.

Finally, P_i sends

$$O_{i+1} = (a_{i+1}, b_{i+1}, c_{i+1,1}, c_{i+1,2}, \ldots, c_{i+1,2n+1})$$

to P_{i+1} where $a_{i+1} = D_{k_i}(a_i)$ and $c_{i+1,j} = D_{k_i}(c_{i,j+1})$ for $j = 1, 2, \ldots, 2n$ and $c_{i+1,2n+1}$ is a random ciphertext in the ciphertext space of the employed symmetric encryption algorithm.

7. After the routing by $P_{n+2}, P_{n+3}, \ldots, P_{2n+1}$, the software user S receives

$$O_{2n+2} = (a_{2n+2}, b_{2n+2}, c_{2n+2,1}, c_{2n+2,2}, \ldots, c_{2n+2,2n+1})$$

and operates as follows.

(a) S calculates $k = b_{2n+2}^{x} \bmod p$ where x is his own private key.

(b) S tries to use k to decrypt $c_{2n+2,1}$ but does not obtain a legal identity. He knows that he is not a router or software provider of the onion packet. The only possibility is that his own onion packet is returned by the software provider.

(c) S calculates $(\rho, \tau) = E_{k_{n+2}, k_{n+3}, \ldots, k_{2n+1}}(a_{2n+2})$. If $\tau = H(m)$, he is ensured that the software provider P_{n+1} returns him an encrypted inquiry result. He can extract the inquiry result as $R = D_m(\rho)$ where $D_m()$ denotes symmetric decryption using key m.

The new key exchange mechanism improves efficiency of the two-way onion routing technique. As most of its operations depend on symmetric encryptions and decryptions and employ small (in comparison with the large integers in asymmetric cipher operations) integers and the number of asymmetric cipher operations is minimized, efficiency of onion routing is not compromised after it is extended to support two-way anonymous communication.

5.3.4   Security Analysis

Security of the optimised two-way onion routing scheme depends on hardness of the Diffie-Hellman problem as its key exchange mechanism is an extension of Diffie-Hellman key exchange. Its main trick is combining key exchanges into a compact chain such that every router can obtain his session key with the help of previous routers. As security of Diffie-Hellman key exchange has been formally proved and hardness of the Diffie-Hellman problem is widely accepted, no further proof of security is needed except for Theorem 22, which shows that the session keys can be correctly exchanged.

Theorem 22 *For $i = 1, 2, \ldots, 2n + 1$, the same session key k_i is generated, respectively by the software user as $k_i = y_i^{s_i} \bmod p$ and by P_i as $k_i = b_i^{x_i} \bmod p$.*

To prove Theorem 22, a lemma has to be proved first.

Lemma 13 *For $i = 1, 2, \ldots, 2n + 1$, $b_i = g^{s_i} \bmod p$.*

Proof: Mathematical induction is used.

1. When $i = 1$, $b_1 = g^{s_1} \bmod p$.

2. Suppose when $i = j$ and $j \geq 1$ it is still satisfied that $b_i = g^{s_i} \bmod p$. Then a deduction can be made in next step.

3. When $i = j + 1$, $b_{j+1} = b_j g^{k_j} = g^{s_j} g^{k_j} \bmod p$ as expected in the last step that $b_i = g^{s_i}$ when $i = j$,

$$b_{j+1} = g^{s_j} g^{k_j} = g^{s_j + k_j} = g^{s_{j+1}} \bmod p$$

Therefore, $b_i = g^{s_i} \bmod p$ for $j = 1, 2, \ldots, 2n + 1$ as a result of mathematical induction. □

Proof of Theorem 22:
According to Lemma 13,

$$y_i^{s_i} = g^{x_i s_i} = b_i^{x_i} \bmod p$$

for $i = 1, 2, \ldots, 2n + 1$. □

The new solution allows users caring about their privacy to use paid cloud software online anonymously. The users buy anonymous tokens to access the softwares they need and employ an efficient two-way onion routing network to communicate with the software providers.

Chapter 6

Practical Systems to Achieve Anonymity: How to Use Them

Suppose there is a user who wants to be anonymous when using the Internet. There are several anonymous communciation systems he can employ. Besides Tor which has been extensively discussed in this book, there are some similar tools as alternatives. They include I2P, JAP/JonDo and QuickSilver. A brief guide is provided in this chapter on installation and usage of these tools. Their usability can be evaluated according to the following standards.

- CT1 Successfully install the anonymization software and the components.

- CT2 Successfully configure the browser (email client in Mixmaster/QuickSilver case) to work with the anonymization software.

- CT3 Confirm that the web-traffic/email is anonymized.

- CT4 Successfully disable the anonymization software and return to a direct connection.

- G1 Users should be aware of the steps they have to perform to complete a core task.

- G2 Users should be able to determine how to perform the steps.

- G3 Users should know when they have successfully completed a core task.

- G4 Users should be able to recognize, diagnose, and recover from non-critical errors.

- G5 Users should not make risky errors from which they cannot recover.

- G6 Users should be comfortable with the terminology used in any interface dialogues or documentation.

- G7 Users should be sufficiently comfortable with the interface to continue using it.

- G8 Users should be aware of the status of the application at all times.

6.1 Installation and Usage of Tor

Tor is the most famous and frequently used anonymous communication network and it is provided through http://www.torproject.org/.

6.1.1 Download and Installation

Tor's project website presents a good starting point to achieve anonymity in the Internet, i.e., to accomplish the tasks CT-1 to CT-3. A user can choose on the website between many languages. The website itself has a clear layout. Additionally, the operators of the site use a simple and natural language (conforms with G6). A general explanation on how Tor works is given directly on the first page. Furthermore, a user can find some helpful examples of typical Tor users as well as some links to more detailed information. The start page of Tor contains three statements under the title "three pieces of fine print". They clearly state that anonymity in the Internet via Tor may only be achieved if and only if Tor is used correctly. A link to a list of some warnings is given with the aim to prevent the user from fatal errors (conforms with G5).

The statements declare that despite a correct use of Tor, there are still possible attacks that compromise user's protection (conforms with G5). Further, the statements make it clear that no anonymity system is perfect and thus users with a demand for strong anonymity should not rely on Tor. Both last declarations provide clarity. However, some users might become scared. This is a dilemma which is not easy to solve. We believe that a good explanation of the circumstances the Tor site provides is the best way to deal with the dilemma.

The "Summary" navigation on the right side of the first page contains a button labeled "Download Tor". A click on the button leads to a download page (conforms with G1, G2). Next, users have the opportunity to choose between two Windows installation bundles and one for OS X. An inconsistent point to G1 and G2 is reflected in the absence of a hint to an installation manual. However, if the user clicks on "See advanced choices" she gets to

Figure 6.1: Installing Tor

another site which contains links to a step-by-step installation manual as well as more download choices.

A filename for the download "Vidalia-bundle" is suggested. The same name is also used during the installation process for the Tor package (see Figure 6.1). The name is not announced and therefore a novice user might be scared away due to a missing explanation on the link between the terms of "Vidalia" and "Tor". In the first dialog of the installation the user can choose between nine different languages. Unfortunately, not every one of the following dialogs is fully translated. Moreover, not every dialog provides the same level of detail, e.g., the Italian version does not provide detailed information on the purposes of the different components on the second dialog. However, even the possibility to choose between different languages greatly contributes to the usability (conforms to G2, G6).

The installation process asks the user to install Vidalia (a GUI for Tor, http://www.vidalia-project.net/), Privoxy (an application layer filtering web proxy) and Torbutton (a Firefox extension). The purpose of the components is briefly explained during the installation process. In addition, the installation manual on the project's website also contains a brief description. The rest of the installation is straightforward. All this supports the user to achieve CT1 (conforms with G1, G2).

G8 is implemented through the realization of an installation progress bar which shows the progress of unpacking the program packages. Once the progress bar reaches 100%, the Firefox standard dialogue for installing extensions pops up and provides a recommendation to install add-ons only from trusted sources. With the conformation to install the extension, the installation of the Vidalia Bundle is completed. This will be illustrated in an extra dialogue together with the standard check box "Run installed components now" and link to https://www.torproject.org/docs/tor-doc-windows. At this point the confirmation screen signals the user that CT1 is completed (conforms with G3).

6.1.2   Configuration

When the Tor program is started by the user, the Vidalia control panel (see Figure 6.2) opens and connects to the Tor network. The duration of establishment of such a connection is about two minutes. However, the user is not aware of the application status (violates G8). Moroever, a window pops up to confirm successful connection to Tor as shown in Figure 6.3 In addition, there are two new icons in the task-bar installed:

- A green onion (alternative-text4: "connection to the network established")

- An animated blue circle with a white "P" (Privoxy)

In Firefox the newly installed plugin adds a cue to the status bar indicating "Tor deactivated". Once a user clicks on the cue, the message changes and the following message is displayed if the current Firefox (version 3) is used:

- Warning! Torbutton on Firefox 3 is known to leak your timezone and livemark feeds during Tor usage.

- In addition, it has not been as extensively tested for Tor security and usability as Firefox 2. Do you wish to continue anyway?

Due to the warning, a user might not know how to proceed (violates G2, G6). Through clicking on the OK button the cue switches to "Tor activated". Now the user knows that his traffic is anonymized (conforms with G8). With the standard settings Tor works immediately. No further configuration is necessary and thus CT2 is completed.

Up to now, the user receives feedback by the "green onion" that Tor is working properly. Unfortunately, the user cannot easily check if her traffic is actually relayed through the Tor network (CT3). Tor does not provide an easy to find reference like a button or bookmark to such a service, e.g., a website which checks whether the traffic is anonymized or not, although a server of the Tor project hosts a webservice which checks, if traffic was relayed through the Tor network.

CT4 can also be easily performed by clicking the cue in Firefox. After the click the traffic will no longer be relayed through the Tor network. The fact that the user has to click on the cue again can be considered as G2 compatible.

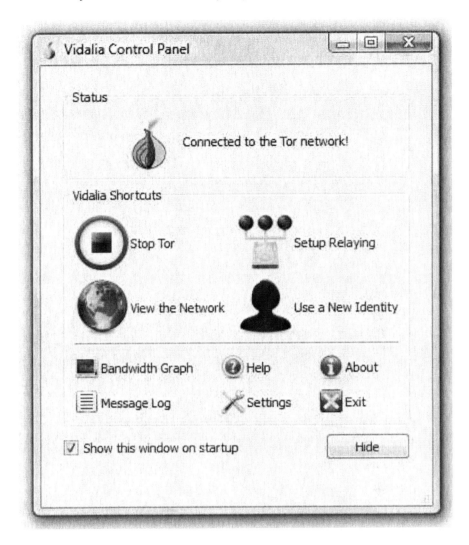

Figure 6.2: Vidalia Control Panel

6.2 Installation and Usage of I2P

I2P is another frequently used anonymous communication network and it is provided through http://www.i2p2.de.

6.2.1 Download and Installation

The Website of the I2P project is available in English and German. The page is clearly arranged and welcomes the visitor with an introduction on I2P. The introduction presents some of the supported applications, gives a brief

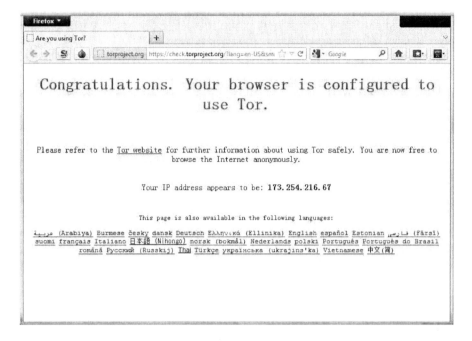

Figure 6.3: Successful Connection to Tor

statement about anonymity and mentions the fact that I2P is evolving over time and should only be used for testing and development purposes.

In the introduction are several notable aspects. Firstly, it is strange that the list of possible applications does not contain web browsing even though it is supported and one of the most important applications in the Internet. The language is technical and maybe too technical for a novice user (violates G6). The picture which explains the function of I2P is also not easy to understand (violates G1, G2). Secondly, the statement that the current software should only be used for testing and development purposes can be seen as a problematic aspect. Without an explanation of the background, the statement can distract users.

In order to complete CT1 a user needs to find the link "Download". We assume that a novice user can achieve this due to the common layout of I2P's website. After user opens the download site, she is confronted with three different downloadable versions: graphical installer, headless install and source install. The descriptions given for each version might direct novice users to download the graphical version (conforms with G2). Nevertheless, G2 and G6 are violated since the statement regarding the precondition for the installation of I2P (Sun Java 1.5 or higher, or equivalent JRE) does not refer to any manual or explanation. It is uncertain if a novice user knows Java and even knows how to install it without any help. If Java is missing, the

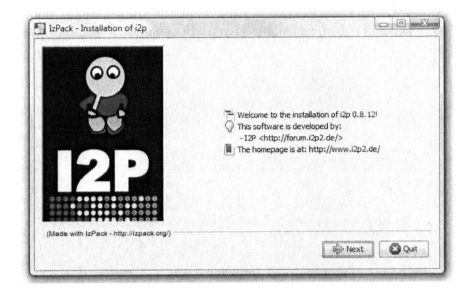

Figure 6.4: Attempted Installation of I2P

execution of the downloaded file will show "Cannot find Java 1.5.0". When the user confirms the error the installer terminates and opens the website of Sun, where the user can download Java (conforms with G1). At the same time it disregards G6, due to the too brief error description. Beginning and end of the installation of a graphical version of I2P are shown in Figure 6.4 and Figure 6.5.

In case Java is installed correctly, the installer shows in its first dialogue a small welcome message. The following procedure is similar to typical installation processes. The installation progress is as in the case of Tor displayed by a progress bar. Afterwards the user needs to decide if she wants the setup routine to create shortcuts on the user's desktop. In the last dialog, I2P signals the user that the installation process is finished. This installation procedure is straightforward and complies with G1, G2, G3 and G6; CT1 is reached.

After the user closes the installer, Windows displays a dialogue. It informs the user that the program she wanted to install has maybe not been correctly installed. In addition the dialogue offers the user two different options (see Figure 6.6). This incident clearly violates several guidelines such as G1, G2 and G8.

If a user selects the default options of the I2P installer, three icons are created on the user's desktop: "Start I2P (no window)", "Start I2P (restartable)" and "I2P router console". The same shortcuts are created in the start menu of Windows. In addition, a shortcut to an uninstall procedure is added in the start menu.

Figure 6.5: Successful Installation of I2P

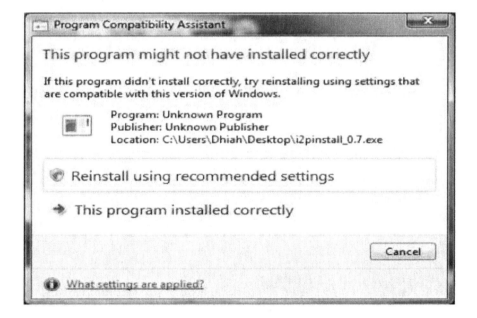

Figure 6.6: Warning Message

In order to complete CT2, with regard to the manual, the user should simply click on the "Run I2P" button which will bring up the router console with further instructions. Because there is no button or shortcut named "Run I2P" (see above which shortcuts have been created) the user does not know how to proceed (violates G1, G2). It also cannot be assumed that a novice user knows what a router console is, so G6 is disregarded. Since a router console is mentioned in the instruction, a user might click on the "I2P router console" shortcut. If the user had managed to open the I2P configuration site, the browser presents a welcome page to the user. The page has three different parts that contain a lot of information. Thus, the page appears (quite) complex. The first part is a sidebar on the left. The sidebar is divided in seven categories. Each presents information to the user, e.g., the status of the established tunnels.

The navigation bar is on the top of the page. It contains links to various services of I2P, e.g., Susimail, SusiDNS. The content area is placed under the navigation bar. The content area itself is again divided into two scopes. The first scope shows the phrase "Congratulations on getting I2P installed!" and gives further instructions on how to proceed and configure I2P. The information is displayed in English as well as in German. The second scope of the welcome page provides instructions how to use and configure different services in the I2P net as well as the Internet. This instruction is only displayed in one language, but the user is able to pick one of four languages. However, the confirmation of the successful installations fits G3 and signals again that CT1 is completed.

6.2.2 Configuration

To complete CT2 a user needs to read both instructions on the welcome page. The instructions of the first scope are similar with those on the download page. They may fulfill G1 and G2 in order to perform CT2. Unfortunately, the instructions are written in a technical language. The user is asked to adjust the bandwidth, to open port 8887 on the user's firewall and to enable "inbound TCP" on the configuration page. The instructions do clearly not address novice users (violates G6). Hence, errors in the configuration are more probable (violates G5). If the user had completed the tasks (adjusting the firewall and bandwidth settings), I2P neither provides feedback nor clearly states how the user can check if she has finished successfully the configuration of the first scope. This disregards G3.

The second scope of the content area deals with configuration of different applications and services. However, for a novice user the separation may not be understandable. Therefore it does not support users in achieving CT2 (violates G1, G2). The "browse the web" instruction refers to another part. The referred part states that the user should tell the browser "to use the HTTP proxy at localhost port 4444". Clearly, the description is not suited for a novice user:

it uses technical language (violates G6) and a user might not know how to complete the task (violates G2).

After the user finishes the instructions in both scopes, she has completed CT2. However, I2P does not present any information that the user has achieved CT2 (violates G3). Beside the mentioned shortcomings, I2P currently also presents too many tasks and options to the user. It hinders her from using I2P comfortably (violates G7) and safely; the latter is due to the fact that the more users tweak their settings, the more likely they can be identified by an adversary because of their individual behaviour.

Now, if the user finishes the configuration within a short time frame, she might receive the following error message, after she has requested a website:

> The WWW Outproxy was not found. It is offline, there is network congestion, or your router is not yet well-integrated with peers. You may want to retry as this will randomly reselect an outproxy from the pool you have defined here (if you have more than one configured). If you continue to have trouble you may want to edit your outproxy list here.
> Could not find the following destination:
> http://some-URL/
> WWW proxy: false.i2p.

The message displayed is another example that the authors of I2P fail to use a non-technical language (violates G6). A novice user might not understand the message. Thus, she does not know how to proceed (violates G1, G2). Just by waiting some minutes the user will be able to open the same website successfully. This behaviour might not be understandable for the user (violates G8).

Verification and deactivation of I2P: Since I2P offers neither an application nor a link to the user, she cannot check if her traffic is anonymized or not (CT3). In order to check whether CT3 was successfully finished, the user needs to compare her own (real) IP address with the one a receiver gets with her request. Again, this is probably too difficult for a novice user. CT4 can be performed by clicking a "shutdown" link the configuration page. But as this just turns off I2P, the user additionally has to reverse the configuration in the browser, too. Due to the fact that the initial configuration step violated G2 and G6, it is clear that the reverse action does the same.

6.3   Installation and Usage of JAP/JonDo

The JAP/JonDo anonymizer is known under various names and is called JonDo here. The name was established by the commercial anonymization service JonDonym. The service as well as the software build upon the AN.ON project and its client. The client software of the AN.ON project is JAP. Even though JonDonym is a commercial service some of the mix cascades are freely available. It is provided through http://www.jondos.de/.

6.3.1   Download and Installation

The JonDo website is available in English and German. G6 is satisfied through an explanation and an illustration of how JonDo works. The illustration can be found directly on the first website. An issue worth mentioning is that there are no hints on possible dangers or attacks, contrary to other examined websites (violates G5).

A download button is visible on the left-hand side, so the user is aware of the next steps she has to do (conforms with G1, G2). With a click on the button a user can choose between different JonDo versions, namely for Windows, Linux and MacOS X. At this point an explanation is given that no registration is required and "the software and simple services it provides access for, are free of charge". Further, it is clearly declared that payment is only required for the optional premium services. The premium services offer a higher speed and better security by allocating enough cascades for the connection, providing longer mix cascades which are typically spread over several countries and offer all Internet ports for usage, whereas the free services only allow web surfing.

On the download site some additional information can be found. Firstly, some installations hints and an easy to use "download button" are presented to the visitors of the website (conforms with G2). Secondly, an announcement is made that the installation process of JonDo does not make any changes that affect the user's computer. It simply copies the JonDo packages to a default directory or to another directory the user may choose. Thirdly, an introduction to browser configuration is given for the reason that each browser used along with JonDo has to be individually configured. This declaration refers to a wizard that helps the user through such a configuration. The wizard starts when the application is executed for the first time (conforms with G1, G2). Alternatively, users have the option to use a preconfigured browser named JonDoFox instead of configuring the browser on their own. The JonDoFox browser is recommended by the JonDo provider in order to eliminate non-recoverable errors (conforms with G5). Fourthly, the website provides users with some information about the downloadable files. Fifthly, the download page provides some information how to update the JonDo software. Sixthly, a recommendation is given to the user to check the authenticity of the down-loaded file. Beside the recommendation, the download page provides the user with a reference how she can perform the authenticity check. The last part of the page briefly states that the user is allowed to distribute the software (conforms to G1, G2).

The user is directed to another web page if she chooses to install the Windows version. On this page she has the choice to install the JonDo desktop or the JonDo portable version. Both versions require Java 1.3 or higher to

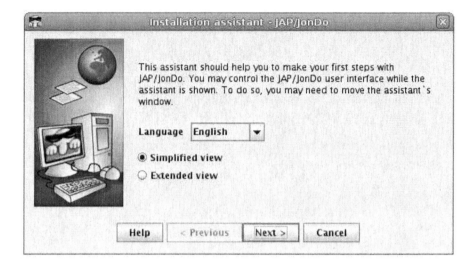

Figure 6.7: Installation Assistant

work. For this purpose, a link to the Java homepage (http://java.com/) is given. However, if the user has not installed Java, the installer will install Java 1.3 on the user's computer. There is no indication about the purpose of Java (violates G6). The default name for the installation package is given as japsetup.exe. Such a name may not be expected since JAP is the name of the client software in the AN.ON project which might be confusing for some users (violates G6). The application version number is specified above the navigation menu on the left side, but the version number is specified neither on the download page nor on the package name. This is not contradictory to any of the guidelines as presented earlier. However, more clarity on the version number can be useful for users, for example, when checking for updates.

The installation process starts with a dialogue where the installation components can be chosen. As a preselected configuration JAP, Swing and Java 1.3 are set. In the dialogue, the JAP name is used five times instead of JonDo. It may bother the users and thus be in conflict with G6, because it is not necessary to know that JAP is a different name of JonDo. Moreover, it might violate G2. A clearly defined name which can be used continuously will be more comprehensible. After the installation process, the installer informs the user that the installation was successful. CT1 is reached. Two installation interface pictures are shown in Figure 6.7 and Figure 6.8.

6.3.2   Configuration

At the first start of the JonDo application a wizard starts to configure JAP/JonDo in the respective browsers. An explanation is given on how to use the JAP/JonDo proxy settings for each of the browsers. The used language is

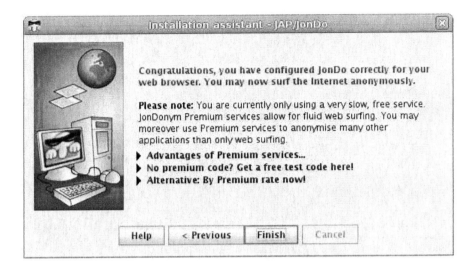

Figure 6.8: Configuration Confirmation

non-technical (conforms with G6) and offers a straightforward description of the single steps (conforms with G2). Warnings are displayed once the user tries to open a website, if JAP/JonDo is switched off. In order to test the connection to the anonymity service, the user will be directed to switch anonymity on and to surf the Internet. Due to the interface (see Figure 6.9) this is straightforward. In our examination, the test was not achievable because a timeout limitation had occurred. The fact that a connection was established, but no website has been presented, indicates to the user that she should choose the option "Connection established but web surfing impossible" in the configuration wizard. Subsequently, the wizard requests to choose the cascade with the name "Dresden Dresden" and prompt browsing in the web becomes possible.

Guidance to disable Java, JavaScript, ActiveX, Flash, etc. according to the type of browser is given in the next dialogue of the wizard, as these web technologies threaten the user's privacy and can be used by adversaries to circumvent network layer anonymization. Next, a dialogue is presented with the option to run JonDo in either a simple or an extended view. A link is given to the JonDo FAQ and at last a confirmation screen of a successful configuration of JAP/JonDo is shown by the wizard. Thus, it gives the user a feedback that CT2 is achieved (conforms with G3). The step-by-step wizard has been proven as a good way to prevent users from making errors throughout the configuration of JonDo (conforms with G4, G5) and is simple to understand (conforms with G6). Further, the wizard can be restarted from the JonDo application and in this manner supports G4.

Verification and deactivation of JonDo: An anonymity test is available on the JonDo website which shows transmitted information from the visiting system (conforms with G3). CT4 can be achieved by clicking the "anonymity

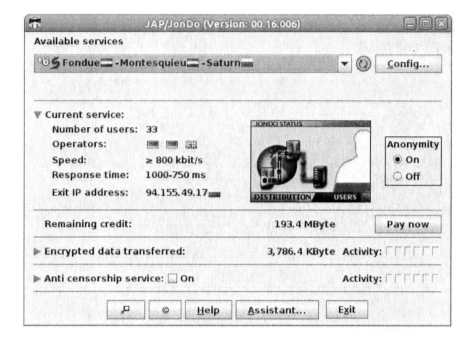

Figure 6.9: JonDo Anonymity Switch

off" switch. When a user clicks on the button a message is displayed that JonDo does not support any protection further on (conforms with G1, G2, G3).

6.4   Installation and Usage of QuickSilver

QuickSilver is a kind of so-called Mixmaster client, which is used for email messaging and usenet. It is provided through http://mixmaster.sourceforge.net.

6.4.1   Download and Installation

The QuickSilver website uses a simple layout and consists of pure textual content. An introduction about QuickSilver, how it works and why it is interesting to use is given at the beginning of the website. The author of the site states that QuickSilver provides complete privacy. Therefore, a message which is sent via the QuickSilver client cannot be traced backward in order to identify the sender. The language of the website is simple and non-technical (conforms with G6). The fact that QuickSilver is just a user interface for Mixmaster is explained on the website. In addition, it is stated that only one person, Richard Christman, develops the client. In order to download the package a hyperlink is given in conjunction with a hint to read the welcome.txt file of

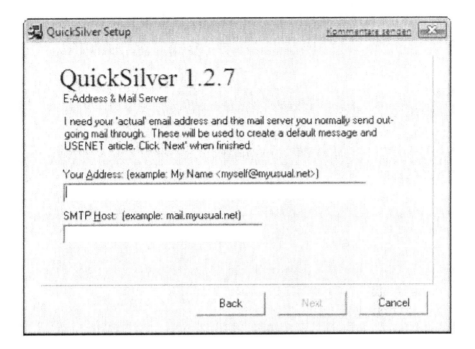

Figure 6.10: QuickSilver Warning Message

the client packages. Thus, a user can determine how to perform the remaining steps (conforms with G2).

The installation process can be started after downloading the file QS1.2.7.exe. A dialogue pops up and by pressing the setup button a wizard installation program starts. The user has the opportunity to select an installation directory or to use the default suggestion offered by the wizard. In addition, she can decide whether a shortcut to her desktop should be added as well as whether a program group should be created. Such a step is known by users (conforms with G2).

The second dialogue demands the user to provide her email address and an SMTP host (Figure 6.10). To help the user to fill in the required information a text and two examples are given. The text explains for what purpose the email address and the mail server are used. In addition, some examples are provided. Both the text and the two examples illustrate a violation to G6 because users may feel confused (violates G6). Considering the examples alone, the user cannot find out how to complete the step (violates G2).

The last dialogue of the installation process gives an overview of the options which have been chosen in the configuration. A confirmation will be given as soon as the installation is completed. Thus a user recognizes that she reached CT1 (conforms with G3). The wizard style installation helps to avoid nonrecoverable errors. Due to the "next" and "back" options, a user can easily change incorrect statements made during the installation process (conforms with G5).

6.4.2 Configuration

As soon as QuickSilver has been started, a prompt pops up to inform the user that Mixmaster is not installed despite being an essential component. A button labelled with non-technical language (conforms with G6) "Get Mixmaster" indicates the next step (conforms with G2). If the user clicks on "Get Mixmaster" a wizard is started. In the first dialogue some information is presented to the user. The information points to the source code of QuickSilver and provides the user with an email address in case a bug is discovered. The user's only possibility is to confirm this information. Afterward the installer asks the user to pick an FTP site from a dropdown list. If the user does not know the word FTP, she cannot proceed from this point (violates G6). Once the user chooses the default site, the wizard shows a list of available updates among other Mixmaster (Mix29b39.zip). A user might be swamped due to the possibilities offered by the list (violates G2, G6).

After downloading the Mixmaster package of QuickSilver, the user can start the install routine which is similar to the QuickSilver installer. Unfortunately, some very technical terms are used without a good explanation (violates G6):

> In actual use, this will be the directory where Mixmaster looks for 'mix.cfg' and QuickSilver looks for 'mixlib.dll' and 'libeay32.dll'.

In order to obtain some random data for the initialization of the random mix pool, the install routine asks the user in the next dialogue to write her name using the mouse. This illustrates a distinct instruction even if the user does not know its purpose (conforms with G6). The user can observe the progress of the pool initialization via an indicator that displays the progress in percentage. The progress advances according to the user's mouse writing. As soon as the indicator reaches 100% an "install" button becomes available. Once the Mixmaster setup is completed, it will be announced by a confirmation screen (conforms with G3).

Consequently, the QuickSilver interface opens and indicates that QuickSilver is ready to be used. Unfortunately, the GUI offers various buttons whose functionality is unclear (violates G7). The help system of QuickSilver provides a Quickstart section; sadly the steps specified in the section take a lot of time to be performed. This might appear as the opposite of quick. Chapter "I-8 Anonymous Messages" of the help system describes how to use QuickSilver to send anonymous messages. Additionally, it explains the interface "New Message". Unfortunately, the interface has a non-standard design. Thus, users are probably not familiar with its handling from other programs or applications. In essence, it contains a text field with predefined values where users have the possibility to edit or add some parameters. CT214 cannot be achieved with such a design. It is not intuitive. In addition, it does not prevent the user from making erroneous inputs (violates G5, G7).

As soon as the user has composed a test message and pressed the "Send" button, a dialogue appears with the note "Mixmaster Remailer Document is missing". This means that CT2 is not fulfilled yet. Up to this point, the user had no chance to recognize this problem (violates G1). In order to lead the user through the configuration step, a "Get documents" button is offered (conforms with G2). After clicking on the button, a dialogue with several other options is displayed. Here the user has the opportunity to specify URLs for the download of the missing files, e.g., "mlist.txt" or "pubring.mix". In addition, a reference is provided, where the user can get a brief explanation about the needed files (conforms with G2). After reading the help notes, executing the instructions (check mlist.txt and rlist.txt) and clicking update, the application fetches new remailers and keys.

The whole procedure is too complicated and opaque for a user who has not read the complete manual. After a user has managed to receive the files and tries to send a message, the process quits with an error message: "No reliable remailers!". In order to solve the problem, the user needs to seek new sources of so-called remailer stats and keys. However, even for an average user the procedure is too demanding (violates G2, G6). Moreover, the software fails to send the message through the mail server entered during the installation process. The reason for the failure was that no credentials were specified for the mail server. Thus, a user needs to enter her credentials for the outbound mail server to send anonymous email. Unfortunately, there is no hint given where to enter such information. Therefore, a user has to find it herself (violates G2). The whole configuration process is very complex and normal users have no chance to master this task.

References

[1] Complaints and enquiries statistics to end of december 2005. 2005. Available as `http://www.privacy.gov.au/about/complaints/index.html`.

[2] Information technology and internet issues. 2005. Available as `http://www.privacy.gov.au/internet/index.html`.

[3] Privacy act regulations. 2005. Available as `http://www.privacy.gov.au/publications/PSRegs17122005.pdf`.

[4] Protecting your privacy on the internet. 2005. Available as `http://www.privacy.gov.au/internet/internet_privacy/#2`.

[5] M Abe. Mix-networks on permutation net-works. In *ASIACRYPT '98*, Volume 1716 of *Lecture Notes in Computer Science*, pages 258–273, Berlin, 1999. Springer-Verlag.

[6] Masayuki Abe and Fumitaka Hoshino. Remarks on mix-network based on permutation networks. In *Public Key Cryptography 2001*, Volume 1992 of *Lecture Notes in Computer Science*, pages 317–324, Berlin, 2001. Springer-Verlag.

[7] Masayuki Abe and Hideki Imai. Flaws in robust optimistic mix-nets and stronger security notions. In *IEICE Transactions on Fundamentals of Electronics, Communications and Computer Sciences*, 2006, E89-A(1), pages 99–105.

[8] Masayuki Abe and Hideki Imai. Flaws in some robust optimistic mix-nets. In *ACISP 2003*, Volume 2727 of *Lecture Notes in Computer Science*, pages 39–50, Berlin, 2003. Springer-Verlag.

[9] James M. Adler, Wei Dai, Richard L. Green, and C. Andrew Neff. Computational details of the votehere homomorphic election system. Technical report, VoteHere Inc, 2000. Available from http://www.votehere.net/technicaldocs/hom.pdf, last accessed 22 June 2002.

[10] B Adida and D Wikstrom. How to shuffle in public. In *Theory of Cryptography 2007*, Volume 4392 of *Lecture Notes in Computer Science*, pages 555–574, Berlin, 2007. Springer-Verlag.

[11] R Avanzi, H Cohen, C Doche, G Frey, T Lange, K Nguyen and F Vercauteren. Handbook of Elliptic and Hyperelliptic Curve Cryptography. HEHCC, 2005.

[12] Olivier Baudron, Pierre-Alain Fouque, David Pointcheval, Guillaume Poupard, and Jacques Stern. Practical multi-candidate election system. In *PODC '01*, pages 274–283, 2001.

[13] Z Beerliova-Trubiniova and M Hirt. Efficient multi-party computation with dispute control. In *TCC '06*, Volume 3876 of *Lecture Notes in Computer Science*, pages 305–328, Berlin, 2006. Springer-Verlag.

[14] P Bogetoft, D Christensen, I Damgard, M Geisler, T Jakobsen, M Kroigaard, J Nielsen, J Nielsen, K Nielsen, and J Pagter. Secure multiparty computation goes live. In *Financial Cryptography and Data Security 2009*, volume 5628 of *Lecture Notes in Computer Science*, pages 325–343, Berlin, 2009, Springer-Verlag.

[15] Dan Boneh and Philippe Golle. Almost entirely correct mixing with applications to voting. In *Proceedings of the 9th ACM Conference on Computer and Communications Security*, pages 68–77, 2002.

[16] E. Goh D. Boneh and K. Nissim. Evaluating 2-dnf formulas on ciphertexts. In *TCC '05*, volume 3378 of *Lecture Notes in Computer Science*, pages 325–341, 2005, Berlin, 2005, Springer-Verlag.

[17] Fabrice Boudot. Efficient proofs that a committed number lies in an interval. In *EUROCRYPT '00*, volume 1807 of *Lecture Notes in Computer Science*, pages 431–444, Berlin, 2000. Springer-Verlag.

[18] D Brin. The transparent society: will technology force us to choose between privacy and freedom? In *Perseus BooksReading, 1999*.

[19] J Camenisch, R Chaabouni, and A Shelat. Efficient protocols for set membership and range proofs. In *ASIACRYPT '08*, Volume 3089 of *Lecture Notes in Computer Science*, pages 234–252, Berlin, 2008. Springer-Verlag.

[20] J Camenisch and A Mityagin. A formal treatment of onion routing. In *CRYPTO '05*, Volume 3089 of *Lecture Notes in Computer Science*, pages 169–187, Berlin, 2005. Springer-Verlag.

[21] J Camenisch and A Mityagin. A formal treatment of onion routing. In *CRYPTO '05*, Volume 3089 of *Lecture Notes in Computer Science*, pages 169–187, Berlin, 2005. Springer-Verlag.

[22] Ran Canetti, Cynthia Dwork, Moni Naor, and Rafail Ostrovsky. Deniable encryption. In *CRYPTO '97*, Volume 1294 of *Lecture Notes in Computer Science*, pages 90–104, Berlin, 1997. Springer-Verlag.

[23] R Chaabouni, H Lipmaa, and A Shelat. Additive Combinatorics and Discrete Logarithm Based Range Protocols. In *ACISP '10, LNCS6168*, pages 336-351.

[24] A Chan, Y Frankel, and Y Tsiounis. Easy come - easy go divisible cash. updated version with corrections. 1998. Available as http://www.ccs.neu.edu/home/yiannis/.

[25] D Chaum. Untraceable electronic mail, return address and digital pseudonym. *Communications of the ACM, 24(2)*, pages 84–88, 1981.

[26] D. Chaum, A. Fiat, and M. Naor. Untraceable electronic cash. In *CRYPTO '88*, Volume 403 of *Lecture Notes in Computer Science*, pages 319–327, Berlin, 1989. Springer-Verlag.

[27] D Chaum and T Pedersen. Wallet databases with observers. In *CRYPTO '92*, Volume 740 of *Lecture Notes in Computer Science*, pages 89–105, Berlin, 1992. Springer-Verlag.

[28] R Cramer, I Damgård, and B Schoenmakers. Proofs of partial knowledge and simplified design of witness hiding protocols. In *CRYPTO '94*, Volume 839 of *Lecture Notes in Computer Science*, pages 174–187, Berlin, 1994. Springer-Verlag.

[29] Ronald Cramer, Ivan Damgård, and Jesper Buus Nielsen. Multiparty computation from threshold homomorphic encryption. In *EUROCRYPT '01*, Volume 2045 of *Lecture Notes in Computer Science*, pages 280–299, Berlin, 2001. Springer.

[30] I Damgård and M. Jurik. A generalisation, a simplification and some applications of Paillier's probabilistic public-key system. In *PKC '01*, Volume 1992 of *Lecture Notes in Computer Science*, pages 119–136, Berlin, 2001. Springer-Verlag.

[31] I Damgård, M Geisler, M Kroigaard, and J Nielsen. Asynchronous multiparty computation: Theory and implementation. In *Eurocrypt '09*, Volume 5443 of *Lecture Notes in Computer Science*, pages 160–179, Berlin, 2009, Springer-Verlag.

[32] I Damgård, Y Ishai, M Kroigaard, J Nielsen, and A Smith. Scalable multiparty computation with nearly optimal work and resilience. In *Crypto '08*, Volume 5157 of *Lecture Notes in Computer Science*, pages 241–261, Berlin, 2008. Springer-Verlag.

[33] Yvo Desmedt and Kaoru Kurosawa. How to break a practical mix and design a new one. In *EUROCRYPT '00*, Volume 1807 of *Lecture Notes in Computer Science*, pages 557–572, Berlin, 2005. Springer-Verlag.

[34] R. Dingledine, N. Mathewson, and P. F. Syverson. Tor: The second-generation onion router. In *USENIX SecuritySymposium*, page 303–320, 2004.

[35] R Granchib F Martinellib M Petrocchib F Baiardia, A Fallenib and A Vaccarellib. Seas, a secure e-voting protocol: Design and implementationstar, open. In *Computers & Security*, Volume 24, Issue 8, November 2005, pages 642–652.

[36] P Feldman. A practical scheme for non-interactive verifiable secret sharing. In *FOCS '87*, pages 427–437.

[37] Pierre-Alain Fouque, Guillaume Poupard, and Jacques Stern. Sharing decryption in the context of voting or lotteries. In *Financial Cryptography 2000*, Volume 1962, pages 90–104, Berlin, 2000, Springer-Verlag.

[38] AM Froomkin. Flood control on the information ocean: living with anonymity, digital cash and distributed databases. In *University of Pittsburgh Journal of Law and Commerce* 15, pages 395–515, 1996.

[39] M Froomkin. Legal issues in anonymity and pseudonymity. In *The Information Society*, Volume 15, Issue 2, pages 113–127, 1999.

[40] J. Furukawa. Efficient, verifiable shuffle decryption and its requirement of unlinkability. In *PKC 2004*, Volume 2947 of *Lecture Notes in Computer Science*, pages 319–332, Berlin, 2004. Springer-Verlag.

[41] J. Furukawa. Efficient and verifiable shuffling and shuffle-decryption. In *IEICE Transactions 88-A(1)*, pages 172–188, 2005.

[42] Jun Furukawa and Kazue Sako. An efficient scheme for proving a shuffle. In *CRYPTO '01*, Volume 2139 of *Lecture Notes in Computer Science*, pages 368–387, Berlin, 2001. Springer-Verlag.

[43] R Gennaro, S Jarecki, H Krawczyk, and T Rabin. Secure distributed key generation for discrete-log based cryptosystems. In *EUROCRYPT '99*, pages 123–139.

[44] Oded Goldreich, Silvio Micali, and Avi Wigderson. How to play any mental game or a completeness theorem for protocols with honest majority. In *Proceedings of the Nineteenth Annual ACM Symposium on Theory of Computing, STOC 1987*, pages 218–229, 1987.

[45] D. M. Goldschlag, M. G. Reed, and P. F. Syverson. Onion routing for anonymous and private internet connections. *Communication of the ACM*, 42(2), page 84–88, 1999.

[46] Shafi Goldwasser and Silvio Micali. Probabilistic encryption. In *Journal of Computer Security*, Vol. 28, No. 2, pages 270–299, 1984.

[47] Philippe Golle and Ari Juels. Parallel mixing. In *CCS '04*, pages 220–226, 2004.

[48] Philippe Golle, Sheng Zhong, Dan Boneh, Markus Jakobsson, and Ari Juels. Optimistic mixing for exit-polls. In *ASIACRYPT '02*, Volume 1592 of *Lecture Notes in Computer Science*, pages 451–465, Berlin, 2002. Springer-Verlag.

[49] J Groth. Non-interactive zero-knowledge arguments for voting. In *ACNS '05*, Volume 3531, pages 467–482, Berlin, 2005. Springer-Verlag. *Lecture Notes in Computer Science*.

[50] J Groth and Y Ishai. Sub-linear zero-knowledge argument for correctness of a shuffle. In *EUROCRYPT '08*, Volume 4965 of *Lecture Notes in Computer Science*, pages 379–396, Berlin, 2008. Springer-Verlag.

[51] J Groth and S Lu. Verifiable shuffle of large size ciphertexts. In *PKC '07*, Volume 4450 of *Lecture Notes in Computer Science*, pages 377–392, Berlin, 2007. Springer-Verlag.

[52] Jens Groth. A verifiable secret shuffle of homomorphic encryptions. In *Public Key Cryptography 2003*, Volume 2567 of *Lecture Notes in Computer Science*, pages 145–160, Berlin, 2003. Springer-Verlag.

[53] L. C. Guillou and J. J. Quisquater. A "paradoxical" identity-based signature scheme resulting from zero-knowledge. In Shafi Goldwasser, editor, *CRYPTO '88*, Volume 403 of *Lecture Notes in Computer Science*, pages 216–231, Berlin, 1989. Springer-Verlag.

[54] Alejandro Hevia and Marcos Kiwi. Non-interactive zero-knowledge arguments for voting. In *LATIN '02*, Volume 2286 of *Lecture Notes in Computer Science*, pages 415–429, Berlin, 2002. Springer-Verlag.

[55] Martin Hirt and Kazue Sako. Efficient receipt-free voting based on homomorphic encryption. In *Advances in Cryptology—EUROCRYPT 00*, pages 539–556, 2000.

[56] M Jakobsson. Flash mixing. In *PODC '98*, pages 83–89, 1998.

[57] M Jakobsson. A practical mix. In *EUROCRYPT '98*, Volume 1403 of *Lecture Notes in Computer Science*, pages 448–461, Berlin, 1998. Springer-Verlag.

[58] M Jakobsson and A Juels. Mix and match: Secure function evaluation via ciphertexts. In *ASIACRYPT '00*, Volume 1976 of *Lecture Notes in Computer Science*, pages 143–161, Berlin, 2000. Springer-Verlag.

[59] M Jakobsson and A Juels. An optimally robust hybrid mix network. In *PODC '01*, pages 284–292, 2001.

[60] Markus Jakobsson, Ari Juels, and Ronald L. Rivest. Making mix nets robust for electronic voting by randomized partial checking. In *Proceedings of the 11th USENIX Security Symposium 2002*, pages 339–353. USENIX, 2002.

[61] A. Juels and M. Szydlo. A two-server, sealed-bid auction protocol. In *The Sixth International Conference on Financial Cryptography 2002*, Volume 2357 of *Lecture Notes in Computer Science*, pages 72–86, Berlin, 2002. Springer-Verlag.

[62] Ari Juels and Markus Jakobsson. An optimally robust hybrid mix network. In *Proc. of the 20th annual ACM Symposium on Principles of Distributed Computation*, pages 284–292. ACM, 2001.

[63] N Sastry C Karlof and D Wagner. Cryptographic voting protocols: A systems perspective. In USENIX Security Symposium 2005, Volume 3444 of *Lecture Notes in Computer Science*, pages 33–50, Berlin, Springer-Verlag.

[64] Jonathan Katz, Steven Myers, and Rafail Ostrovsky. Cryptographic counters and applications to electronic voting. In *Advances in Cryptology—EUROCRYPT 01*, pages 78–92, 2001.

[65] Aggelos Kiayias and Moti Yung. Self-tallying elections and perfect ballot secrecy. In *Public Key Cryptography, 5th International Workshop— PKC 02*, pages 141–158, 2002.

[66] D Kesdogana and C Palme. Technical challenges of network anonymity. In *Computer Communications*, Volume 29, Issue 3, 2006, pages 306–324.

[67] Byoungcheon Lee and Kwangjo Kim. Receipt-free electronic voting through collaboration of voter and honest verifier. In *JW-ISC 2000*, pages 101–108, 2000.

[68] Byoungcheon Lee and Kwangjo Kim. Receipt-free electronic voting scheme with a tamper-resistant randomizer. In *Information Security and Cryptology, ICISC 2002*, Volume 2587 of *Lecture Notes in Computer Science*, pages 389–406. Springer-Verlag, 2002.

[69] H. Lipmaa. On diophantine complexity and statistical zero-knowledge arguments. In *ASIACRYPT '03*, Volume 2894 of *Lecture Notes in Computer Science*, pages 398–415, Berlin, 2003. Springer-Verlag.

[70] M McGaley and J Gibson. A critical analysis of the council of Europe recommendations on e-voting. In *USENIX/Accurate Electronic Voting Technology Workshop 2006*, page 9, 2004.

[71] A. Menezes, P. van Oorschot, and S. Vanstone. *Handbook of Applied Cryptography*. CRC Press Inc., 1996.

[72] M Michels and P Horster. Some remarks on a reciept-free and universally verifiable mix-type voting scheme. In *ASIACRYPT '96*, Volume 1163 of *Lecture Notes in Computer Science*, pages 125–132, Berlin, 1996. Springer-Verlag.

[73] C. Andrew Neff. Conducting a universally verifiable electronic election using homomorphic encryption. White paper, VoteHere Inc, 2000.

[74] C. Andrew Neff. A verifiable secret shuffle and its application to e-voting. In *ACM Conference on Computer and Communications Security 2001*, pages 116–125, 2001.

[75] C. Andrew Neff. Verifiable mixing (shuffling) of elgamal pairs. 2004. Available as http://theory.lcs.mit.edu/~rivest/voting/papers/Neff-2004-04-21-ElGamalShuffles.pdf.

[76] Juan Manuel Gonzalez Nieto, Colin Boyd and Ed Dawson. A public key cryptosystem based on a subgroup membership problem. *Designs, Codes and Cryptography*, Issue 3, pages 301–316, 2005.

[77] L Nguyen, R Safavi-Naini, and K Kurosawa. Verifiable shuffles: A formal model and a paillier-based efficient construction with provable security. In *ACNS 2004*, pages 61–75.

[78] L Nguyen, R Safavi-Naini, and K Kurosawa. A provably secure and effcient verifiable shuffle based on a variant of the Paillier cryptosystem. In *Journal of Universal Computer Science*, 11(6), pages 986–1010, 2005.

[79] Lan Nguyen, Rei Safavi-Naini, and Kaoru Kurosawa. Verifiable shuffles: a formal model and a Paillier-based three-round construction with provable security. *Internatioanl Journal of Information Security*, 4, pages 241–255, 2006.

[80] W Ogata, K Kurosawa, K Sako, and K Takatani. Fault tolerant anonymous channel. In *Proceedings of International Conference on Information and Communication Security 1997*, Volume 1334 of *Lecture Notes in Computer Science*, pages 440–444, Berlin, 2000. Springer-Verlag.

[81] Miyako Ohkubo and Masayuki Abe. A length-invariant hybrid mix. In *ASIACRYPT '00*, Volume 1976 of *Lecture Notes in Computer Science*, pages 178–191, Berlin, 2000. Springer-Verlag.

[82] T Okamoto and S Uchiyama. A new public-key encyptosystem as secure as factoring. In *CRYPTO '98*, Volume 1403 of *Lecture Notes in Computer Science*, pages 308–318, Berlin, 1998. Springer-Verlag.

[83] P Paillier. Public key cryptosystem based on composite degree residuosity classes. In *EUROCRYPT '99*, Volume 1592 of *Lecture Notes in Computer Science*, pages 223–238, Berlin, 1999. Springer-Verlag.

[84] C. Park, K. Itoh, and K. Kurosawa. Efficient anonymous channel and all/nothing election scheme. In *EUROCRYPT '93*, Volume 765 of *Lecture Notes in Computer Science*, pages 248–259, Berlin, 1993. Springer-Verlag.

[85] T Pedersen. A threshold cryptosystem without a trusted party. In *EUROCRYPT '91*, pages 522–526.

[86] Kun Peng. A secure and efficient batched shuffling scheme. In *ICICS*, 2007.

[87] Kun Peng and Feng Bao. An efficient range proof scheme. In *IEEE PASSAT '10*, pages 826–833.

[88] Kun Peng and Feng Bao. Batch range proof for practical small ranges. In *AFRICACRYPT 2010*, Volume 6055 of *Lecture Notes in Computer Science*, pages 114–130, 2010, Berlin, 2010. Springer-Verlag.

[89] K Peng E Dawson, and F Bao. Modification and optimisation of a shuffling scheme: stronger security, formal analysis and higher efficiency. In *International Journal of Information Security*, Volume 10, Number 1, pages 33–47, 2011.

[90] Kun Peng, Colin Boyd, and Ed Dawson. Simple and efficient shuffling with provable correctness and ZK privacy. In *CRYPTO '05*, Volume 3089 of *Lecture Notes in Computer Science*, pages 188–204, Berlin, 2005. Springer-Verlag.

[91] Kun Peng, Colin Boyd, Ed Dawson, and Byoungcheon Lee. Multiplicative homomorphic e-voting. In *INDOCRYPT 2004*, Volume 3348 of *Lecture Notes in Computer Science*, pages 61–72, Berlin, 2004. Springer-Verlag.

[92] Kun Peng, Colin Boyd, Ed Dawson, and Kapali Viswanathan. Efficient implementation of relative bid privacy in sealed-bid auction. In *The 4th International Workshop on Information Security Applications, WISA2003*, Volume 2908 of *Lecture Notes in Computer Science*, pages 244–256, Berlin, 2003. Springer-Verlag.

[93] Kun Peng, Colin Boyd, Ed Dawson, and Kapali Viswanathan. A correct, private and efficient mix network. In *2004 International Workshop on Practice and Theory in Public Key Cryptography*, Volume 2947 of *Lecture Notes in Computer Science*, pages 439–454, Berlin, 2004. Springer-Verlag.

[94] B. Pfitzmann. Breaking an efficient anonymous channel. In *EUEOCRYPT '94*, Volume 950 of *Lecture Notes in Computer Science*, pages 339–348, Berlin, 1994. Springer-Verlag.

[95] M Reed, P Syverson and D Goldschlag. Anonymous connections and onion routing . In *IEEE Journal on Selected Areas in Communications*, Volume 16, Issue 4, pages 482–494, 1998.

[96] K. Sako and J. Killian. Receipt-free mix-type voting scheme–a practical solution to the implementation of a voting booth. In *EUROCRYPT '95*, Volume 921 of *Lecture Notes in Computer Science*, pages 393–403, Berlin, 1995. Springer-Verlag.

[97] Berry Schoenmakers. Fully auditable electronic secret-ballot elections. *XOOTIC Magazine*, July 2000.

[98] C Schnorr. Efficient signature generation by smart cards. *Journal of Cryptology, 4, 1991*, pages 161–174, 1991.

[99] S Ross. *Introduction to Probability Models*. 8th ed. Academic Press, New York, 2002.

[100] D Wikstrom. Five practical attacks for optimistic mixing for exit-polls. In *SAC '03*, Volume 3006 of *Lecture Notes in Computer Science*, pages 160–175, Berlin, 2004. Springer-Verlag.

[101] D Wikstrom. A universally composable mix-net. In *Theory of Cryptography 2004*, Volume 2951 of *Lecture Notes in Computer Science*, pages 317–335, Berlin, 2004. Springer-Verlag.

[102] D Wikstrom. A sender verifiable mix-net and a new proof of a shuffle. In *ASIACRYPT '05*, Volume 3788 of *Lecture Notes in Computer Science*, pages 273–292, Berlin, 2005. Springer-Verlag.

[103] D Wikstrom. A sender verifiable mix-net and a new proof of a shuffle. 2005. Available as `http://eprint.iacr.org/2005/137`.

[104] D Wikstrom and J Groth. An adaptively secure mix-net without erasures. In *ICALP '06*, Volume 4052 of *Lecture Notes in Computer Science*, pages 276–287, Berlin, 2006. Springer-Verlag.

[105] Akihiro Yamamura and Taiichi Saito. Private Information Retrieval Based on the Subgroup Membership Problem. In *ACISP '05*, page 206–220, 2005.

Index

Note: Page numbers ending in "e" refer to equations. Page numbers ending in "f" refer to figures. Page numbers ending in "t" refer to tables.